TESTED
ADVERTISING
METHODS

FIFTH EDITION

The John Caples International Awards

Andi Emerson, President of The Emerson Marketing Agency, founded the Caples Awards in 1978. They were established as a way to honor John Caples by giving creative individuals their moment in the spotlight. Today, entries are received and individual creatives are honored from 30 countries worldwide. (For the 1994 winner, see page 152.)

TESTED ADVERTISING METHODS

FIFTH EDITION

JOHN CAPLES
REVISED BY FRED E. HAHN

Foreword by
DAVID OGILVY

Introduction by Gordon White

PRENTICE HALL

Library of Congress Cataloging-in-Publication Data

Caples, John.
    Tested advertising methods / John Caples. — 5th ed., rev. and
enl. / revised by Fred E. Hahn.
      p.   cm.
    Includes index.
    ISBN 0-13-244609-X (cloth)
    1. Advertising.   I. Title.
    HF5823.C18   1997   96-47752
    659.13′2—dc21   CIP

Printed in the United States of America

10 9 8 7 6 5 4 3 2 1   10

ISBN 0-13-244609-X (C) ISBN 0-13-095701-1 (P)

PRENTICE HALL
Paramus, NJ 07652

On the World Wide Web at http://www.phdirect.com

CONTENTS

ILLUSTRATIONS

vii

PREFACE

When I was asked to prepare a new edition of John Caples' *Tested Advertising Methods*, I did what I am certain he would have done. I read the book before giving an answer. It was an eye-opener. Here was the only copywriter who deserves to be called a genius and judging by his book, I knew everything he did!

It took very little time for the euphoria to subside and the truth to sink in. Of course I knew everything he'd put into his book. He had taught it to me. He had shared his hard-won insights with all those who were willing to learn from him and it was from their books and articles, seminars and conversations, I had learned during the past 35 years. I had finally discovered where so much of my own success as a copywriter had originated. I owe him my long belated thanks. I hope this edition conveys them.

John Caples became one of America's most famous copywriters by combining immense natural gifts with the determination to learn *why* successful ads worked and unsuccessful ads failed. His three-step systems for advertising creativity and advertising success revolutionized the way much advertising was written, designed, and tested. They were fine-tuned by him throughout his long working life and shared with us in many articles and books, especially in his four revisions of *Tested Advertising Methods*, which this fifth edition is proud to continue.

CAPLES' THREE-STEP APPROACH TO CREATIVITY

1. Capture the prospect's attention. Nothing happens unless something in your ad, your mailing, or your commercial makes the prospect stop long enough to pay attention to what you say next.

2. Maintain the prospect's interest. Keep the ad, mailing, or commercial focused on the prospect, on what he or she will get out of using your product or service.

3. Move the prospect to *favorable* action. Unless enough "prospects" are transformed into "customers," your ad has failed, no matter

how creative. That's why you don't stop with A/I/A (Attention, Interest/Action), but continue right on with testing.

CAPLES' THREE-STEP APPROACH TO TESTING

1. Accept nothing as true about what works best in advertising until it has been objectively—what Caples called "scientifically"—tested.

2. Build upon everything you learn from testing to create an ever-stronger system that you return to with each new project. (Even a slow learner should not have to invent the wheel more than twice.)

3. Treat every ad as an ongoing test of what has been learned before. When something new works better—or something old stops working—be ready to admit you were wrong about what you thought you "knew." But don't just accept it. Find out why and apply it the next time.

   Or to put it the way Caples taught us:

   ■ Include in every ad a way to learn (quantify) the exact results of each promotion.

   ■ But don't just include it. Take the time and effort to actually learn it!

   ■ Base your future writing and design for the same product or service on what you learn.

   A third way of putting this is the LALALAL . . . rule:
   Learn/Adapt/Learn/Adapt/Learn/Adapt/Learn . . .

ABOUT "SCIENTIFIC" ADVERTISING

John Caples spent his long life learning more than anyone else had known about how to make advertising successful through "scientific" testing. We must all be grateful that he not only did, but also shared it with us.

The Direct Mail Revolution. The consumer direct-by-mail magazine advertising in which Caples found success and fame has changed little in the past 50 years. Today, the products sold are largely collectibles, clothing, health and beauty aids, self-help books, and audio and video cassettes, and, of course, everything electronic. Though many newspapers and magazines carry some direct-by-mail advertising, comparatively few specialize in this type of promotion. But those that do—*Parade* (a newspaper insert), *TV Guide*, and *Readers Digest* among others—are some of the largest circulation publications we have.

What has changed is the transformation of "direct-by-mail" and "direct mail" into Data-based Direct Response Selling . . . next to computer electronics, the fastest growing nonarmament industry of the past 20 years. Although many newspaper and magazine advertisers still ignore John Caples' principles of scientific advertising, the data-based community has boomed, building upon and practicing what he preached.

Beginning in the 1970s, there has been an explosion of direct response selling. Practically every major "regular" agency—primarily because of client demand—has established a direct-response division, and smaller direct-response agencies, in-house direct response advertising departments, and one-person do-it-yourselfers now number in the thousands. The "scientific advertising" revolution may not have come quite the way Caples expected, but the results are everything he could have hoped for . . . and more!

Nothing in this new edition departs from the basic techniques and principles he taught. They are as true today as when he first shared them. Equally true are the insights in the quotations at the end of each chapter. The quotations were selected by Caples and have not been changed by the editor. There are, however, a number of additions and changes that make his book even more valuable for today:

WHAT'S NEW IN THIS EDITION

- **Wider application**. Much of Caples' discussions assumed the resources of a major agency. But his insights can be applied equally well by smaller advertising departments or one-person do-it-yourselfers. These applications have been added without further comment.

- **More varied illustrations**. In addition to outstanding newspaper and magazine ads from the 1990s, this edition includes current tested direct mail and multimedia campaigns that show the validity of Caples' "scientific" approach to *all* advertising.

- **Terminology and nomenclature**. Caples wrote to persuade advertising professionals to his scientific approach. He used their—and his—terminology without further explanations. To make this edition more accessible to beginners, trade terms now are defined immediately, in context, the first time used.

- **Case histories**. Hundreds of case histories are updated or replaced to show contemporary usage and application, such as no longer assuming that all women are "housewives" or an oil change costs $3.20.

- **The story behind the man behind history's most famous ad**. Gordon White, John Caples' biographer, friend, and fellow BBDO worker, tells how an Annapolis graduate became America's most famous copywriter just one year out of the Academy.

WHERE SCIENTIFIC ADVERTISING STANDS TODAY

The approach to "scientific" advertising that John Caples preached and practiced for half a century has largely been accepted. But like every other art and science, it must be retaught to every new practitioner.

Gordon White, author of the Introduction to this fifth edition, deserves the final word. Says White:

> "*Tested Advertising Methods* is so clear, so complete, and so easy to follow, that if a creature from outer space came to Earth and read it, that visitor could produce excellent advertising. That hardly leaves any excuse for our not doing the same."

Fred E. Hahn
November 15, 1996

FOREWORD TO THE FOURTH EDITION

In this book John Caples writes, "I have seen one advertisement sell 19-1/2 times as much goods as another." This statement dramatizes the *gigantic* difference between good advertisements and bad ones. You will increase your chances of writing good ones if you read this book, and commit its conclusions to memory.

An earlier edition taught me most of what I know about writing advertisements. For example:

1. The key to success (maximum sales per dollar) lies in perpetual testing of all the variables.

2. What you say is more important than how you say it.

3. The headline is the most important element in most advertisements.

4. The most effective headlines appeal to the reader's self-interest or give news.

5. Long headlines that say something are more effective than short headlines that say nothing.

6. Specifics are more believable than generalities.

7. Long copy sells more than short copy.

These discoveries, and dozens like them, have been made by John Caples in the course of his long and distinguished career as a writer of mail-order advertising. He has been able to measure the results of every advertisement he has ever written.

The average manufacturer, who sells through a complex system of distribution, is unable to do this. He cannot isolate the results of individual advertisements from the other factors in his marketing mix. He is forced to fly blind.

Experience has convinced me that the factors that work in mail-order advertising work equally well in *all* advertising. But the vast majority of people who work in agencies, and almost all their clients, have never heard of these factors. That is why they skid hopelessly about on the greasy surface of irrelevant brilliance. They waste millions on bad advertising, when good advertising could be selling 19 1/2 times as much.

John Caples is the only graduate of the Naval Academy at Annapolis I have encountered in the advertising business. Before he became a copywriter, he was an engineer with the New York Telephone Company. These disciplines predisposed him to the analytical methods that have made him such an effective advertising man. He has no theories; only facts.

His methods are empirical and pragmatic. He is also highly *creative*. He has written scores of remarkable advertisements. Every anthology of famous advertisements includes his classic for the U.S. School of Music, with the headline "They Laughed When I Sat Down at the Piano. But When I Started to Play!—"

In short, John Caples is a very rare bird. He is not only an indomitable analyzer and teacher of advertising, he is also a first-rate copywriter—one of the most effective there has ever been.

Most of the other great copywriters—including Raymond Rubicam, Claude Hopkins, Rosser Reeves, Harry Scherman and Art Kudner—abandoned the hard slog of writing advertisements to become administrators. Not so John Caples. He has stuck to his knitting—*for 49 years*. That is how he has been able to accumulate his unique body of knowledge.

This is, without doubt, the most *useful* book about advertising that I have ever read.

David Ogilvy
Chairman, Ogilvy & Mather, International

INTRODUCTION TO THE FIFTH EDITION

THE STORY BEHIND THE MAN BEHIND
HISTORY'S MOST FAMOUS AD

In the mid-roaring-twenties, at age 25, the same age as the century, a shy young man in New York City was about to make advertising history. A recent graduate from, of all places, the Naval Academy, in his rookie try-out as an advertising copywriter, he sat at the typewriter and wrote this headline:

> THEY LAUGHED WHEN I SAT DOWN AT THE PIANO.
> BUT WHEN I STARTED TO PLAY!—

Four pages of single-space copy followed. Unsuspected by the writer, history was being born.

The young writer's name was John Caples, born in Manhattan, son of a doctor and a highly cultured mother.

At age 18, Caples entered Columbia University as a Naval Reservist, but soon dropped out. A year later he enlisted in the Navy as an ordinary seaman, but with an extraordinary goal. He would study, prepare himself, and take the competitive examination for Annapolis. So he polished brass, went to class, passed handily, and entered the United States Naval Academy, class of 1924.

At Annapolis he had to study engineering and did well. But he also contributed a few poems to the *Annapolis Log*, the school's magazine, and eventually became associate editor.

But in post-World War I, as in the 1990s, the Navy was downsizing. John was given, and took, the option to forgo the ensign's commission and to work for the B.S. degree in electrical engineering—a degree that led to his employment by the New York Telephone Company, a job he soon found totally boring.

Rescue came in the form of Dr. Katherine Blackford, an early practitioner of adult vocational guidance. For her advice he had to pay $25 *in advance*—a staggering sum in those days—and wait a month for a meeting and her written report.

In five typewritten pages she pointed out a variety of negative factors about his employment future. But there was a terse recommendation at the end. "I would not discourage you in your ambition to develop yourself as a writer."

John took her advice. Concluding there was more money to be made in writing advertising than in his childhood ambition of newspaper reporting, he entered Columbia's evening program and took courses in advertising principles and copywriting. The latter course, especially, proved invaluable. His samples from class made a hit with the copy chief of a leading mail-order agency. He was offered a job at $25 a week, $6 less than he made as an engineer. He grabbed it!

That was in the fall of 1925. Newspaper and magazine mail-order advertising flourished, as it had since the beginning of the century. High among the many items bought by mail in those days—as now—was self-improvement. Correspondence schools did well. By mail you could improve your mind, learn a language, improve your memory, learn to dance, improve your physique, learn executive skills, learn the niceties of etiquette and, of course, learn to play the piano.

John loved his new job and learned fast. His first ad to see print, on October 3, 1925, was for Arthur Murray Dance Studios. Its headline: "How a Faux Pas Made Me Popular." From those early assignments and the response the ads generated he learned two things: People very much want to be popular, and they are always seeking a quick, easy way to solve their problems.

Then came the assignment to write an ad selling a home study course offered by the U.S. School of Music.

The copy ran to four typewritten pages, single-spaced. But it was the headline that captured the imagination: "They laughed when I sat down at the piano. But when I started to play!—" Overnight it became a fixture on the American scene. Vaudeville comedians made jokes about it with such knee-slappers as "They laughed when I sat down at the piano. Someone had stolen the stool." Newspaper columnists lampooned it. Other copywriters "borrowed" from it, copied it, paraphrased it.

"They laughed . . ." was hugely successful as an ad. Within a month Caples reworked the formula for a correspondence school course in French. "They grinned when the waiter spoke to me in French—but their laughter changed to amazement at my reply" was the headline. It too both rang the bell as an advertisement and caught the public fancy.

The John Caples ad that started a new school of advertising. To see how it still flourishes, turn to the illustration at the end of this Introduction—and to practically every other ad and direct mail package shown in this fifth edition.

In spite of his almost instant, industry-wide fame as a mail order copywriter, Caples began to yearn for a job with more prestige. "I yearned for the day," he explained years later, "When I would see my ad in *Harper's Monthly, The Atlantic,* or *The Saturday Evening Post,* instead of *Physical Culture* magazine."

So in 1927 he joined the agency known as BBDO. It was an association that was to last well over 50 years, interrupted only by his return to the Navy in World War II. Via mail-order advertising he had learned about testing copy. He went on to pioneer other forms of testing, then shared what he learned in articles and books such as *Tested Advertising Methods*, in my opinion as a teacher and author, still the best basic book on advertising copy.

I was John's fellow BBDO employee and friend for two decades, and our friendship continued for 20 more after I left the agency to teach at the University of Illinois. He was amused—and I think flattered—when he became the subject of my dissertation, especially its later publication (without all the footnotes) as a popular book for the trade. Much of the material here comes from our conversations and reminiscences throughout that time.

But let me close by returning to that magical year of 1925 when Dr. Caples' young son was dazzling the world of advertising. At Christmas, he proudly took home his proof book to show his mother. The reception was hardly what he expected. She asked him questions such as, can people really learn to play the piano by mail? and does this book really give people a magnetic personality? "She read my headlines aloud," he later recalled, "with growing concern in her voice:

'Fat men . . . try this new reducing belt.'

'Overnight I stopped being the underdog!'

'60 days ago they called me "baldy"!'

"She closed my proof book, returned it to me, and said, `You'd better not let your father see this.'"

John finished the story with a grin, then added, "Talk about being a prophet without honor in your own mother's kitchen!"

Gordon White
Professor Emeritus, University of Illinois

Six decades young and still going strong. Sixty years after John Caples developed this first-person-story appeal, it still produces superb results. But the headline alone isn't all. Subheads feature "Free," "50% Savings," and the offer to "See for Yourself," with an even bigger "FREE" offering sample portfolios (note the plural "s"). There's a big toll-free number too, still there after the coupon is removed. No wonder the ad increased lead generation by 26 percent over the prior year, with a much higher conversion rate. Surely John Caples smiles down from copywriters' heaven!

ACKNOWLEDGMENTS

WE COULDN'T HAVE DONE IT WITHOUT . . .

Here, in alphabetical order, are the advertisers that illustrate this new edition. Wherever possible, we have identified the men and women who did the ads and direct mail packages so that they can see their names as well as their work in print. Where the examples are award winners from result-based competitions, they are identified. Two such identifications are "CADM Tempo Awards" given by the Chicago Association of Direct Marketing, and the "Benny," the Philadelphia Direct Marketing Association's Benjamin Franklin awards.

The following categories are used for accreditation:

1. **Advertiser.**

2. Key Advertiser Person (*KAP*).

3. Copywriters (*Copy*).

4. Creative direction/Design/layout (*Art*).

5. Agency or in-house group.

Our heartfelt thanks to each and all!

American Federation of Teachers
KAP/Copy: Albert Shanker
American Federation of Teachers, Washington, D.C.

Andersen Consulting
KAP: Christine Cherry
Copy/Art: Client/Agency staffs
Madison & Summerdale, Inc., Deerfield, IL

Bell Atlantic
Initial package:
Copy: Scott Armstrong
Art: Gema Kreivanas

Follow-up package:
Copy: Elliot Simmons
Art: Michael Rowinski
Devon Direct Marketing & Advertising, Inc., Berwyn, PA

Canyon Ranch
KAP: Brian R. Shultz
Copy/Art: Weiss Whitten Stagliano/Canyon Ranch

Caples Award
KAP: Andi Emerson
John Caples International Awards, Inc., New York, NY

Carnation Baby Formula
KAP: Patti Kirk
Copy/Layout: Cara Lipshie, Viv Alter
Concept: Michael Cancellieri
McCann Direct, New York, NY

Chemical Bank
KAP: Don Hogle
Copy/Art: Client/agency creative and marketing staffs
McCann Erickson, New York, NY

Dayton's, Marshall Field's, Hudson's
KAP: Connie Soteropulos
Copy: Heidi Rose
Art: Bryan Pohl
D-MF-H Advertising Department, Minneapolis, MN

Evans, Inc.
KAP: Rob Steffen
Copy: Paul Benson, Anne McInnis
Art: Dale Stackler
State Advertising, Chicago, IL

Evanston Hospital
KAP: Jean Benzies, David Loveland
Copy: Tom Bartholomew
Art: Dick Prow, Curt Ippensen, Dave Grinnell, Kim Callaway
Rhea & Kaiser Advertising, Naperville, IL

Fabrikant Fine Diamonds, Inc.
KAP: Andrew & Peter Fabrikant
Copy: Sheldon J. Kravitz
Art: Richard Corralde
Ultimo Advertising, Inc., New York, NY

Foley-Belsaw
KAP: John Baenish
Copy: John Baenisch, Lavonne Hanshaw
Art: Lavonne Hanshaw
Field Advertising, Kansas City, MO

Franklin Mint
KAP: Bill Molnar
Copy/Art: Franklin Mint staff
The Franklin Mint, Franklin Center, PA

Grizzard
KAP: Claude Grizzard
Copy: John Davies
Art: Terry Greer, John Sillesky
Grizzard—The Agency Team, Atlanta, GA

Guess?, Inc.
KAP: Paul Marciano
Art: Paul Marciano
Paul Marciano Advertising, Los Angeles, CA

Helmsley Hotels
KAP: Joyce Beber
Copy: Joe Perz, Agency creative team
Art: James Hale, Joe Perz
Beber/Silverstein and Partners, Miami, FL

Jaguar Cars LTD
KAP: Jaguar USA Marketing
Copy: Jim Herbert, Nancy Vecilla, Steve Diamond
Art: Rob Cohen, Peter White, Joe Cupani
Ogilvy & Mather Direct, New York, NY

Land Rover
KAP: Elizabeth A. Schama
Copy: Ari Merkin
Art: Allen Richardson
Grace and Rothschild Advertising, New York, NY

Lands' End
KAP: Reta Brown
Copy/Art: Biederman, Kelly & Shaffer
The Peer Group, Dodgeville, WI

Lenox
Copy/Art: Lenox creative staff
Lenox Creative, Langhorne, PA

Lufthansa
KAP: Jennifer Kinzinger
Copy/Art: Steve Cowles, Birgit Schwarz, Gary Scheiner,
Tom Drymalski, Leila Vuorenmaa, Michael Cancellieri,
Joe Cipani Ogilvy & Mather Direct, New York, NY

MCI
Copy/Art: Stan Bennett
Devon Direct Marketing & Advertising, Inc., Berwyn, PA

Mobi! Corporation
Copy/Art: Mobil staff
Mobil Public Affairs, Fairfax, VA

Original Pet Drink Co.
KAP: Eric Zurbuchan, Marc Duke
Copy: Eric Zurbuchan
Art: Eric Zurbuchan, Marc Duke
O. P. D. Advertising, Fort Lauderdale, FL

OXY Brand
KAP: T. S. Lenyg
Copy: Patricia Schirmer
Art: Armanda Parton, NG Pei Pei
Ogilvy & Mather Direct, Singapore

Pitney Bowes Copier Systems
KAP: Gary C. Battaglia
Copy/Art: Alan Fonorow
Ogilvy & Mather Singapore

Pitney Bowes Copier Systems
KAP: Gary C. Battaglia
Copy/Art: Alan Fonorow, Bob Schemmel
Kobs Gregory Passavant, Chicago, IL

S&S Mills Carpet
KAP: Elena Finizio
Copy: Nancy Thornton
Art: Nancy Thornton, Elizabeth Rushing
Bennett Kuhn Varner, Atlanta, GA

Sandoz Agro, Inc.
KAP: Jeff Cook
Copy: Jon Basinger, agency staff
Art: Nancy Pesile
Basinger & Associates, Inc., Atlanta, GA

Select Comfort
KAP: Susan Lichtenwalner
Copy: Dan von der Embse, Chuck Dorsey
Art: Dan von der Embse, Von Direct
Von Direct, Minneapolis, MN

Smith Barney
KAP: Catherine Kapta
Copy/Art: Client, agency staff
McCann Ericksen New York

Toyota
KAP: Jon Bucci
Copy: Steve Wilson
Art: Terri Balagia, Al Abbott, Eric Gardner, Doug Van Andel
Saatchi & Saatchi DFS/Pacific, Torrance, CA

United Airlines
KAP: Trudy Havens
Copy: Tim Pontarelli
Art: Tom Walker, Ted Naron
Leo Burnett, Chicago, IL

. . . and thanks to:

Michael Snell, my literary agent; the Prentice Hall editorial staff; Mariann Hutlak and Marlys Lehmann, Prentice Hall's great production/copyeditors; Nancy Willson, for her work on the illustrations. And, extra special thanks to my wife, Alice Joan Hahn, who outspells SpellCheck™, outgrammars Fowler, and tolerates a husband who insists on working at home.

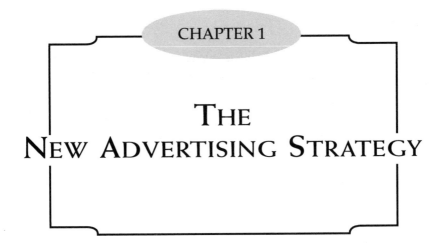

THE
NEW ADVERTISING STRATEGY

The most difficult things to discover in the study of advertising are facts. For example:

- What kind of advertising headlines attract the most readers?
- What kind of pictures get the most attention?
- What sales appeals sell the most merchandise?
- What kind of advertising copy is most effective in selling your product or service?

It is easy to get opinions on these questions. It is hard to get facts. The purpose of this book is to answer questions of this kind. And the answers are based on the traceable results from advertising that can be tested and measured.

TWO CLASSES OF ADVERTISING

1. *The Testers*: Those who are continually testing their advertisements to find out how much actual business each advertisement brings in, for example, mail order advertisers, classified advertisers, and department stores.

2. *The Non-testers:* The advertisers who, for one reason or another, do little or no testing or measuring of advertising results.

In a classic booklet on advertising, "Blind Advertising Expenditures," John W. Blake states:

> There is just one justification for advertising: Sales! Sales! Sales! Sales that are immediate, sales that are abundant, sales that are profitable. These are the results that mail order houses demand and get from advertising. Why don't you?

1

In the general publicity field too much copy is judged solely by opinion and appearance. Costly campaigns are launched, and often pay the advertiser well. Yet the advertiser never knows the individual performance of each advertisement. In a campaign of a dozen pieces of copy it is possible for most of the achievement to be accomplished by just one or two advertisements. All the rest could be duds. Not only is this possible, it is very probable. All mail order men who are onto their job know this. Too many literary faddists, and not enough salesmen, write advertising. The general advertiser may question the above statement; yet he knows that in a sales force of a dozen untried men, not all will succeed.

General advertising greatly needs the cold-blooded, analytical, scientific methods of mail order practice.

Perhaps in years to come, even more advertisers will use scientific methods. Perhaps even more advertisers will run tested copy in tested media. In answer to the question, "What will advertising be like 30 years hence?" a famous advertising man replied, "It will be more exact, more scientific, and therefore produce more results." The fact that the nonscientific advertisers have derived benefit from their efforts is a tribute, not to their methods, but to the extraordinary power of advertising.

MY FIRST TWO TEACHERS

The first week I worked in advertising, an artist said to me, "Drawings are just the thing to illustrate these furniture advertisements. Pen and ink sketches are so modern. They give the product just the style that it needs."

A copywriter said, "We don't use headlines in these perfume advertisements. Headlines would spoil the effect. Besides, headlines are unnecessary for short copy."

I believed these statements. I believed that these men had a real foundation for what they said. I tried to remember the rules they laid down. "Pen and ink drawings are good in furniture advertisements." "Headlines are not needed where short copy is used." Every time I heard an advertising person talk about advertising I listened carefully. I thought I was learning the rules of the business.

Not long after that I began to work on mail order advertising. Each advertisement was tested. Results were tabulated. Not only each advertisement, but each publication had to prove itself in actual sales.

I quickly learned that much of the talk abut advertising I had listened to and believed in was just talk. Too often the speakers were stating opinions they mistook for facts. And in many cases the opinions were merely personal and did not even reflect industry rules-of-thumb.

If those opinions could have been subject to hypnotic recall, their real source would often have been laughable. An artist might favor blue backgrounds in advertising because blue was his current fiancee's favorite color. A copywriter might recommend short copy because her first boss had told her, "I would never read all that small print and I don't think anyone else will either." An advertising manager might put a newspaper on the list because he liked its editorials, or because the space sales representative had a great personality.

FIRST STEPS IN PLANNING A CAMPAIGN

The steps outlined here are followed today by practically all major advertisers. Smaller advertisers, with more limited resources, should follow them as far as time and budgets permit, using tested guidance such as that given throughout this book.

In planning an advertising campaign, the first step should be to clear the decks of all opinions, all theories, all conjectures, all prejudices.

The next step should be to find a scientific method of testing the real strength of the different advertisements and the various advertising media, such as publications, broadcasting, direct mail advertising, and so on.

This takes a three-pronged approach:

1. *Initial testing*. Test different ads, commercials, direct mailings (what the industry calls direct mail "packages") against one another in their own media.

2. *Expand testing of winners*. Once you have found what works best in each medium, test a much expanded list of individual publications, radio stations, or direct mail lists against one another.

3. *Learn from the results*. As you do this, you will be testing whole media such as newspapers, magazines, broadcasting, direct mail and so forth, against one another for future attempts at selling similar products or services. In other words, you are not only testing individual newspapers or radio stations against one another, you are, at the same time, testing newspapers as a class against magazines against direct mail, and so on, to learn how they rank in providing cost-effective sales results.

This preliminary three-step research takes time. Let it!

The time is well spent. To get started on the right foot—to find the right appeal and the right place to advertise—is so important that other considerations are insignificant by comparison.

HOW PRELIMINARY RESEARCH PAYS OFF

I have seen one mail-order advertisement actually sell, not twice as much, not three times as much, but 19-1/2 times as much merchandise as another ad for the same product. Both advertisements occupied the same space. Both were run in the same publication. Both had photographic illustrations. Both had carefully written copy. The difference was that one used the right appeal and the other used the wrong appeal.

If I were a manufacturer and I hired an advertising agency or had an in-house advertising staff, I would be vitally concerned about getting the right appeal. I would much rather have a hastily prepared advertisement based on the correct appeal than 20 beautiful pieces of copy with beautiful pictures featuring an ineffective appeal.

Discovering the most effective appeal is often difficult. Often there are many seemingly attractive appeals, yet only one right one. If my advertising department or agency had a year in which to prepare a campaign for my product, I would be perfectly satisfied if they spent 11 months in search of the right appeal and one month—or one week, for that matter—preparing the actual advertisements.

"APPEAL" ONLY ONE OF MANY ASPECTS THAT NEED TESTING

But finding the right appeal is only one of many instances in which facts must replace *unfounded* opinions:

- Time and budget permitting, every logical advertising medium should be tested.

- Season or other specific dates should be checked. "Christmas" catalogs, for instance, were mailed two months earlier in 1996 than they were 20 years ago.

- Location of advertising, both geographically and within each medium, should be tracked for results.

- Every single element in an advertisement—headline, subhead, illustration, and copy—must be put there not because it looks good, not because it sounds good, but because testing has shown that it works best! See Figure 1.1 for an example of a campaign that got them all right.

WHEN YOU CAN'T PRETEST

There are cases in which pretesting is difficult, if not impossible; for example, single-use advertisements and advertising with very limited budgets. And even when time and budget permit, it is difficult to test in advance the long-term effect of repeating an advertising slogan over and over again. Faced with this problem, learn from those who *have* tested and apply their results. Instead, all too many advertisers decide by opinion or unproven theory in setting their "Three W's" advertising policies:

1. Where to advertise
2. When to advertise
3. What to say in advertisements

Often the person whose opinion is final is not even an advertising man or woman. It may be a vice president with a flair for writing interoffice memos, or a manufacturer who knows production from A to Z and nothing at all about advertising. What a wasteful, inefficient state of affairs! Compared with the insistence on ever more efficient manufacturing and sales techniques, many advertising methods are still in the dark ages.

NOT THEORY, BUT FACTS!

Now let us look at the other side of the picture. There are many advertisers who waste not a penny on theory, who deal only with facts. These advertisers test every advertisement and every publication on a small scale before they use them on a large scale. Every advertisement and every advertising medium must prove itself by producing inquiries from interested prospects, or leads for the sales staff or mail order and telephone sales, or sales in stores. Some of these scientific advertisers spend comparatively small sums in advertising. Yet they have made their products as well known as certain advertisers who spend far more. They make one advertising dollar do the work of several dollars. How do they do this? What is their secret?

Figure 1.1: *Eye-opening blind response.* Research showed that first-time mothers viewed having a baby as three distinct and perhaps stressful events (getting pregnant, being pregnant, and giving birth) rather than one enjoyable experience in their life. In addition, research showed that women were "information seekers" who were actively pursuing help in what to expect during their pregnancy. Through a "blind" mailing, the agency and Evanston Hospital targeted 15,000 25–35-year-old married women without children. A phenomenal 44 percent response identified 3,500 likely new mothers. They then developed an inte-

grated print/direct-mail campaign to invite the information-seeking women to free maternity seminars, which, incidentally, introduced the women to the hospital and obstetrician referral service. Mailing was coordinated with advertisements in selected zip/zone editions of *The Chicago Tribune's* "Women's News" section. The campaign increased seminar registration by 50 percent, obstetrical referral by 40 percent, and increased hospital births by 10 percent. *Winner, 1st Place, Marketing: Integrated Media Campaign, CADM 1995 TEMPO Award.*

The answer is testing, testing, testing. For example, mail order advertisers, supermarkets, and department stores watch with eagle eyes the sales that result from every advertisement and every publication. Based on proven results, they then spend the bulk of their advertising dollars on tested copy in tested media.

HOW TO TEST YOUR ADS

For anyone unfamiliar with advertising testing, here are three of the easiest and most common methods:

1. *Retail sales.* When department stores or other retailers run an advertisement for a certain article, they can judge their advertising's effectiveness by the increase in sales over previous days on each article advertised. Computer-recorded laser-scanned checkout provides instant sales comparisons and even automated reordering, if wanted.

   Long before laser scanning, your editor worked on one of the first such systems, at Orbach's in New York City. Every sales tag had a detachable number key that was manually keypunched, then laboriously—and noisily—sorted by the earliest "programmers." Twelve of us worked throughout the evening to provide buyers the detailed overnight records they now get instantly at the click of a mouse.

2. *Test cities.* Certain national advertisers use test cities or test neighborhoods. They try out copy and design appeals there, then compare the resulting sales with comparable cities or neighborhoods that use the regular ads. Depending on the increase in sales, additional, more widespread tests will check the results before the new ads are "rolled out"; that is, run nationally.

3. *Key numbers.* Other advertisers use key numbers in the coupon of their advertisements. Notice the coupon in a typical mail-order advertisement. Here is how the address in the coupon might read:

Acme Products Co.
200 Park Avenue, Dept. R-44-1-7
New York, N.Y. 10017

The key number in this advertisement is "Dept. R-44-1-7." The letter "R" is the code for the publication in which the advertisement ran. The number "44" designates the specific ad and that ad only. It is used to identify that ad *no matter where it appears*! The number "1" shows the month, January in this case, and "7" the day of the month. If, on the same day, Acme Products also runs that ad in a different medium and the code for that publication is T, the key will read "T-44-1-7." A different advertisement will change "44" to that ad's number. The part of the key identifying a specific advertisement is never changed as long as that advertisement remains the same. Equally important, it is always changed when *anything* within the ad is made different, no matter how seemingly trivial.

To keep the tracking—and understanding—of test results simpler, use letters rather than numbers for changes on specific ads: 44A . . . 44B . . . 44G, rather than 44 . . . 45 . . . 51. Both systems will tell you that there have been six changes in the original advertisement, but only 44G shows this without having to discover the number with which you began.

The key number was an invention that has done as much for the science of advertising as the X-ray has done for the science of medicine. It has made it practical, simple, and inexpensive to know exactly how many inquiries or how many sales came from each advertisement. The importance of this is far-reaching. It is one of the greatest steps ever made toward taking the guesswork out of advertising.

For instance, one of the important things you can learn through the use of key numbers, as shown in Figure 1.2, is which advertisements gain the most attention. By running two or more advertisements for the same product, each with a different key number, in the same publication, you can discover by simply counting inquiries or telephone and coupon orders which advertisement attracted the most readers. How to do this without giving the first ad the reader sees a special advantage is discussed in Chapter 18. Naturally, in a test of this kind, the coupon and/or toll-free number must not be featured in some advertisements and hidden in others. They must be given the same prominence throughout the test.

Figure 1.2: *Doing everything right!* Begin with a prospect-targeting headline plus to-the-point subheads, one asking the key question, the other promising the answer. Use show-and-tell pictures to illustrate and explain key benefits . . . with captions that mention the product name three times. Write fact-packed, benefit-laden copy with a large 800 number that has the same extension as the coupon code. Put a really tiny picture of the FREE video and brochure in the coupon, just as Caples taught us. Finally, add a "violator" to tie in radio commercials with a popular personality. Using Caples as its copywriting bible, this "totally reengineered" advertising is proving the all-time winner! No one is surprised.

VALUE OF INQUIRIES

"But I don't care about coupon returns!" you exclaim. "What I want is sales." This brings up a fundamental point. It has been proven many times and by many advertisers that in a properly controlled test the advertisements that bring the most inquiries—what our profession calls the first step in "two-step" or "multistep" selling—usually bring in the most sales.

Daniel Starch of "Starch Reports" fame, reached this conclusion decades ago in his analysis of five million inquiries received by 165 firms over a period of 12 years. Today, when the average business-to-business sales call costs more than $300, it is more true than ever, and many advertisers "qualify" responses through telephone follow-up before the salesperson goes to visit.

There are, of course, exceptions to the value of inquiries. An advertisement with a picture of a free booklet or other attractive premium at the top of the page and the headline "Send for this FREE gift" may bring an avalanche of inquiries, but very few worthwhile leads. In this case, the huge response has little relationship to the true value of the advertisement.

There is also the compulsive coupon-clipper to contend with, the man, woman, or child who goes through a magazine and clips any coupon that offers *anything* free—sample, booklet, or premium. Fortunately, this group is not large and what there is remains fairly constant. Legally, however, anything offered as "free" must be provided unless clearly qualified in immediate conjunction to the offer. Some advertisers eliminate coupon-clippers by omitting the coupon and using a "hidden offer" buried in the copy. The value of this method—if any— is explained later.

The important thing to remember in testing a series of advertisements is to keep the booklet, premium, or sample offer subordinated and identical in all advertisements. If this is done, you will find that in general the advertisements that bring the most inquiries also bring the most sales.

THE TWO MOST IMPORTANT THINGS YOU WILL LEARN IN THIS BOOK

In the following chapters of this book, an effort will be made to do two things:

1. To explain the scientific principles of advertising that have been learned by advertisers who know by actual test which kind of advertisements sell the most goods, which headlines attract the most readers, which publications are best, and which kind of advertising illustrations and layouts are most effective.

2. To explain the methods of testing so that you may determine for yourself just which headlines, appeals, illustrations, copy, and media are best for you.

I read but one newspaper and that more for its advertisements than its news.

Thomas Jefferson

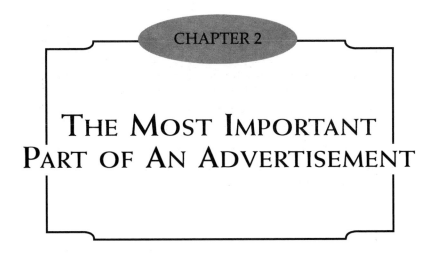

CHAPTER 2

THE MOST IMPORTANT
PART OF AN ADVERTISEMENT

There are 18 chapters in this book. Four of these chapters, or more than one fifth of the entire book, deal with headlines of advertisements. But four chapters are not too much space to devote to this vital subject. In most advertisements, no matter how striking the illustration, the headlines are critically important. The majority of the public reads little else when deciding whether or not they are interested. Exactly like the headlines in newspaper stories and articles, they are the telegraphic messages that the advertiser puts into big print for the public to read what follows.

The success of an entire advertising campaign may stand or fall on what is said in the headlines of the individual advertisements. In an article in a trade magazine, Don Belding wrote:

> Inquiry returns show that the headline is 50 to 75 percent of the advertisement. So, selling punch in your headline is about the most important thing. It competes with news and articles and other headlines in picking out readers. In fact, your single headline, in the average big-town newspaper, competes with 350 news stories, 21 feature articles, and 85 advertisements. And it competes in time, because, seen for a second, it is heeded, or passed up, and there is no return by readers. . . .

In discussing the importance of headlines, Bruce Barton told how results were increased by a change of headline on a correspondence-school advertisement. Mr. Barton said:

> The old headline was, "John Smith made $110,000 the first year writing motion picture scenarios." The new headline was "John Smith sold his first motion picture scenario for $9,000 one month after completing this Course." The advertisement with the new headline drew enormously, and the explanation is, of course, easy.

Every reader could imagine himself or herself making $9,000, but few could imagine themselves making $110,000.

I feel we are in a period when the interesting headline is more indicated than ever before. I believe that all copywriters ought to put on it the best headline they can and then say to themselves, "How can that headline be changed to be more interesting or appeal to more people?"

AN AD THAT FAILED . . . AND ONE THAT DIDN'T

Following are two headlines that were tested by a mail order advertiser. One was a success, the other a failure. You probably know which one won, but do you know why?

ARE YOU AFRAID OF MAKING MISTAKES IN ENGLISH?

DO YOU MAKE THESE MISTAKES IN ENGLISH?

The advertisements bearing these headlines were the same in general appearance. And they both had the same copy appeal. The difference in pulling power was due largely to the headline.

The second headline produced far more inquiries and orders. Why? What quality does the second headline possess that the first one lacks?

The word "these" in the second headline is what makes the difference. The headline, "Do you make these mistakes in English?" says in effect to the reader, "There are described below certain blunders in English. Read the copy and see if you make these blunders."

This arouses the readers' curiosity and self-interest. Here is free information. They can read about these mistakes in English and learn to avoid them. They may also find entertainment and self-satisfaction in reading about the blunders of other people and saying to themselves, "I would never make such silly mistakes as that."

Now consider the other headline, "Are you afraid of making mistakes in English?" This headline fails to even suggest to the reader that there are some interesting blunders described below. It merely suggests that the copy will be a sales talk for a book on English grammar or a course in English. And who wants to read a sales talk?

Today, most experienced advertising people realize how much of the effectiveness of an advertisement depends on the headline.

Every copywriter knows what it is to struggle with copy for hours, for days—fixing it, polishing it, rearranging it. We have all been guilty of leaving the headline until the last and then spending half an hour on it—or perhaps only ten minutes. I did just that before I had any experience with keyed copy and traceable results. Now, I spend hours on headlines—days if necessary. And when I get a good headline, I know that my task is nearly finished. Writing the copy can usually be done in a short time if necessary. And that advertisement will be a good one—that is, if the headline is really a "stopper."

What good is all the painstaking work on copy if the headline isn't right? If the headline doesn't stop people, the copy might as well be written in Greek.

If the headline of an advertisement is poor, the best copywriters in the world can't write copy that will sell the goods. They haven't a chance. Because if the headline is poor, the copy will not be read. And copy that is not read does not sell goods. On the other hand, if the headline is a good one, it is a relatively simple matter to write the copy.

WHEN NOT TO WRITE THE HEADLINE FIRST

Of course, writing the headline first is based on your knowing what you are selling so well that the copy will flow naturally no matter where you begin. When that is not the case, begin by learning about the product or service. Then, before starting on possible headlines, write a first draft of the copy to help organize what you now know. Somewhere in that copy you are likely to find the key selling point on which to base your headline—not its words, but the concept on which your headline will be based. Now spend all the time you need to get the best headline possible, then rewrite and polish your copy to flow naturally from final headline to the logo.

What do people see of advertising? Headlines! What do you yourself see of advertising as you glance through a newspaper or magazine? Headlines! What decides whether or not you stop a moment and look at an advertisement, or even read a little of it? The headline!

Of course, the illustration counts, too. Sometimes a striking picture will make an advertisement good even if the headline is only ordinary. But a good headline can make an advertisement good even if the picture is poor. The combination of a good headline and a good picture, as in Figure 2.1, is irresistible.

Figure 2.1: *Moving your 4/wd out of the pack.* PROBLEM: With practically every manufacturer entering the tough-guy 4/wd market, give yours additional appeal. SOLUTION: Translate a higher-price monthly lease into a $17-a-day exotic vacation. The inventive "800-Fine 4WD" is a sure winner too!

THREE CLASSES OF SUCCESSFUL HEADLINES

Advertisers who work with keyed copy find the majority of their most successful headlines can be divided into three classes:

1. *Self-interest.* The best headlines are those that appeal to the reader's self-interest, that is, headlines based on *reader benefits*. They offer readers something they want—and can get from *you*. For example:

ANOTHER $50 RAISE

RETIRE AT 55

2. *News.* The next-best headlines are those that give news. For example:

NEW FEATURES OF THE FORD TRUCK

DISCOVERED—A NEW KIND OF HAND CLEANER

3. *Curiosity.* The third-best headlines are those that arouse curiosity. For example:

LOST: $35,000

ARE YOU PLAYING FAIR WITH YOUR WIFE?

However, the effectiveness of the average curiosity headline is doubtful. For every curiosity headline that succeeds in getting results, a dozen will fail.

Why is it that self-interest headlines are best and the curiosity headlines only third best? You can answer this question for yourself. Suppose you are looking through a newspaper. You see a headline that arouses your curiosity. You will read the copy if you have time. But suppose you see a headline that offers you something you want. You will make time to read the copy.

The headline that makes a definite offer of something people want has a further advantage. It conveys its message to people who read only headlines. And as every advertising pro knows, there are scores of people who read only headlines for every person who reads both headlines and copy.

Note this: The following curiosity headline and logotype (company name) convey practically no message to the newspaper glancers who read only the large print:

HERE'S ONE QUESTION YOU SHOULDN'T ASK YOUR WIFE

[Copy and illustration]

ABC Life Insurance Company

Notice the difference in the following self-interest headline and logotype:

YOU CAN LAUGH AT MONEY WORRIES
IF YOU FOLLOW THIS SIMPLE PLAN

[Copy and illustration]

ABC Life Insurance Company

By merely reading the headline and logotype of this second advertisement, the readers learn that a certain company has a plan that will help them solve their money problems. Actual returns show that this second advertisement brought twice as many coupon inquiries as the first advertisement and twice as many sales.

Occasionally, a curiosity headline is produced that does compete successfully with self-interest headlines. For example, an advertisement for a book of etiquette with the headline, "What's wrong in this picture?" was an excellent puller.

Here is an astounding fact. Even today you can look through almost any consumer or professional publication and find headlines that possess not a single one of the necessary qualities, such as self-interest or curiosity. Here are some examples of meaningless headlines taken from magazines:

YOUTH CRIES UNTO YOUTH

BLOW HOT—BLOW COLD

AND THIS LITTLE GIRL WENT TO MARKET

NO REASON NOW

JUST ONE QUESTION, PLEASE

Test these headlines yourself. Do they give news? Do they offer you anything you want? Do they arouse your curiosity? No. Absolutely no. These headlines might have some value if they mentioned the name of the product advertised. Yet they don't even do that.

But those headlines came from the 1950s. We've all learned better by now, right? So let's look at some headlines from a 1995 computer magazine:

TOMORROW'S HIGH-BANDWIDTH APPLICATIONS ARE GOING TO DEMAND
A NETWORK THAT CAN FLY

THE WEAPON OF YOUR DREAMS

PUT UP. OR SHUT UP.

AND ON THE SEVENTH DAY . . .

IF PATIENCE IS A VIRTUE, THEN WE MUST BE GOING TO HELL

What do these headlines mean, *simply as selling statements*, even to the computer hack? What reason do they give you for reading the copy when other advertisers use headlines like this:

INTRODUCING FIVE *NEW* WAYS APC SMART-UPS INCREASES
NETWORK RELIABILITY

or

GET THE ROUTER THAT PAYS FOR ITSELF

Then why are so many headlines like the first two groups still used? Probably because somewhere, somehow, some advertisers or copywriters thought they were clever and cleverness would lead to readership and sales.

Quite obviously those headlines do not offer anything. Then they must be intended to arouse curiosity. Do they? Read them over and see for yourself. Does the headline, "Put Up. Or Shut Up." arouse your curiosity? You may reply, "Combined with the illustration, the headline may have meant something." The answer is that this particular advertisement had no illustration. And the illustration of almost all the other advertisements, then and now, while clever, were of little or no value in making the headline message clear.

The purpose of headlines must be to convey a message to people who read only headlines, then decide whether or not they will look at the copy. But do the first two groups of the preceding headlines convey any reason to read further? None whatever.

Perhaps the writers of these advertisements would say, "But you should read the entire advertisement. Then you will see how beautifully the headline ties up with the copy." This is laughable. What reader cares how well the headline ties up with copy? Do people read advertisements backwards? No. They read the headline first. Only then, if they are interested, do they read the copy. The business of judging a headline after you read the copy is wrong. It takes for granted that everybody reads the copy.

For example, the headline of the following advertisement taken from *The New York Times* means little or nothing until you read the copy:

IT'S SURE!

IT'S PERMANENT!

IT'S ALL MINE!

This is the feeling you get when the monthly Life Income starts under a Retirement Annuity.

The monthly income can begin at any time between 50 and 70. It is a most attractive self-pension plan.

Retirement Annuities are obtainable in $100 investment units. Income is also guaranteed in event of total and permanent disability. A substantial cash return is guaranteed if you do not reach retirement age.

ABC LIFE INSURANCE COMPANY

Compare that meaningless headline—which was probably mistaken for a permanent wave advertisement—with this homely but effective mail order headline/picture caption:

CORN GONE IN 5 DAYS OR MONEY BACK

There's a headline that says something. There's a headline that stands up on its hind legs and talks to its audience in a language they understand. The picture of a man's foot with a corn plaster helped to make the meaning of the headline absolutely clear.

Analyze the headline. "Corn Gone!" Instantly the man with foot troubles knows he is being spoken to. "In 5 Days!" "Better yet," he says. . . . "Or Money Back." . . . "Sold!" he cries.

The best headlines are the ones that aim at a specific audience and offer that "target market" something its readers want and want badly.

Another thing: In order to impress your offer on the mind of the reader or listener, it is necessary to put it into brief, simple language. Your prospective customers may be in a hurry. They may be half asleep as they turn the pages, or browsing the channels of their TV sets. Their thoughts are a thousand miles from you and your product. No far-fetched or obscure statement will stop them. You have got to hit them where they live—in the heart or in the head. You have got to catch their eyes or ears with something simple, something direct, something they want.

A QUICK FIRST TEST FOR HEADLINES

For consumer products or service, read your suggested headlines to several people without telling them what you are trying to sell and get their reactions. For technically sophisticated products, use an audience familiar with the field. If they would not *immediately* look at the copy, try again . . . and again . . . and again. In his autobiography, David Ogilvy tells of writing 104 headlines and trying them out on his associates before he came up with the classic: "At 60 miles an hour the loudest noise in the new Rolls-Royce comes from the electric clock." If Ogilvy needed help in picking a headline winner, you certainly needn't be bashful in following in his footsteps.

> *Given a good product, the American advertising industry does an efficient, imaginative and essential job of information and promotion and makes an important contribution.*
>
> Dwight D. Eisenhower

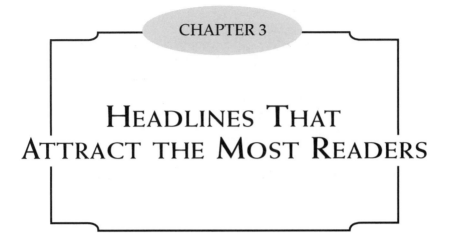

CHAPTER 3

HEADLINES THAT
ATTRACT THE MOST READERS

As Caples often pointed out, *few, if any, headlines work forever.* But the lessons to be learned from his analyses of *why* these examples worked—very well and very long—are fully applicable today. We can take them with us and apply them, regardless of media innovations, into the twenty-first century—and probably beyond.

This chapter discusses ten successful headlines and tells what made them successful. Here is headline No. 1.

1. HOW A FOOL STUNT MADE ME A STAR SALESMAN

The advertisement bearing this headline sold a large number of correspondence courses in salesmanship. The ad was repeated many times in many publications. Obviously the success of the ad was due largely to its unusual headline. Let us, therefore, examine the headline and see what special qualities it possesses. Perhaps we can inject some of these good qualities into our own future headlines.

This particular headline does two things: (1) It arouses the readers' curiosity by making them want to know what the fool stunt was. And (2) it appeals to their self-interest by offering to tell them how to become a star salesman.

The copywriter could have written the headline this way:

HOW I DID A FOOL STUNT

This is a good curiosity headline and would have attracted a number of readers.

On the other hand, the copywriter could have written the headline this way:

HOW I BECAME A STAR SALESMAN

This is a good self-interest headline and would have captured the interest of many prospects.

By combining the two features, curiosity and self-interest, into a single headline—"How a fool stunt made me a star salesman"—the copywriter produced one of the most successful mail-order advertisements of its day.

One other point: In addition to curiosity and self-interest, the headline possesses a third important quality. It suggests that here is a quick and easy way to become a star salesman. If the headline had read, "How two years' training made me a star salesman," it would not have been so attractive.

Let us look at a few other tested, successful headlines and see if we can discover the secret of their success. Take, for example, the headline of one of the best advertisements for a book of etiquette:

2. WHAT'S WRONG IN THIS PICTURE?

The illustration in the advertisement showed two women walking along the street escorted by a man. The man was shown walking between the two women.

The chief virtue of this headline is its curiosity value. It is a challenge to the reader. Readers suspect that they know what is wrong in the picture, but they have to read the copy to make sure. Thus the headline accomplishes its main purpose. It gets the reader into the copy.

Another virtue of the headline is its appeal to the self-interest of the reader. Readers take it for granted that they will find in the text of the advertisement the answer to the question, "What's wrong in this picture?" Thus they will get free information, a free lesson in etiquette.

Here is a successful headline for a course in memory training:

3. HOW I IMPROVED MY MEMORY IN ONE EVENING

This is primarily a self-interest headline. A great many people think they have poor memories. Hence, a method of improving one's memory is bound to be attractive. The headline also suggests that the method is quick and easy, that results may be obtained in a single evening.

Next is a successful headline for a mail order book on the subject of personality development. Although the value of a book of this kind may be questioned by some people, this caption proved to be a powerful one:

4. GIVE ME 5 DAYS AND I'LL GIVE YOU A MAGNETIC PERSONALITY . . . LET ME PROVE IT—FREE

This is a self-interest headline. People want to be liked by other people. They want to be popular with their friends. This advertisement offers to tell the reader how to accomplish this by means of a magnetic personality.

The headline also suggests that here is a quick, easy way to become magnetic. The method is apparently quick because the headline says it takes only five days. The method seems easy, because there is apparently no effort required on the customer's part. The headline does not say, "How you can develop a magnetic personality." It says, "Give me 5 days and I will give you a magnetic personality."

Here is a headline that was used with excellent results to introduce a new business course for executives:

5. ANNOUNCING

A NEW COURSE AND SERVICE FOR MEN AND WOMEN WHO WANT TO BE INDEPENDENT IN THE NEXT FIVE YEARS

This is primarily a news headline. It announces something new. It also strikes a strong self-interest note with the words "for men and women who want to be independent in the next five years."

Here is the headline for an advertisement selling a device for people who are hard of hearing. This advertisement brought a large number of orders.

6. THE DEAF NOW HEAR WHISPERS

This is primarily a self-interest headline. It appeals directly to the proper audience and offers them the thing they want; namely, an invention that aids the deaf. There is also curiosity value in this headline. The reader wonders, "What can this device be that enables formerly deaf people to hear whispers?"

Here is a headline for a mail-order course in selling real estate. The advertisement bearing this headline was highly successful and was repeated many times.

7. WANTED—YOUR SERVICES AS A HIGH-PAID REAL-ESTATE SPECIALIST

This is purely a self-interest headline. It offers jobs—highly paid jobs. There are plenty of men and women in this country who are dissatisfied with their work and their pay. It would be difficult for these men and women to pass this advertisement without reading it.

It should be further noted that the word "wanted" has always been a good attention-getter. Readers instinctively stop to find out what is wanted. They think perhaps they can furnish the thing that is wanted and make a profit for themselves.

Here is the headline of an advertisement that brought excellent results:

8. ANNOUNCING A NEW HOME MONEY-MAKING PLAN

This headline is a combination of news and self-interest. The words "announcing" and "new" give the news flavor. The self-interest element is expressed in the words "Home Money-Making Plan."

Here is the headline for an advertisement that was notably successful in selling a set of books containing the World's Greatest Literature:

9. "NO TIME FOR YALE—TOOK COLLEGE HOME," SAYS WELL-KNOWN AUTHOR

This is primarily a self-interest headline. It is aimed at those who never had a college education and who would welcome an opportunity to continue their studies.

Sometimes a mail-order advertisement can be run for years without wearing out. Here is the headline of just such an advertisement. The product being sold is a course in self-improvement.

10. I GAMBLED A POSTAGE STAMP AND WON $35,840 IN 2 YEARS

Here again is a headline that appeals primarily to the reader's self-interest. Who wouldn't like to gamble a postage stamp and win $35,840?

This headline also contains curiosity appeal. The reader would like to know how on earth it is possible to gamble so little and win so much. Furthermore, the plan seems easy. There is no suggestion in the headline that any effort is required on the part of the reader. All you have to do is to gamble a postage stamp and the same big winnings may be yours.

Anyone experienced in advertising can probably guess the plot of this advertisement, yet it proved phenomenally successful. Even readers who know about "the headline game" may well want to play! The postage stamp the reader is asked to risk is the stamp necessary to send for the free booklet that tells about the self-improvement course.

WHAT MAKES CERTAIN HEADLINES SUCCESSFUL?

Having discussed ten headlines, all of which were outstandingly successful in their respective fields, let us see what qualities they possess in common. Then, perhaps we can formulate the test of a good headline. Here are the qualities: Two of the headlines were news headlines. Four employed curiosity as a means of getting the reader into the copy. Four suggested that here is a quick and easy way to accomplish certain results. Ten of the headlines—or, in other words, every single headline— offered the readers something they wanted and therefore appealed to their self-interest.

This analysis suggests that there are four important qualities that a good headline may possess. They are:

1. Self-interest

2. News

3. Curiosity

4. Quick, easy way

Self-interest is by far the most important of these headline qualities. News comes next in importance. Department stores and other users of tested copy employ the news angle to a large extent in their newspaper advertising.

Another important point, which has not been mentioned, is believability. In striving to produce an attractive headline, the copywriter should not emphasize the "quick, easy way" to such an extent that the headline becomes unbelievable. One aid to believability is to use specific figures. Note the frequent use of specific figures in the aforementioned successful headlines. For example: "Give me 5 days. . . ," ". . . in one evening." ". . . $35,480 in 2 years."

DO ADVERTISING AWARDS INDICATE TRUE MERIT?

In considering advertising awards, always remember this: If you want a real judgment of the selling power of an advertisement or direct-response mailing, that judgment must be based on scientific, measurable results. *All advertisements shown in this edition are based on such documentation.*

WHY NONSCIENTIFIC ADVERTISING WINS ADVERTISING AWARDS

Unless results are based on such scientific evaluation, there are a half dozen reasons why judges are apt to select poor headlines:

Reason Number One: Before voting on a headline, the members of the jury read the copy. Thus, the meaning of many an obscure headline is made clear to them.

The reading public uses the reverse method. If the headline is obscure, they do not bother to read the copy.

Reason Number Two: Advertising juries are usually composed of men and women who want to raise the image of the advertising business. This is a praiseworthy undertaking. Nevertheless, every advertising professional must answer this question: Shall I spend my clients' money to raise the image of the advertising business? Or shall I spend the money to increase their sales?

Reason Number Three: The following two life insurance headlines were judged by an advertising jury:

WHAT WOULD BECOME OF YOUR WIFE IF SOMETHING HAPPENED TO YOU?
GET RID OF MONEY WORRIES FOR GOOD!

The jury favored the first headline because it seemed to be the more logical for life insurance. Also because it is more altruistic and higher toned. Yet actual sales results showed that the second headline was more effective.

Reason Number Four: Advertising juries give too much weight to fine writing. As a matter of fact, there is little sales value in fine writing. It is what you say that counts, not how you say it. A valid argument presented in blunt language will sway the reader more than a less valid argument beautifully presented.

Reason Number Five: The business of judging advertisements in a conference room creates a false atmosphere. The judges are not buyers. They are advertising critics, and as such they cannot always tell which advertisements would sell them.

Reason Number Six: Advertising effectiveness can usually be judged only by sales or by some action that may lead to a sale, such as writing for a booklet or a sample. The real judge of advertising is the woman who says to her grocer, "No, I don't want Blank's Soap. I want that kind I saw advertised in the newspapers last week."

More and more advertising professionals and manufacturers are becoming sold on the idea that there should be less guessing and more testing in the advertising business. The anecdote that follows is typical of the reasons why:

> A set of mail order ads of known results were submitted to 14 advertising clubs. Each club was requested to present these ads to its members and ask them to pick out the best-selling ads.

> About 50 percent of the judgments of these experienced advertising men and women in the 14 advertising clubs were wrong when compared with the actual sales results of the ads.

> Therefore, it must be reasonable to assume that 50 percent of all advertisements are ineffective and that even expert advertising judgment *without testing* is unsafe in prejudging the selling power of an ad.

Do not depend on opinions. Use some kind of objective test to determine the relative effectiveness of advertisements.

The spider looks for a merchant who doesn't advertise so he can spin a web across his door and lead a life of undisturbed peace!

Mark Twain

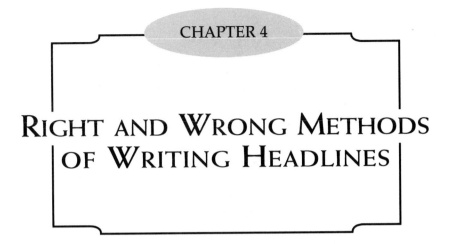

RIGHT AND WRONG METHODS OF WRITING HEADLINES

In the preceding chapter, we analyzed ten outstandingly successful headlines and found that self-interest was the principal quality they all had in common.

Following are the headlines of ten advertisements that were outstanding failures. Each of these ten advertisements was tested by running it in a magazine or newspaper in which previous advertisements had been tested. These advertisements brought so few inquiries and so few sales that they were never used again. Let us consider the headlines of these failure advertisements so that we will know what sort of headlines not to write.

TEN HEADLINES THAT FAILED

"NO . . . NO . . . DON'T CALL ON ME!"
[Course in Public Speaking]

THE ODDS ARE 9 TO 1 AGAINST YOU
[Business Training Course]

"I'LL NEVER GIVE ANOTHER PARTY," SHE SOBBED
[Book of Games for Parties]

A TEST OF HOW "WELL READ" YOU ARE
[Book of Literary Gems]

IS WORRY ROBBING YOU OF THE GOOD THINGS OF LIFE?
[Life Insurance]

THE TROUBLE WITH MANY MARRIED MEN IS . . .
[Life Insurance]

ARE YOU PLAYING FAIR WITH YOUR WIFE?
[Life Insurance]

ARE YOU LIVING IN A CIRCLE?
[Budget Book]

THE YEARS THAT THE LOCUST HATH EATEN
[Business Training Course]

LETTERS WIVES DON'T WRITE TO THEIR UNSUCCESSFUL HUSBANDS
[Business Training Course]

In reading over these unsuccessful headlines, perhaps you decided in your own mind what made them unsuccessful. See if you agree with the following analysis:

1. All ten headlines are primarily curiosity headlines. For example, the headline, "The Trouble with Many Married Men Is . . ." attempts to get the readers into the copy by making them want to find out what, if anything, is the trouble with many married men.

2. None of the headlines gives news.

3. None of the headlines contains an offer of a benefit that appeals to the reader's self-interest.

4. Seven of the headlines are negative. They paint the dark side of the picture. For example, "`I'll never give another party,' she sobbed."

Having analyzed ten successful headlines in the previous chapter, we should now be able to set down a few fundamental rules for writing a good headline.

FIVE RULES FOR WRITING HEADLINES

1. First and foremost, try to get self-interest into every headline you write. Make your headline suggest to the readers that here is something they want. This rule is so fundamental that it would seem obvious. Yet the rule is violated every day by scores of writers.

2. If you have news, such as a new product, or a new use for an old product, be sure to get that news into your headline in a big way.

3. Avoid headlines that merely provoke curiosity. Curiosity combined with news or self-interest is an excellent aid to the pulling power of your headline, but curiosity by itself is seldom enough. This fundamental rule is violated more often than any other. Every issue of every magazine and newspaper contains advertising headlines that attempt to sell the reader through curiosity alone.

4. Avoid, when possible, headlines that paint the gloomy or negative side of the picture. Take the cheerful, positive angle.

5. Try to suggest in your headline that here is a quick and easy way for the readers to get something they want.

In using this last suggestion—as mentioned previously—be sure to make your headline believable. Here is the headline of an advertisement that was tested by a correspondence school:

TO MEN AND WOMEN WHO WANT TO WORK LESS AND EARN MORE

This seems to sum up in a few words what people have wanted ever since the world began. Yet the advertisement did not bring many replies, probably because the headline was unbelievable. It seemed too good to be true.

ADDITIONAL AIDS TO HEADLINE WRITING

Having set down five fundamental rules for writing a good headline, let us now consider a few other aids to headline writing that have been proven by actual sales tests. Here are 13 proven pointers for writing successful headlines:

1. A sensible point of view to take in writing a headline is this: Try to decide what would make you buy the product. Actually try to discover in your own mind what argument would make you, the writer of the headline, part with good money in order to buy the product or service you are advertising. Then express in a few words this reason for buying. That is your headline.

2. Do not try to make your headline so short that it fails to express your idea properly. Brevity in headlines may be an excellent quality, but it is not so important that all else should be sacrificed for it. It is more important to say what you want to say—to express your complete thought even if it takes 20 words to do it—or 12 or 24, as in the very successful ads in Figure 4.1.

When Lisa Cooper Sold Her Mother's Jewelry For $12,000, She Made A $4,000 Mistake.

Visit The Fabrikants And You Won't Make The Same Mistake.

*or four generations the Fabrikant fa
for integrity, fair dealing and the pi
watches, gold, diamonds and other fin
For your private, no obligation co
and a free appraisal by a GIA graduat
or Brian Fabrikant at (212) 382-2270.
If you're calling from out of town
1-800-581-GEMS (4367).*

abrik
FINE DIAMO

The Jewelers Building / 576 Fifth A
New York, NY 10036 / (212

Don't Even Think About Selling Jewelry Without An Offer From The Fabrikant Family.

*or four generations sophisticated collectors have made the
Fabrikant Family their primary resource for fine watches,
diamonds, gold and other valuable signed and unsigned jewelry.
This constant demand enables the Fabrikants to pay you more.
Assure yourself of getting the most for your jewelry by calling
Andrew, Peter, Sherry or Brian Fabrikant at (212) 382-2270 or
if you're calling from out-of-town 1-800-581-GEMS.*

abrikant
FINE DIAMONDS, Inc.

The Jewelers Building / 576 Fifth Avenue (Bet. 46th & 47th St.)
New York, NY 10036 / (212) 382-2270

~ OPEN SATURDAYS ~

NYC Dept. of Consumer Affairs Lic. #0897408

Figure 4.1: *What's in a [newspaper] name?* Though the Fabrikant name was established in the diamond community, it was unknown to the general public. Therefore the creation of a personalized approach featuring a single person, Lisa Cooper, with whom the prospects could relate. That ad and its "Don't even think about selling" companion ran in *The New York Times* and were instant successes, leading to a twelve-fold increase in advertising in just three years. Since many respondents lived in upscale New Jersey communities, the schedule was expanded to include their suburban papers . . . with practically zero additional response. When it came to diamonds: the medium was, and is, the message!

Here is a lengthy but excellent headline for a travel bureau. It tells a complete story:

THIS SUMMER THE WEST IS YOURS FOR AS LITTLE AS $827 AND UP . . .

ALL-EXPENSE TOURS
14 THRILLING VACATIONS TO CHOOSE FROM

This headline would have been far less effective if the writer, for the sake of brevity, had merely said:

THIS SUMMER THE WEST IS YOURS

Here is another lengthy but effective headline. It appeared at the top of an advertisement for the New York Telephone Company:

A 3-HOUR TRIP FOR A $10 ORDER! . . .
IT WOULD HAVE TAKEN 3 MINUTES BY TELEPHONE

3. Avoid the "dead" headline—the type of headline that sounds as if it were written to be carved on a bronze tablet or uttered in a solemn conclave by the chairman of the board of directors. Here are examples:

UNUSUAL TIMES
UNUSUAL VALUES

THE VALUE IN QUALITY

TRUE OPTIMISM

4. Avoid the "too smart" headline—the headline that instead of making the readers want to buy your product simply makes them exclaim "How clever!" Examples:

WOMEN! READ THIS SUMMERY SUMMARY

BANQUET SIZE
FAMILY WISE

WHY NOT GIVE EMERALDS AWAY?

5. Avoid the meaningless headline. Examples:

A PLAIN FACT FOR PLAIN PEOPLE
WHEN, AS AND IF . . .

6. One way to persuade people to read an advertisement is to suggest in the headline that the copy contains useful information. Examples:

ADVICE TO WIVES WHOSE HUSBANDS DON'T SAVE MONEY

7. Get the big point of your advertisement into your headline. Use your headline as a hook to reach out and catch the special group of people you are trying to interest. It is an old saying that shoemakers' children usually have poor shoes. Below is an example of a modern parallel—a poor advertisement for an advertising consultant. The advertisement occupied a full page in a trade magazine. The reason it is poor is because the idea that should have been expressed in the headline is not expressed in the headline, but in small print in the last paragraph of the advertisement. Here is the actual advertisement:

ADVERTISER'S NOTE

Mr. A.B. Jones
Director of
X.Y.Z., LTD.
London, England

the well-known and old established international advertising agency responsible for handling a number of American advertising accounts in various parts of the world, will be in New York from May 12th to 20th. Advertisers and agents wishing to consult them with regard to overseas markets should write to:

Mr. A.B. Jones
c/o Blank Agency, Inc.
Fifth Avenue
New York

The last line of this advertisement contains the words "overseas markets." That is the point of the entire advertisement. It is addressed to advertisers and agencies who want data regarding overseas markets. Yet this fact is not mentioned until the end. It should have been mentioned in the headline in order to attract the proper audience. An advertiser who was actually looking for data regarding overseas markets might read the headline of this advertisement and turn the page, not realizing that the copy contained the very data he wanted.

8. Although curiosity alone is seldom enough to make a good headline, it is an excellent idea to get curiosity into your self-interest headlines. For example, here are two purely self-interest headlines:

HOW I SAVED MYSELF FROM BALDNESS

MAKE $200 A DAY

Notice how these headlines are improved by revising them so that they arouse curiosity in addition to offering the reader something he or she wants:

HOW A STRANGE ACCIDENT SAVED ME FROM BALDNESS

IS $200 A DAY WORTH A POSTAGE STAMP?

Advertisements bearing these headlines were used in magazines. The advertisements were extremely successful and were repeated over and over again for years before sales fell off to a point where the cost of the advertising space was greater than the profits from the sales.

Compare the aforementioned tested headlines with the following headlines taken from untested advertisements:

MEN MAY NOT ADMIT IT, BUT . . .

CHILDREN SHRIEK WITH JOY

LOOK TO THE SEA!

What hopeless, useless, senseless headlines! They say nothing, mean nothing, sell nothing. Yet scores of advertisers are using headlines that are just as bad. It is unfortunate that these advertisers do not test their copy. Or is it fortunate perhaps? Sometimes ignorance is bliss.

9. Headlines that are merely a statement of fact are not effective in getting people to read copy. For example:

WHEN DULL FILM COVERS TEETH, SMILES LOSE FASCINATION
[Toothpaste manufacturer]

NOTHING ROLLS LIKE A BALL
[Ball bearing manufacturer]

The reason that these headlines are not effective in getting people into the copy is that the reader knows what the copy is going to say without reading it. It is going to say, "Use Brand X Toothpaste" . . . "Use Brand Y Ball Bearings." However, this type of headline does have the advantage of getting a brief message across to people who read only headlines.

10. The advertiser's logotype at the bottom of the ad can be considered as part of the headline. After reading the headline, the reader instinctively looks down at the logotype to see what company the message is from. Thus, the headline writer can count on the name of the company to supplement and make clear the meaning of the headline. For example, the following four advertisements all have the same headline, but the headline means something different in each case, owing to the different logotypes.

END MONEY WORRIES

[copy and illustration]

The New York Business Training Institute

This advertisement suggests that here is a method of ending money worries either through (1) some system of accounting, or (2) through a course of training that will enable a man or woman to earn more money.

END MONEY WORRIES

[copy and illustration]

Life Insurance Company

This advertisement suggests that here is a plan for ending money worries by means of life insurance.

END MONEY WORRIES

[copy and illustration]

Macy's Department Store

This advertisement suggests that you may end money worries by means of the money you save through Macy's reduced prices.

END MONEY WORRIES

[copy and illustration]

First National Bank

This advertisement obviously is a suggestion to end money worries through some plan for saving money.

The effect of the advertiser's logotype must be considered when writing a headline.

11. What is true of the logotype is also true of the picture used to illustrate the advertisement. The picture may be used to supplement and help make clear the meaning of the headline. For example, a successful mail order advertisement had the headline, "Fat Men." This headline would not be entirely clear if it weren't for the fact that the illustration showed a fat man being pulled in at the waistline by a reducing belt.

12. Avoid the "hard-to-grasp" headline—the headline that requires thought and is not clear at first glance. Here are examples:

DEPENDABILITY—A WORD THAT GREW OUT OF A FACT

COMING AND GOING THROUGH NEW ORLEANS,
THE TOURING THOUSANDS PAUSE AND REFRESH THEMSELVES

IF EVERY WIFE KNEW WHAT EVERY WIDOW KNOWS,
NO HUSBAND WOULD BE WITHOUT LIFE INSURANCE

Remember that the readers' attention is yours for only a single, involuntary instant. They will not use up their valuable time trying to figure out what you mean. They will simply turn the page.

13. Do not run advertisements without headlines. Some advertisers do this in the mistaken notion that it is smart, modern, and sophisticated. Because they do not test their advertising, these advertisers do not realize that about the only person who reads their copy is the proofreader who is paid to read it.

You can't expect people to read your message unless you first give them, in the headline, a powerful reason for reading it. To run an advertisement without a headline is like opening a store without hanging out a sign to tell people what kind of store it is. A few customers may come into the store, but many prospective customers will be lost.

If there is any exception to this rule, it is one in which an excellent picture of the product is used. For example, a beautiful, four-color picture of a bowl of delicious peaches with the name Del Monte at the bottom of the page conveys a message without a headline.

HEADLINE-WRITING TECHNIQUES

Write a number of headlines for every advertisement and then select the best one. The person who submits a dozen answers in a prize contest has a better chance of winning than the person who writes only one answer. In the same way, the copywriter who writes a dozen headlines has a better chance of writing a good one than the copywriter who writes only one headline.

If you have time to write as many as 25 headlines, you increase still further your chances of writing a good one. Put the headlines away and read them over the next day. Try to take the point of view of the bored customer. Try to decide which headline would be most likely to stop you if you were turning the pages of a magazine or a newspaper and you were not interested in the advertising at all.

Before you make your final decision as to which headline to use, it is a good idea to show your list of possible headlines to someone who has never seen them before. Let some person whose judgment you have found good in the past act as copy chief.

You should not trust your own judgment entirely. You may be prejudiced. You are too close to the headlines you have just written. A headline whose meaning may be perfectly clear to you may be puzzling to someone else.

If you could put your headlines away for a month and then read them, you might be able actually to view them from the customer's angle. But you can't wait a month. Therefore, get the customer's reaction today by showing your headlines to someone else.

Often a headline may have two meanings, one of which you do not suspect. For example, a copywriter recently showed me an allegorical piece of copy, the first sentence of which was:

DAVID DROPPED GOLIATH

This sentence gave me a mental picture of David holding Goliath up in the air and suddenly dropping him to the ground. That is not the impression the copywriter wanted me to get. He wanted to say that David knocked out Goliath or that David felled Goliath.

HOW TO HANDLE LONG HEADLINES

As mentioned previously, a long headline that really says something is more effective than a brief heading that says nothing. It is important, however, to handle the long headline correctly. Here are two headlines taken from a national magazine showing examples of the wrong way to handle the long headline.

WHY
MY SECOND DUPLEX IS THE ONLY CAR
I HAVE EVER BEEN ABLE TO PAY CASH FOR

THERE'S SATISFACTION IN
KNOWING
THE APPEARANCE OF YOUR BATHROOM
IS PLEASING TO GUESTS

The trouble with the arrangement of these headlines is that the words in large print are words that by themselves mean nothing. If you are going to emphasize certain words in the headline, be sure that they are words that say something.

Here are two headlines taken from a national magazine showing examples of the correct way to handle the long headline. Notice that the emphasized words are words that mean something.

NO MATTER WHERE YOU LIVE YOU NEED AMPLE
WINDSTORM INSURANCE

BRAND X'S
FINE COFFEE
IS SERVED IN THE HOME
OF EACH OF THESE SURPRISINGLY DOMESTIC BACHELORS

Two ways to handle the long headline are

1. Print the entire headline in the same size type.

2. Play up one or more important words of the headline in capitals, or extra-large, or extra-bold type.

The trouble with the first method is that a long headline all printed in the same size type gives the effect of a gray tone across the page. It is flat, uninteresting. Nothing sticks out to stop the reader.

The second method is the better. It overcomes this disadvantage. It has three factors in its favor:

1. By their very size, these words act as a "stopper."

2. The words in large or bolder print, if they are the right words, help to select from the audience your "target audience," the special group who are prospects for your product.

3. These words in large or bolder print get a brief message across to these prospects—a message that is almost impossible to miss, no matter how fast the reader turns the page.

Here is another example of the correct application of this method of handling headlines. Consider the following headline, which sells subscriptions to a weekly book review magazine:

CAN YOU TALK ABOUT BOOKS
WITH THE REST OF THEM?

When this headline was used, it was printed this way:

CAN YOU TALK
ABOUT BOOKS
WITH THE REST OF THEM?

The proper audience was targeted, and their interest aroused by the message that appeared in larger or bolder type.

Some headlines do not lend themselves to this sort of emphasis. It is impossible to pick out two or three or even five words that tell the story briefly. In cases of this kind, there are two things you can do:

1. Recast the headline.

2. Put half the headline in larger or bolder type and subordinate the rest of it.

Here are some more examples of the right way—as in Figure 4.2—and wrong ways to emphasize certain words in headlines:

Wrong	**THE SECRET** OF HOW TO BE TALLER
Right	THE SECRET OF HOW TO **BE TALLER**
Wrong	**THE FINEST QUALITY** ALUMINUM RAILINGS MONEY CAN BUY
Right	**ALUMINUM RAILINGS** THE FINEST QUALITY MONEY CAN BUY
Wrong	**NOW IS THE TIME** TO BUY GOOD FURNITURE
Right	**GOOD FURNITURE** NOW IS THE TIME TO BUY IT
Wrong	**AT LAST** A HAIR SPRAY MADE FOR DRY HAIR
Right	AT LAST A HAIR SPRAY MADE FOR **DRY HAIR**
Wrong	**HI-POWER** AUTOMATIC ELECTRIC PAINT SPRAYER
Right	HI-POWER AUTOMATIC ELECTRIC **PAINT SPRAYER**

Figure 4.2: *Emphatically CAPS!* The only problem with John Caples' suggestion to capitalize individual words for emphasis is knowing which words to pick. Few advertisers do this as well as Toyota. (Why not capitalize "good" in the headline? Because GOOD . . . GOLD is a stopper, not a start-up to the rest of the copy.) Individual words and short phrases such as BEST . . . AMERICA . . . REP-UTATION . . . GOLD STANDARD . . . AIR BAGS . . . POWER . . . RESTYLING . . . and BROCHURE add the emphasis of 19 subheads without using even one. Placing the headline beneath the main illustration and putting the product name in both captions are selling bonuses too often forgotten.

Some of the wrong emphasis that you will find in ad headlines is because an ad writer has handed to the designer or layout artist a typed piece of copy and left it up to the artist to decide which headline words to emphasize. This is unwise. The writers should sit down with the artists and help them to select meaningful words to emphasize. Artists tend to think in terms of tone values and masses of light and shade. If the balance of a layout is helped by putting the first word or the last word of the headline in large letters, the artist may do it regardless of the meaning or lack of meaning. I once heard the following amusing exchange between a writer and an artist:

"The trouble with artists is that they think ads should be looked at but not read," said the writer.

"The trouble with writers is that they think ads should be read but not looked at," said the artist.

The net of it is that the best ads are produced when writer and artist work together as a team.

LESSONS FROM CURRENT PUBLICATIONS

It is instructive to look through current magazines and newspapers and compare the headlines being used by some of the general advertisers with the headlines being used by the mail order advertisers—the advertisers who can trace the sales results from every ad.

The headlines below are taken from a single copy of a magazine. Notice the vagueness and supposed cleverness of the general headlines (List No. 1) as compared with the simple directness of the mail order headlines (List No. 2).

List No. 1—Headlines used by General Advertisers

YOUR LUNCHEON ON MANY A SUMMER'S DAY!

WHAT'S RIGHT WITH THE WORLD WHEN GIRLS JUST WILL BE BOYS?

THIS NOSE BELONGS TO A THRIFTY WOMAN

BLANK'S CANDY—THE FIFTH THAT MAKES THE FOURSOME

LUCKY BABY

FIRST YOU LISTEN! THEN JUST DIP IN YOUR SPOON

IT WON'T GO OFF!

List No. 2—Headlines used by Mail Order Advertisers

BE A HOTEL HOSTESS

BANISH TEETERING FURNITURE

LIFETIME FLOOR COATING

SPARE-TIME CASH

KILL ANT COLONIES AT THEIR SOURCE

SPRAY YOUR WEEDS AWAY WITH WEED OUT

MATERNITY FROCKS

START A $10,000 LIFE INSURANCE POLICY FOR $1

THE FABULOUS FORD MODEL T FIRE ENGINE (SEE FIGURE 4.3)

HOLLYWOOD'S MAKE-UP SECRET

Could anything be more simple or more direct than these mail order headlines? They are telegraphic. They get the story to you in a few short words. They are absolutely clear and understandable.

Mail-order ads of this kind are repeated again and again. Sometimes they last for years before their effectiveness is worn out.

Advertising nourishes the consuming power of men. It creates wants for a better standard of living. It sets up before a man the goal of a better home, better clothing, better food for himself and his family. It spurs individual exertion and greater production.

Winston Churchill

Figure 4.3: *The most valuable list of all.* First, test to your own "house" list of proven, satisfied direct response buyers. If you can't sell them, why would you advertise? No one does such testing better than the marketers at The Franklin

Mint. Quick response from personalized mailings tell the likelihood of success and final ads incorporate changes (can you find five?) to make it even better. Note the "Please mail by . . ." date in both reply card and coupon. It works.

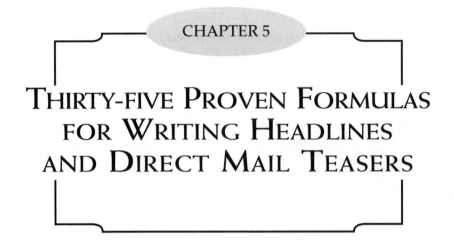

THIRTY-FIVE PROVEN FORMULAS FOR WRITING HEADLINES AND DIRECT MAIL TEASERS

Formulas are applied to the writing of stories, plays, and popular songs, and to the creation of dramas that are broadcast daily on television. Can formulas be applied to writing headlines and teasers for advertisements?

The answer is yes. Many successful headlines have been written by this method. This chapter presents a checklist of 35 headline formulas that have worked successfully in the past and may be expected to work successfully in the future.

As you review these formulas, with your product or service in mind, you may find a formula that will give you a good headline you can use. If not, you may be stimulated to invent a new formula. New formulas are being invented all the time. Or you may find that an old formula can be reworked into a new pattern. This list of formulas is not intended to hamper your creative thinking, but to guide your thinking into profitable channels. Use the formulas not as a crutch but as a springboard!

And remember, if you create a good headline, your task is more than half completed. It will be a relatively easy matter to write the copy. On the other hand, if you use a poor headline, it doesn't matter how hard you labor over your copy because your copy will not be read.

The headline formulas listed here can be applied, not only to advertisements in publications, but also to headlines printed on the outer envelopes of direct mail pieces. The same formulas can be used in writing the opening sentences of radio and television commercials.

NEWS HEADLINES

Let's begin with news headlines. One of the most important functions of advertising is to present new products and to tell about new uses and new improvements of old products. Department stores use news head-lines because they bring people into the stores. Mail-order advertisers use news headlines whenever possible because they are good pullers. News headlines are effective in getting attention and promoting sales. Therefore, the first eight of these headline formulas are devoted to the presentation of news.

Here is the first formula:

1. BEGIN YOUR HEADLINE WITH THE WORD "INTRODUCING"

INTRODUCING [Brand Name]. A NEW GENERATION OF AFFORDABLE ART MATERIALS FOR STUDENT ARTISTS.

INTRODUCING POLARFLEECE FOR THE HOME [Note Product Name]

INTRODUCING ASPEN-GPS SYSTEMS

INTRODUCING A SPECIAL GIFT FOR A SPECIAL TIME OF YEAR

INTRODUCING THE ALL-NEW FORD TAURUS

INTRODUCING FOUR NEW WAYS TO SAY I LOVE YOU EVERY DAY [Cat Food]

INTRODUCING A NEW WAY TO HELP BRIDGE THE GAP BETWEEN WHAT YOU'VE SAVED AND WHAT YOU'LL NEED DURING RETIREMENT

2. BEGIN YOUR HEADLINE WITH THE WORD "ANNOUNCING"

ANNOUNCING A GREAT NEW CAR

ANNOUNCING A NEW DICTIONARY

ANNOUNCING A NEW SELECTION OF [Brand Name] VIDEO CAMERAS

ANNOUNCING NEW FIRESTONE TIRES

ANNOUNCING A NEW HELP IN SOLVING THE HOMEOWNER'S PROBLEM

The word "Announcing" can take different forms. For example:

GULF ANNOUNCES A NEW AND DIFFERENT GASOLINE

AN IMPORTANT ANNOUNCEMENT TO HOMEOWNERS

3. USE WORDS THAT HAVE AN ANNOUNCEMENT QUALITY

FINALLY AN EXCITING NEW LOOK THAT ISN'T RETRO ANYTHING

THANK YOU FOR MAKING US AMERICA'S TRUCK COMPANY

PRESENTING NEW 36" TALL BALLERINA DOLL

TODAY'S DUPONT SPONGE WITH MOP-UP ACTION

GOOD-BYE . . . OLD-FASHIONED AIR CONDITIONERS

JUST PUBLISHED . . . A NEW ENCYCLOPEDIA

Whenever a new product or a new improvement of an old product arrives on the market, you should announce that fact. Announce it in a big way—as in Figure 5.1. Spread the word "Introducing" or "Announcing" clear across the page in large type. People are interested in announcements. They will often read an announcement of a new improvement or a new product regardless of whether or not they have any immediate need for the product.

Announcement copy is not a recent invention. The ancients used it. Many ancient advertisements were announcements in the form of proclamations.

After you have introduced your new product or your new improvement, you can continue to retain the news element in later advertisements by using formula four.

4. BEGIN YOUR HEADLINE WITH THE WORD "NEW"

NEW LEMON BLOSSOM PIE

NEW STANDARD DRIVER AIR BAG. NEW ERGONOMIC INTERIOR. NEW 4-WHEEL AB5. NEW 6-CD CHANGER. MORE POWERFUL ENGINE.

NEW PROGRESSO 100% WHITE MEAT CHICKEN SOUP

NEW 10 CHANNEL HAND-HELD GPS ONLY FROM MAGELLAN

NEW BLACK & DECKER ELECTRIC DRILL

NEW METHOD OF KEEPING YOUR PERSONAL FINANCES

When you have used the word "New" for all it is worth, you can continue to give a news flavor to advertisements by employing formula number five.

5. BEGIN YOUR HEADLINE WITH THE WORD "NOW"

NOW IN PAPERBACK!

NOW . . . LEARN BOTH WAYS TO WRITE FOR PUBLICATION

NOW EVEN-DEPTH TILLAGE IS EVEN EASIER

BOSTON AND L.A. NOW HOURLY [Airline]

NOW ON HOME VIDEO

United Airlines proudly introduces something shockingly amazing...

Nothing.

Figure 5.1: *The only thing better than everything.* How do you introduce the new airline paperless "E Ticket"? Use a seven word teaser to fill the full newspaper page . . . followed by a single word on page two. That's sure to get the reader to the not-so-small type at the bottom. Note that these were two *consecutive right-hand* pages, not a spread.

E-Ticket℠ The new ticketing service involving no paper ticket whatsoever.
Purchase now for flights on or after September 18. Then just flash a picture I.D. at the gate and you're on.
How in the world can we do that? It's nothing.

✈ UNITED AIRLINES

Here is a successful headline which contains both "Now" and "New":

NOW THERE'S A SYSTEM! NEW SERIES LEADS TO GED SUCCESS

6. BEGIN YOUR HEADLINE WITH THE WORDS "AT LAST"

AT LAST! A STEAM IRON WITH A "MAGIC BRAIN"

AT LAST—YOU CAN DRIVE ALL OVER EUROPE
WITH ONE EASY-TO-FOLLOW ROAD ATLAS

AT LAST—A TOOTHBRUSH GUARANTEED FOR 6 MONTHS

Using the words "At last" creates the impression that here at last, after long preparation, is a product that many people have been waiting for.

A variation is to put the words "at last" at the end of your headline, like this:

HAS A REMEDY FOR THE COMMON COLD BEEN FOUND AT LAST?

Here are two approaches to "at last" news quality without using the actual words:

FINALLY PROFESSIONAL FLEA CONTROL AT A FAIR PRICE

IMAGINE AN AUTOMOBILE SO PRECISELY ENGINEERED IT FEELS AS IF IT
WERE FORMED FROM A SINGLE PIECE OF STEEL

7. PUT A DATE INTO YOUR HEADLINE

BEGINNING JUNE 1 . . . LOW SUMMER RATES AT THE MIAMI BILTMORE

ONE DAY ONLY. SUNDAY, AUGUST 6TH. 10:00 AM TO 6:00 PM
[Piano Sale]

JULY SALE OF FASHION GLOVES

MONDAY SAVE 30% TO 60% ON THESE BOOKS

WHY G.E. BULBS GIVE MORE LIGHT THIS YEAR

A 19— [InsertYyear] WARNING FROM THE WALL STREET JOURNAL

REDUCE YOUR GOLF HANDICAP WITH THESE NEW 19— [Insert Year]
GOLF CLUBS

HOW TO KEEP AHEAD THIS SUMMER

YOU CAN SPEAK FRENCH BY OCTOBER 15

8. WRITE YOUR HEADLINE IN NEWS STYLE

THE WINES YOU LOVED IN PARIS ARE HERE

BETTER HEARING IS SUDDENLY HERE

THE WORLD'S FIRST ATOMIC WATCH

MODERN GIFT FROM OLD MEXICO

DISCOVERED—AMAZING WAY TO GROW HAIR

ALL BIPOLARS ARE NOT CREATED EQUAL [Awards Story]

COMFORT, WARMTH, QUIET AND SAFETY. A REMARKABLE HEATER.

THE MYTHS ABOUT BABIES ARE GONE. AND THESE INNOVATIVE TOYS HAVE TAKEN THEIR PLACE

Other words and phrases that give a news flavor are "Just invented," and "Just off the press."

Here is a successful news headline that appeared at the top of an advertisement selling business courses by mail:

JUST PUBLISHED

A NEW BOOKLET ANNOUNCING

A NEW SERIES OF BUSINESS COURSES

This headline uses the news formula no less than four times: (1) Just Published, (2) new booklet, (3) announcing, (4) new Business Courses.

HEADLINES THAT DEAL WITH PRICE

Sales tests show that one of the most important factors in any sale is price. Readership surveys show that readers will often skip copy set in big type in order to get to the bottom of an ad and read prices set in small type.

The next three formulas are devoted to price. It is not always practical to mention price in national magazine ads because prices may vary in different areas. However, it is often practical and desirable to mention price in local newspaper ads and in local broadcast ads.

9. FEATURE THE PRICE IN YOUR HEADLINE

LIGHTWEIGHT G.E. PORTABLE MIXER DOES ALL MIXING JOBS . . . ONLY $27.95

MAGNIFICENT ALL-MAHOGANY DINING ROOM . . . $749

GUARANTEED 17-JEWEL QUALITY WATCHES . . . $16.95

WOULD YOU SPEND $5 TO FEEL LIKE A MILLION?

IT'S TRUE—GENUINE KIDSKIN LEATHER ONLY $29.95 [Shoes]

"KILLER $500 CD PLAYER" [Note strengthening of price value through use, of quoted testimonial.]

10. FEATURE REDUCED PRICE

This formula, as seen in Figure 5.2, is constantly used by retail advertisers, as follows:

WITH UP TO $2,000 IN OPTIONS SAVINGS, IT'S MORE ATTAINABLE THAN EVER [Auto]

WOOL TWIST BROADLOOM USUALLY $12.95 SQ. YD. . . . SALE $8.88 SQ. YD.

PIGSKIN EXECUTIVE FILE CASE $19.80 (Reg. $35)

WAMSUTTA SUPERCALE SHEETS . . . SLIGHTLY IRREGULAR . . . $3.95 (If Perfect $6.95)

National advertisers also use this formula sometimes. For example:

WHALE OF A COFFEE SALE . . . $2.00 OFF

LESS THAN HALF PRICE . . . STAINLESS STEEL KITCHEN SETS

11. FEATURE A SPECIAL MERCHANDISING OFFER

In this type of headline, you often make an offer that actually causes you to lose money. You do this in order to entice a customer to start using your product. Examples:

FOR BIG THIRSTS. 48 OZ. 49¢

DOUBLE THE TRADE-IN VALUE ON YOUR FUR

BIG PERENNIAL OFFER . . . 10 DELPHINIUMS $1

SPECIAL 1/2 PRICE INTRODUCTORY OFFER . . . 8 MONTHS $8

30-DAY SUPPLY OF VITAMINS FOR $2.65

ANY 4 BOOKS (VALUE UP TO $43.95) FOR ONLY $1 EACH [Note that you must mention "shipping and handling," if there is such a charge.]

Figure 5.2: *Make eight words do the work of eight hundred!* While not technically a "rebus," the use of the illustrations in Hudson's ad has much the same effect by "telling" the breadth of the clearance without having to go into wordy detail. Note that three of the four figures look straight out to catch the eyes of the reader. In communities with only a single Hudson's, the address appears below the store name.

12. FEATURE AN EASY PAYMENT PLAN

Sales tests show that the offer to sell merchandise on the installment plan creates many sales that otherwise would be lost. Many ads mention easy payments in the copy. Some successful ads have featured this appeal in the headline. Examples:

ORDER NOW . . . PAY AFTER JANUARY 10

ONLY $2 A WEEK BUYS THIS NEW CASSETTE PLAYER

NO MONEY DOWN . . . EASY PAYMENTS WHEN YOU BUY CYCLONE FENCE

13. FEATURE A FREE OFFER

A free offer is a device that frequently leads to future sales. The free offer may take several forms as follows: (1) a free trial; (2) a sample of the product or service; (3) a booklet about the product; or (4) a premium that requires the purchase of the product, (5) or a combination of any of the four. (See Figure 5.3). Examples:

FREE 10-DAY TRIAL OF THREE-RECORD ALBUM

FREE PLATO AND ARISTOTLE

FREE TRIAL LESSON

FREE CONSULTATION

FREE TO BRIDES . . . $2 TO ANYONE ELSE

FREE GRAY HAIR TREATMENT

FREE PLANS FOR A CLEVER VALENTINE'S DAY PARTY

"Free" does not have to be the first word, but unless you are testing a hidden offer, be sure it gets special emphasis:

WHEN YOU DONATE $10 TO EASTER SEALS, WE'LL DONATE A MOTOROLA PORTABLE TO YOU FREE [Cellular Phone Service]

A SMALL BUSINESS OFFER JUST FOR YOU. GET AUGUST FREE [Telephone]

100 FREE HAIRCUTS. IF YOU'RE FREE SATURDAY, SO ARE WE.

BUY A NEW WHIRLPOOL OVER-THE-RANGE MICROWAVE AND GET THIS [Counter] SPACE FREE [A Different Kind of "Free" Offer]

14. OFFER INFORMATION OF VALUE

People buy newspapers and magazines to read articles that give them information. Therefore, it is possible to get high readership by writing your ad in the form of a helpful article. The copy usually consists of three parts, as follows: Part 1: Information without sales talk, Part 2:

Information interwoven with sales talk, Part 3: All sales talk. Here are examples of headlines of ads of this kind:

ONLY ONE OF THESE SAFETY FEATURES CAN HELP YOU AVOID AN ACCIDENT

INSIDER'S GUIDE TO OLD BOOKS, ETC.

MINISKIRTS AREN'T THE ONLY WAY TO FEEL YOUNG

IF YOU WANT TO SEE WHERE THE WORLD IS GOING, LOOK HERE [University]

DO YOU MAKE THESE MISTAKES IN ENGLISH?

STRAIGHT FACTS ON WHEN TO TAKE PROFITS

TWO EASY TUNA "SHORT PIE" DISHES WITH BISQUICK

BARRON'S TELLS HOW "SOAPLESS SOAP" IS CREATING NEW MARKETS

FOLLOW THIS AGRICO PLAN TO A GREENER LAWN

15. TELL A STORY

People buy magazines in order to read fiction and nonfiction stories. Therefore, you can get high readership by writing a headline that offers the reader a story. In addition to high readership, this method offers the following advantages, as seen in Figure 5.4: (1) A good story makes your message clear; and (2) a good story makes your message compelling. The effectiveness of stories was illustrated long ago by the parables in the Bible.

Some of the following headlines not only sold merchandise or services, but also became famous.

HOW I IMPROVED MY MEMORY IN ONE EVENING

THEY LAUGHED WHEN I SAT DOWN AT THE PIANO

THE DIARY OF A LONESOME GIRL

HOW I BECAME POPULAR OVERNIGHT

OFTEN A BRIDESMAID BUT NEVER A BRIDE

DURING THE FIRST MONTH, WE RECOMMEND YOU PULL OVER EVERY FEW HUNDRED MILES TO GIVE YOUR GRIN MUSCLES A REST [Auto]

MRS. ROGERS' 4TH GRADE CLASS PROVED HEROES REALLY DO LIVE OUTSIDE [Theme Park]

THE TALLEST RECYCLING STORY EVER TOLD

Note: The most successful story headlines (from a sales standpoint) are those that select the right audience. For example, the aforementioned headline selling a memory course contains the word "memory" in the headline.

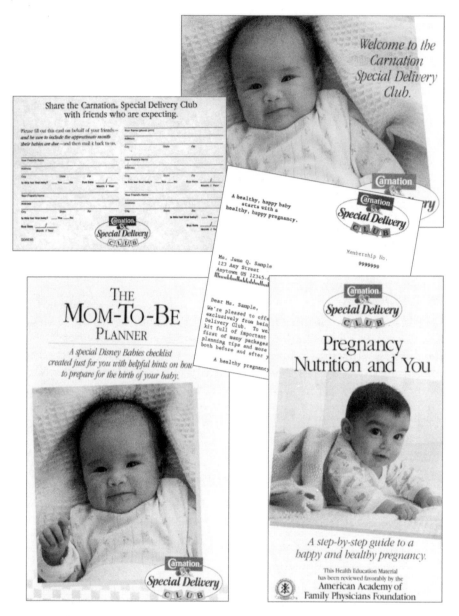

Figure 5.3: *Relationship marketing for success.*

PROBLEM: 90% of the infant formula market was locked into pharmaceutical companies' hospital- or doctor-recommended brands.

SOLUTION: Be the only supplier to use consumer advertising to speak directly to prospective and new mothers. Use magazines, television, and point-of-purchase to extol the benefits of something new and unique: Carnation's FREE "Special Delivery Club."

Enrollment by the hundreds of thousands provided a member-get-member data base at half the single membership cost. Members got personalized mailings that helped in planning from pregnancy through birth, and in caring for infant and mother thereafter.

RESULT: Carnation's relationship marketing effort has been successful far beyond expectation. In a stagnant category between 1992 and 1995, it doubled its market share. Perhaps greatest compliment of all, competitors started their own "clubs" too!

Figure 5.4: *Just the facts, but make it interesting.* Put your facts into story form to make them stick in memory, Begin with the headline (12 miles!) Continue with weave and yarn. (You may not remember what shirtmakers call it, but you're impressed.) Tell about and illustrate a few of the sewing steps (not all 69), about your use of "super durable" buttons (only 62 in the whole world), and 120 lock-stitched buttonholes. Tell a story with about a dozen facts in all, plus the promise of a great price and a free catalog. Put the headline under the picture and give the same code to the 800 number and the coupon. Hear the phones begin to ring off the hook!

USING KEY WORDS IN HEADLINES

The next ten formulas deal with key words.

16. BEGIN YOUR HEADLINE WITH THE WORDS "HOW TO"

Certain key words in headlines not only increase readership, but also have a beneficial effect on copywriters by forcing them to write copy that is in the proper groove. For example, if a headline begins with the words "How to," the copywriter is forced to write copy that tells how to do something, and that is exactly the kind of copy the reader desires.

HOW TO TURN 40 WITHOUT TURNING TO BIFFOCALS [Disposable Contact Lenses]

HOW TO BRING HOME THE RIGHT HOME-THEATER RECEIVER

HOW TO USE THE BATHROOM [Public-Service Water Usage Guide]

HOW TO DO CENTRAL AMERICA ON $17 A DAY [Utility Vehicle]

HOW TO END MONEY WORRIES

HOW TO GET A BETTER POSITION

HOW TO START A BACKYARD GARDEN

HOW TO KEEP YOUR HUSBAND HOME . . . AND HAPPY

People are interested in learning how to do things. They will eagerly read advertisements that tell them how to do the things they want to do.

The words "How to" have also been found valuable in other forms of writing. One time I said to a magazine editor, "Mail order advertisers discovered long ago that advertisements whose headlines begin with the words 'How to' bring a large number of inquiries."

The editor replied, "We discovered the same thing in our work. Magazine articles whose titles begin with the words 'How to' are popular with readers. Such articles actually increase circulation."

Closely related to the above headlines are those beginning with the word "How."

17. BEGIN YOUR HEADLINE WITH THE WORD "HOW"

"HOW DO I CONNECT MY BUSINESS TO THE INTERNET?" 1-800-827-ETC.

HOW MANY A DOWN-AND-OUT KITCHEN HAS BEEN REFORMED

HOW THIS NEW INVENTION IS REVOLUTIONIZING CONCRETE CONSTRUCTION

HOW YOUR ENERGY CURVE RESPONDS TO THE WORLD'S QUICKEST HOT BREAKFAST

HOW I EARN MY LIVING IN 4 HOURS A DAY

HOW I STARTED A NEW LIFE WITH $7

HOW PEPPERIDGE FARMS BREAD HELPS YOU KEEP THAT RADIANT LOOK

HOW CAN THESE MAGNIFICENT NATURE GUIDES BE SOLD FOR ONLY [PRICE]?

18. BEGIN YOUR HEADLINE WITH THE WORD "WHY"

WHY THESE VITAMINS CAN MAKE YOU FEEL PEPPIER

WHY YOUR FEET HURT

WHY G.E. BULBS GIVE MORE LIGHT THIS YEAR

WHY SOME PEOPLE ALMOST ALWAYS MAKE MONEY IN THE STOCK MARKET

19. BEGIN YOUR HEADLINE WITH THE WORD "WHICH"

WHICH STOCKS WILL OUTPERFORM THE S&P 500® OVER THE NEXT 12 MONTHS?

WHICH IS THE BEST BATTERY VALUE FOR YOUR CAR?

WHICH OF THESE FIVE SKIN TROUBLES WOULD YOU LIKE TO END?

A slightly different handling of this formula is seen in the following:

DO YOU HAVE THESE SYMPTOMS OF NERVOUS EXHAUSTION?

This type of headline has two advantages: (1) It is interesting. It appeals to the readers' keen interest in themselves. They like to find out if their own difficulty is among those mentioned. (2) The mentioning of a number of symptoms enables the copywriter to cover much ground. Almost every reader is likely to have at least one of the symptoms.

20. BEGIN YOUR HEADLINE WITH THE WORDS "WHO ELSE"

WHO ELSE WANTS A WHITER WASH—WITH NO HARD WORK?

WHO ELSE WANTS A KISSABLE COMPLEXION WITHIN 30 DAYS?

WHO ELSE HAS HAIR THAT WON'T STAY COMBED?

21. BEGIN YOUR HEADLINE WITH THE WORD "WANTED"

WANTED! MAN OR WOMAN WITH CAR TO RUN STORE ON WHEELS

WANTED. AUTOGRAPHS AND HISTORICAL DOCUMENTS

WANTED. A FEW GOOD MEN [For many years, the recruiting slogan of the U.S. Marine Corps]

WANTED—YOUR SERVICES AS A HIGH-PAID REAL-ESTATE SPECIALIST

WANTED—SAFE MEN FOR DANGEROUS TIMES

The word "Wanted" is a compelling word. It makes the reader curious to know what is wanted. Furthermore, the headline "Wanted—Your services as a high-paid real-estate specialist" suggests a great demand for real-estate specialists. As mentioned previously, this particular headline belonged to a couponed advertisement and appeared again and again in many magazines—proof enough of its effectiveness!

22. BEGIN YOUR HEADLINE WITH THE WORD "THIS"

THIS SOOTHING BEAUTY BATH IS ASTONISHING TO FASTIDIOUS WOMEN

THIS HOLIDAY SEASON, STAY AWAY FROM YOUR RELATIVES [Hotel Chain]

THIS KIND OF LUXURY IS LIKE STEPPING BACK INTO THE 1980S. EXCEPT THIS TIME YOU CAN ACTUALLY AFFORD IT. [Auto]

THIS IS THE QUIETEST DISHWASHER IN AMERICA

THIS FRIENDLY SIGN . . . EVERYWHERE

Beginning a headline with the word "This" has two advantages: (1) It makes the headline specific and, (2) It draws attention to the product you are advertising.

23. BEGIN YOUR HEADLINE WITH THE WORD "BECAUSE"

BECAUSE YOUR PET'S QUALITY OF LIFE IS IMPORTANT TO YOU [Cat Food]

BECAUSE FLEAS COME BACK

24. BEGIN YOUR HEADLINE WITH THE WORD "IF"

IF THEY GAVE AWARDS FOR CASH MANAGEMENT, WE'D BE THANKING THE ACADEMY

IF THEY EVER BUILD AN AUTOBAHN STATESIDE, YOU'LL BE READY

IF PEOPLE SEEM TO BE WORKING FASTER, IT'S NOT THE COFFEE [Office Machine]

IF YOU SAVOR GROWTH AND SECURITY, WE GIVE AN EDGE

IF YOU THINK THE ULTIMATE SPEAKER SYSTEM WOULD HAVE A SUBWOOFER, YOU'RE HALF RIGHT

IF YOU WANT A WORTHY COMPARISON, ASK TO SEE IT IN GREEN [Motorcycle]

Here is an "if" formula that has practically unlimited application:

IF YOU THINK YOU CAN'T AFFORD [Product or Service], YOU HAVEN'T CHECKED [Special Discount, Leasing Terms, etc.]

A formula that has been proved by advertisers who use keyed copy is to offer advice. This is accomplished employing formula number 25.

25. Begin Your Headline with the Word "Advice"

ADVICE TO A YOUNG PERSON STARTING OUT IN BUSINESS

ADVICE TO HUSBANDS

ADVICE TO BRIDES

The word "Advice" suggests to the readers that they will discover some useful information if they read the copy. The headline doesn't ask them to buy anything. It simply offers free advice. Naturally, this is an attractive offer. After you have enticed the readers into the copy, you can include sales talk in addition to advice.

The preceding ten formulas employing key words do not exhaust the list of key words you can use. You can find other key words in the headlines you see in daily newspapers and in the titles of books and magazine articles. For example, in the following titles, the key words are printed in italics:

PLAIN TALKS WITH HUSBANDS AND WIVES

COMMON FAULTS IN ENGLISH

PRINCIPLES OF ELECTRICITY

WHAT EVERY GIRL SHOULD KNOW

FACTS YOU SHOULD KNOW ABOUT SKIN CARE

26. Use a Testimonial-style Headline

Your headline can be an actual testimonial or it can be a testimonial-style headline. Here are three examples of each:

LET ME TELL YOU HOW I REDUCED FOR KEEPS

WHY I CRIED AFTER THE CEREMONY

I WAS GOING BROKE—SO I STARTED READING *THE WALL STREET JOURNAL*

"DISCOVER THE GREATEST VALUE IN HIGH-END LOUDSPEAKERS" [Quoted from Magazine Review]

"AFTER MONTHS IN THE TAKLA MAKAN DESERT, NOT ONLY DO WE SWEAR BY THIS PROTECTION SYSTEM, OUR CAMELS LOVE IT TOO" [Clothing]

"DO YOU HAVE ANY IDEA HOW MUCH FAT IS IN THIS CREAMY CHOCOLATE PUDDING? NONE." [Person Speaking Is Pictured]

27. OFFER THE READER A TEST

CAN YOUR SCALP PASS THE FINGERNAIL TEST?

CAN YOUR KITCHEN PASS THE GUEST TEST?

CAN YOU PASS THIS MEMORY TEST?

A TEST OF YOUR WRITING ABILITY

28. USE A ONE-WORD HEADLINE

Advertisers who run small ads are sometimes able to find a single word that can serve as a headline. This method is successful if the single word is meaningful and selects the right audience. The method has the advantage that the single word can be printed in big type and thus give big display to a small ad. Examples:

ACCOUNTING	LAW
AVIATION	PATENTS
DIAMONDS	NERVES
REDUCE	CORNS
BASHFUL?	VITAMINS

You can take it for granted that these one-word headlines are effective. Otherwise, mail order and patent medicine advertisers would not continue to use them year after year.

Two all-time classics as one-word headlines are HERNIA and SEX. The former sold trusses and appeared for decades in the classified-advertising sections of men's magazines such as *Popular Mechanics*. It was so successful in finding and selling its targeted audience that the Hahn agency begins its analysis of each proposed headline with the words: "Where's the 'hernia'?" The second classic has appeared for more than 50 years in hundreds of college papers just before the end of the school year in a fairly large ad somewhat like this:

SEX
Now that we have your attention, here's how to get the most money for your used text books . . . etc.
(Book Store Logo)

29. USE A TWO-WORD HEADLINE

Sometimes it is impossible to find a single word that will convey a meaningful message about your product or service. In that case, you can use a two-word headline. Thus, the 1996 equivalent of the one-word Hernia now uses the two-word headline: HERNIA TRUSSES. Other examples:

> FREE MONEY (COMPUTER PROGRAM FOR BANKING) For this all-time two-word winner, see Figure 5.5.
>
> BE STRONG [Foods]
>
> ENGINEERING OPPORTUNITIES
>
> FARM ANIMAL
>
> WALK SOFTLY [Hiking Footwear]
>
> GOOD RIDDANCE [Skin Cream]
>
> ABSOLUT PARIS [One of a Series Using Well-Known Place Names]
>
> ITCHY SCALP
>
> DIAPER RASH
>
> PUBLIC SPEAKING
>
> HEAD COLD

30. USE A THREE-WORD HEADLINE

> BURN FAT FASTER
>
> GET AUGUST FREE [Long-Distance Service]
>
> EXPAND WITH STYLE [Home Remodelers]
>
> DOUBLE BONUS SALE!

31. WARN THE READER TO DELAY BUYING

Most headlines urge you to buy something. Therefore, a headline advising "Don't buy" is an effective stopper. Examples:

> BUY NO DESK UNTIL YOU HAVE SEEN THE NEW, ALL-STEEL EXECUTIVE
>
> READ THIS BEFORE YOU ORDER YOUR ZOYSIA GRASS
>
> DON'T BUY CAR INSURANCE UNTIL YOU HAVE READ THESE FACTS
>
> BUY NO MORE SOAP UNTIL YOU HAVE TRIED AMAZING NEW [Name of Brand]

For a limited time, Microsoft® Money for Windows® 95 is yours free from Chemical Bank.

At Chemical, we believe the best way to bank is the way that's best for you. That's why we've introduced Online Banking. It's the most efficient way ever to manage your money, because now you can download your account information directly into Microsoft® Money for Windows® 95. You can even pay your bills and E-mail our Chemical Customer Service Department, right from your PC. And if you sign up before January 31, 1996, we'll give you Microsoft® Money for free.

For more information or to get started with Online Banking today, call 1-800-CHEMBANK.

 **CHEMICAL**

Expect more from us

©1995 Chemical Bank. Member FDIC. Microsoft and Windows are either registered trademarks or trademarks of Microsoft Corporation in the United States and/or other countries.

For the hearing-impaired, call 1-800-48-ASSIST.

Figure 5.5: *Make an offer they can't refuse.* The ultimate in *New York Times* full-page, two-word headlines. Three insertions generated 578 calls and 349 applications the first week. Nuff said.

Sometimes there are totally unexpected—and delightful—consequences. When Rand McNally was forced to delay the introduction of a new line of school maps at the major buyers' convention, advertising manager Jack Heimerdinger (now an independent consultant in Plainfield, IL), rented billboards surrounding the convention site. His message:

> ## DON'T BUY MAPS
> UNTIL YOU SEE THE REP
> FROM RAND MCNALLY IN BOOTH 138

A few weeks later, Andrew McNally III told Jack that several presidents of competing map companies had called to chide him for the negative approach. "I told them I was surprised to hear that, since it was the most successful map sales convention *we've* ever had."

Even more surprises followed. Since no other company immediately purchased the billboards at this popular site, they remained up for four more educational conventions, even though Rand McNally was not exhibiting. At the conclusions of each of those shows, Jack got a call from the advertising manager of the company occupying Booth 138. Each had the same story: "We just want you to know that your billboards gave us the biggest traffic we've ever had. And lots of them bought, once they got over the surprise of finding us there. Let us know when you do that again!"

32. LET THE ADVERTISER SPEAK DIRECTLY TO THE READER

WHY I OFFER YOU THIS NEW KIND OF PIPE FOR $5

I'LL TRAIN YOU AT HOME FOR A GOOD JOB IN COMPUTER PROGRAMMING

YOU'VE EARNED IT. NOW ENJOY IT. [Auto]

CONSIDERING WHAT RUNS THROUGH SEWER PIPES, IT'S A GOOD THING YOU'LL ONLY HAVE TO TOUCH OURS ONCE

BABY TEETH HAVE SPECIAL NEEDS. PEDIATRICIANS RECOMMEND [Name] TOOTH AND GUM CLEANER

I GUARANTEE YOU RESULTS WORTH $2,000 IN ONE YEAR

THEY THOUGHT I WAS CRAZY TO SHIP LIVE MAINE LOBSTERS AS FAR AS 1,800 MILES FROM THE OCEAN

33. ADDRESS YOUR HEADLINE TO A SPECIFIC PERSON OR GROUP

TO A $25,000 MAN OR WOMAN WHO WOULD LIKE TO BE MAKING $50,000

TO CAR OWNERS WHO WANT TO CUT GASOLINE BILLS

FOUR WORDS FOR THE BEST FOREIGN LANGUAGE PROGRAM EVER!
FREE. FAST. FUN. GUARANTEED

TIRED OF THE DAILY GRIND? TRY OUR MONTHLY GRIND. [Coffee]

WE TAKE HEART CASES OTHER HOSPITALS WON'T

ALLERGY SUFFERERS: ASK YOUR DOCTOR FOR AN ALLERGY MEDICINE
THAT UNSTUFFS YOUR NOSE

[Company] IS ALL SET TO HELP YOU MAKE MONEY ON THE INTERNET

YOU TOO CAN BEAT THE MARKET [News Service]

NOBODY MAKES THE NET EASIER THAN [Company]

TWENTY-FIVE MILES. YOU'RE WORKING HARD. BUT COULD YOU BE
WORKING HARDER? [Sports Drink]

YOUR KNEES WILL THANK YOU. [Running Shoes]

GROW UP. NOT OLD.

TO YOUNG MEN AND WOMEN WHO WANT TO GET AHEAD

TO MEN AND WOMEN WHO WANT TO RETIRE ON A GUARANTEED
INCOME

This type of headline does two important things. First, it selects your logical prospects. Second, it offers the prospects a solution to some problem close to their hearts.

34. HAVE YOUR HEADLINE ASK A QUESTION

WHAT GOOD ARE FREQUENT FLYER PROGRAMS IF THE MILES TAKE OFF
BEFORE YOU DO?

DID YOU KNOW YOU CAN GIVE YOUR DOG PERFECT NUTRITION?
[Another ad Substitutes "Cat" for "Dog."]

WILL WE EVER RUN OUT OF TREES? [Forest Products Company]

WOULD YOU BELIEVE THE [Milk] JUG ON THE RIGHT IS 45% LIGHTER?

CAN YOU FIND THE 26 DIFFERENT PRODUCTS FROM AMWAY®
IN THIS PHOTO?

35. OFFER BENEFITS THROUGH FACTS AND FIGURES

[NAME] BURNS UP TO 79% MORE CALORIES THAN ORDINARY TREADMILLS

BECAUSE WE RECYCLE OVER 100 MILLION PLASTIC BOTTLES A YEAR,
LANDFILLS CAN BE FILLED WITH OTHER THINGS. LIKE LAND,
FOR INSTANCE.

FOR $5,000 LESS THAN AN [Auto Model], YOU CAN HAVE A FEATURE
THAT'S PRICELESS.

Here's one that combines testimonial with facts and figures:

JOHN TIMMONS TESTED THE $530 [Bicycle Model] AND DECLARED IT
PERFECT FOR YOU.

SUMMING UP

Headline formulas are selling ideas that have worked again and again
in the past and can be expected to continue to get results in the future.
For example, the formula "Begin your headline with the words `How
to'" will probably last as long as advertising exists. Unless human nature
changes radically, people will never tire of learning how to do the things
they want to do and how to get the things they want to get.

Another form of headline that will probably never wear out is the
announcement. As long as human beings inhabit this earth, they will be
looking for something new, something different, something better.

Just as the physician uses the same prescription many times with
beneficial effect, just as the civil engineer uses the same formulas again
and again for building bridges, so can the advertising copywriter use
formulas that have worked successfully in the past.

Here is a complete list of the 35 formulas discussed in this chapter.
This list can help you in two ways: (1) as a tool to use when you need a
headline in a hurry; and (2) as a stimulus to spur your imagination
toward the invention of new formulas.

1. Begin your headline with the word "Introducing."
2. Begin your headline with the word "Announcing."
3. Use words that have an announcement quality.
4. Begin your headline with the word "New."
5. Begin your headline with the word "Now."
6. Begin your headline with the words "At last."
7. Put a date into your headline.
8. Write your headline in news style.
9. Feature the price in your headline.
10. Feature reduced price.
11. Feature a special merchandising offer.
12. Feature an easy-payment plan.

13. Feature a free offer.
14. Offer information of value.
15. Tell a story.
16. Begin your headline with the words "How To."
17. Begin your headline with the word "How."
18. Begin your headline with the word "Why."
19. Begin your headline with the word "Which."
20. Begin your headline with the words "Who else?"
21. Begin your headline with the word "Wanted."
22. Begin your headline with the word "This."
23. Begin your headline with the word "Because."
24. Begin your headline with the word "If."
25. Begin your headline with the word "Advice."
26. Use a testimonial-style headline.
27. Offer the reader a test.
28. Use a one-word headline.
29. Use a two-word headline.
30. Use a three-word headline.
31. Warn the reader to delay buying.
32. Let the manufacturer speak directly to the reader.
33. Address your headline to a specific person or group.
34. Have your headline ask a question.
35. Offer benefits through facts and figures.

As a profession, advertising is young: as a force, it is as old as the world. The first four words uttered, "Let there be light," constitute its character. All nature is vibrant with its impulse.

Bruce Barton

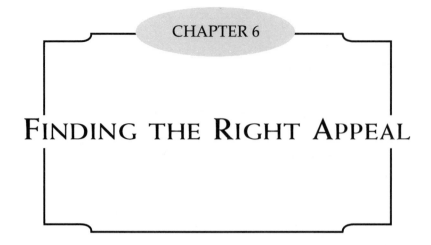

CHAPTER 6

FINDING THE RIGHT APPEAL

Early in Hahn's own advertising career, a supervisor told him that all successful advertising was based on one or more of three appeals: "Sex, greed, or fear." Further discussion brought out the expanded explanation below:

1. *Sex/sex appeal.* Not just—or even primarily—the physical act, but also love, affection, friendship.

2. *Greed.* All the things—physical and emotional—that money can buy.

3. *Fear.* Fear of losing what you have . . . of not gaining what you hope to achieve . . . or both.

4. *Duty/honor/professionalism.* Not what's in it for me, but what is best for those I serve—the right medicine, the longest lasting sewer pipes, the most effective fire engine.

The fourth appeal, that of "duty/honor," is based on Hahn's own experience promoting a Britannica fire-safety educational film. His assignment was to test possible sales to fire departments and also test different premiums to enhance sales. Without having yet heard the term "telemarketing" (you don't have to know the term to do it!), he began to telephone a dozen fire chiefs around the country and asked two questions:

- Would they like to see the film for possible purchase for their safety education programs? Uniformly, the answer was an enthusiastic "Yes!"

■ Would their firefighters prefer a large electric popcorn popper or an excellent set of chef's carving knives as a thank you for reviewing the film? The first two responses were an immediate, loud, and furious "DO YOU THINK WE'D USE A FIRE-SAFETY PROGRAM BECAUSE OF SOME (deleted) POPCORN POPPER!"

Hahn asked no more questions about premiums, but we made children's safety the promotional feature that helped create a long-term bestseller for the film's producer.

Note this. ALL four appeals concentrate on what is best for the buyer. NOT ONE of these appeals mentions what is best for the seller! The most frequent reason for unsuccessful advertising is advertisers who are so full of their own accomplishments (the world's best seed!) that they forget to tell us why *we* should buy (the world's best lawn!) Much more about this difference throughout the rest of the book.

Not too long ago, an advertisement like the following usually brought results:

(Headline) YOU CAN MAKE BIG MONEY EASILY

(Illustration of man or woman pointing finger at reader)

Today the likely attitude of the reader toward such an approach is: "Who are they trying to kid! I'd probably have to work like hell or try to sell some useless junk to my relatives and friends at five times their value."

But this does not mean that you can't use an old standby such as the money appeal. People are as eager as ever to make money. It's our advertisements that had to change. For legal as well as business reasons, they had to become more believable and definitely more honest. In advertising, as exemplified by Figure 6.1, an ounce of belief is worth a pound of half-belief!

Here are some much more believable money headlines for today:

HOW A MAN OR WOMAN OF 40 CAN PLAN TO RETIRE IN 15 YEARS
(Stock Fund)

Note the word "plan" in this headline. Remove it and the advertiser has guaranteed results.

TO THE MAN OR WOMAN WHO WANTS TO BE INDEPENDENT IN THE NEXT FIVE YEARS
(Trade school, MBA program, legal school, etc.)

A STORY OF SPARE TIME AND EXTRA CASH
(Computer training, part time employment service, etc.)

Figure 6.1: *To tell the truth.* No other advertising is regulated and monitored as closely as the financial market's. Yet good copywriting and design still find their way. The bold headline asks the question in every investor's mind. The subhead offers a possible answer without promising what it can't deliver. Text and illustration expand the free offer, with the 800 number stated twice, just in case the reader no longer has letters on a push-button phone. With everything done right, no wonder this became one of the top Smith Barney lead-generating ads in 1995!

There is no element in an advertisement more important than the appeal—the reason you give the reader for buying. If this statement seems to clash with the previous emphasis on the headline, remember that the headline and the appeal are one and the same. In successful ads, the appeal is almost always expressed in the headline.

EFFECTIVE APPEALS

Here are some appeals that continue to increase sales:

- Make more money
- Save money
- Retirement security
- Better health now
- Health care security
- Security in old age
- Advance in profession or trade
- Prestige
- Enjoyment
- Easier chores
- Gain more leisure
- Comfort
- Reduce fat
- Freedom from worry

Other effective appeals are:

The desire to be one of the "in" group. This appeal sells everything from clothing to CDs to what to eat and where to eat it.

The average person's desire for a bargain is another powerful appeal used by discount chains, department stores, supermarkets, and practically every other retailer—from bargain glasses (Buy one, get the second pair FREE!) to luxury automobiles ("Would you believe around $30,000?")

The desire to be popular, to attract attention, sells everything from cosmetics, bathing suits, and shaving cream to sports-team jackets, skiing, and off-the-road bicycles.

The desire to outshine our neighbors—and let them know it!—is an appeal that sells pricey private schools, luxury automobiles, expensive boats, luxurious homes, landscape gardening, fancy swimming pools, and so on. Unlike most other appeals, this one is often best implied rather than spoken.

The money appeal, one of the most effective of all, can be employed in a number of ways. For example, a clothing manufacturer found that of all the appeals they tried, the most effective was "Wear these high-grade clothes and you can command a better income." In a 1980s campaign, a publisher of business books found that their most effective appeal was, "Eight books that can help you make more money." (NOT "will" help . . . *can* help.) Books that got the most coupon and telephone orders were then given large individual ads for just those titles. Thus, the multibook ads were not only successful in themselves, but also became successful low-cost tests for what sold in different media. Insurance companies, banks, investment plans, stockbrokers, and many others all use the money appeal in one way or another.

PROOF OF THE IMPORTANCE OF THE APPEAL

The importance of the appeal used in advertising was brought forcibly to my attention by the following experiment. I had prepared 11 magazine full-page ads for a certain client in one year's time and analyzed the coupon returns from a test point of view. Here is the way the coupon returns looked:

Advertisement	Replies
A	218
B	666
C	240
D	191
E	502
F	511
G	263
H	550
I	867
J	194
K	210

I then arranged these advertisements in order of merit, as follows (the poorest advertisement is listed first and the best one last):

Advertisement	Replies
D (poorest)	191
J	194
K	210
A	218
C	240
G	263
E	502
F	511
H	550
B	666
I (best)	867

Notice that the foregoing 11 advertisements fall into two distinct groups:

Group 1.

The following six advertisements brought 263 coupon returns or less:

Advertisement	Replies
D	191
J	194
K	210
A	218
C	240
G	263

Group 2.

The following five advertisements brought 502 coupon returns or more:

Advertisement	Replies
E	502
F	511
H	550
B	666
I	867

Further analysis revealed this important point: Every advertisement in Group 2—the successful group—had a certain strong, specific appeal expressed in the headline of the advertisement. No advertisement in Group 1—the unsuccessful group—had this appeal expressed in the headline. In other words, the five successful advertisements, without exception, had a definite quality in common. That quality was a certain appeal around which the headlines were built. The headlines of the unsuccessful advertisements were based on several entirely different appeals. *Note this*: The unsuccessful headlines were not written without a strong appeal, but it was the wrong appeal for that product and that audience. TESTING told us which appeal would work, and it continued to work for several years thereafter.

WHAT TO LEARN FROM YOUR HEADLINE ANALYSIS

This analysis pointed to the following logical conclusions:

1. That the appeal around which an advertisement is built is vitally important.

2. That in order to be effective, the successful appeal must be featured in the headline. To get the appeal into the copy is not enough. Some of the unsuccessful advertisements had it in the copy.

One other significant point about this analysis is that Advertisement G, the best of the unsuccessful group, had the result-getting appeal moderately displayed in a subheading. Think of what it might have done, if it had been in both!

This method of analyzing a series of advertisements almost always brings out one or more significant points. It is an easy method to follow. Simply take a set of proofs and mark in the corner of each proof the number of replies or the amount of sales brought in by that advertisement. Then lay the proofs in a row in order of merit and study the advertisements to see what quality the most successful advertisements have in common. But don't just look at them; make a checklist like the one below and document *everything* that is different, or remains the same, ad by ad:

- *Headline/Subheads*. Appeal. Wording. Size. Placement.
- *Illustration(s)*. Subject. Size. Style. Placement.
- *Layout/Colors*. Any overall difference between winner(s) and loser(s).
- *Copy*. Amount. Type size and style.
- *Offer*. Including how to order or purchase.
- *Size*. Size in relation to the page on which ad appears.

- *Medium.* Name. Type. Daily, weekly, monthly.
- *Placement.* Where ad ran in relation to medium as a whole.

You will find that the successful advertisements usually possess one or more definite qualities that the unsuccessful ones do not have. For example, the successful advertisements may all have long copy, whereas the unsuccessful advertisements may have short copy, or vice versa. Or the successful advertisements may all have a certain type of illustration that is lacking in the others. The important thing is that once you have discovered the result-getting quality, you can work on it to make it even better and use it to the fullest possible extent in future advertisements.

BE YOUR OWN GUINEA PIG

One way to realize the importance of getting the right appeal is to consider the effect on yourself of two advertisements for the same product or service. For example, suppose the following two advertisements for toothpaste were shown to you:

Ad No. 1: More people buy A's Toothpaste than any other toothpaste in the world

Ad No. 2: B's Toothpaste comes in a specially patented tube, the cap of which is fastened to the tube and cannot be lost

It is obvious that Ad No. 1 contains the stronger appeal. Logic tells you that if more people buy A's Toothpaste than any other in the world, it must be superior. The other advertisement devotes too much emphasis to a minor point.

Now suppose the advertisement that tells you A's Toothpaste is the largest seller is a carelessly prepared advertisement—poor selection of type, no illustration, no use of color, just black and white. Suppose the advertisement telling you about the cap that cannot be lost is a handsome four-color job with an expensive painting for an illustration. Would you alter your decision? Probably not. The basic appeal would sway you more than the manner in which the appeal was presented.

But now make a small change in Ad No. 2. Have a cap that never has to be twisted off, but flips open effortlessly. If you aim that ad at older men and women who often have difficulty grasping smaller objects, will Ad No. 1 still be the winner? The result now is not nearly as obvious and the way to find out is to test . . . test . . . TEST!

Suppose two advertisements for business schools were presented to you. The first advertisement tells you how this particular business course helps you to make more money. It gives specific examples of men and women who have made more money by taking the course. It tells what their incomes were before they took the course and what their present incomes are.

The second advertisement speaks in general terms about the value of business training. It fails to give you specific facts and figures and proof of results.

Wouldn't you be much more apt to be swayed by the first advertisement—the advertisement that tells you exactly how much more money was made by the men and women who took the course? And again, wouldn't the facts the advertisement gave you be more important than the manner in which the facts were presented?

The layout, the illustration, and the style of type wouldn't have nearly as much effect on you as what the advertisement said. The point of all this is that what an advertisement says is more important than how it is said.

Note this: Your clients or employers are just as likely to insist on using the second version as agreeing to the first. To give yourself a better chance of winning here without a fight, do the following:

- When multiple examples of possible ads (or other promotions) are being considered, ALWAYS give management decision makers a strong recommendation on which one to run. This is *your* expertise. It's why *you* are getting paid. Earn it!

- NEVER show management decision makers your proposed ads in "rough"; that is, in a doodle-appearing version. Advertising professionals can visualize what this will turn into. Others can't!

- NEVER show a decision-maker proposed ads that are not equally "finished"; that is, not equally handsome in appearance.

- NEVER present ads that are not equally well edited. If different versions use different linguistic styles, tell why before they are read.

- If only one ad can be run and management insists it be the version you consider a sure loser, suggest that "we" use an "A/B Split" (covered in Chapter 18) to guarantee the approach. If management proves to be right, congratulate them. If you were right, don't mention it, unless you are asked.

IDEAS THAT SOUND GOOD VERSUS IDEAS THAT ARE GOOD

Another point: Appeals that sound good when described to a client or employer are not always the most effective appeals that can be used. Clever, tricky ideas often sound fine when described in a conference room. But usually some simple, basic, plain-as-the-nose-on-your-face idea will sell more goods.

A nationally advertised business school published an advertisement with this headline:

LETTERS WIVES DON'T WRITE TO THEIR UNSUCCESSFUL HUSBANDS

The advertisement featured the following beautifully written letter.

Dear Fred:

Tomorrow is our eighth wedding anniversary. Haven't the years flown by! How carefree we were, how hopefully we started out just eight years ago! You were going to work so hard and get ahead so fast, remember?

You *have* worked hard. I've seen the tired, worried lines in your face that prove it. And I've worked hard, too, since the children came—worked to make the same old salary enough for the four of us, worked to make one dollar carry the burden of two.

Understand, dear, I'm not complaining. I'm not thinking about *me*—I'm thinking about *you*. Often I've wondered, lying awake at night, why some of the men we know have gone ahead while you haven't—men who haven't any more brains and aren't half as nice as you. Remember that first disappointment when Joe Edwards was made assistant to the president? You wanted that promotion, and you were ahead of Joe. But they told you that he had the all-around training you lacked.

Dearest, it's gone on a long time now. You come home tired at night, and there are bills to pay, and we have a scene, and you say you "simply *must* make more money"—and then you never seem to *do* anything about it. Can't something be done? I want to help you succeed while we are still young. Isn't there a way?

Your loving wife,
Helen

This advertisement brought more praise from advertising professionals than any business-school advertisement in years. Ad pros who read it exclaimed, "Wonderful!" Yet the advertisement was an unqualified failure. The coupon returns failed to come in. Unsuccessful husbands didn't want another lecture from their wives—even in a beautifully written letter.

Highly praised advertisements are not always selling advertisements.

Another type of copy that testing has shown to be ineffective is copy that talks in general terms and fails to get to the point, like this ad for an investment plan:

EVERYONE IS ENTITLED TO FUN IN LIFE.

Everyone is entitled to the things that make the world worth living in.
And yet thousands of people with perfectly normal incomes
think of the good things as luxuries they can't afford.

This advertisement rambled on in this strain for several paragraphs. Finally, the reader was given a few facts. A revision in advertising approach started the copy off by telling the facts right away. *Result*: Increased inquiries and sales.

APPEALS THAT CREATED ILL WILL

Some attempted appeals not only fail to sell a product; they actually create ill will for the advertiser.

A friend once said, "Have you seen the (product) ad that shows a fat, grinning male face? It's perfectly round, with a silly ogling grin. I hate that face! It's so unnecessarily ugly."

A woman complained about a slogan seemingly aimed at her, but that she didn't understand. "That slogan is meaningless to me," she said. "Every time I see it, it annoys me."

Another friend described a point-of-sale display card that bothered him. It was an advertisement for a household insect repellent showing a picture of a woman smiling and winking one eye. The caption was "I'm wise, are you?" "That makes absolutely no sense to me," remarked my friend. "What is it supposed to mean?"

Experiences of this kind indicate that people actually feel resentment toward advertisements they don't understand. They become positively annoyed at slogans and captions whose meaning is not instantly clear.

Note this: A few complaints can crop up about any advertisement. So don't panic, but don't ignore them. Rather:

- Use them to trigger a check on advertising results.
- Determine how widespread the ill will is. If sales are good, will you lose more than you gain by a change?

The reverse of the ill-will feeling is also true. Advertisements that seem good to the readers and actually do sell them create a friendly feeling toward the advertiser.

A friendly feeling toward an advertising campaign is not always enough, however, to make the customer buy the product. An artist told me how much she admired a certain toothpaste's campaign—especially an advertisement that showed the old Greek temples on the Acropolis crumbling away. A line was drawn through the base of the temples and nearby appeared the slogan "Guard the Danger Line." "What kind of toothpaste do you use?" I asked. With a laugh, she mentioned a different brand!

People often have two reactions to advertisements—the conscious and the unconscious. The conscious judgment is their reaction to its visual or verbal impact. The unconscious judgment or real judgment comes to the surface when they go into a store to buy. *There is no better test of an advertisement than whether or not it actually sells the product*! In fact, it is the only true way of determining if your advertisement works.

In regard to the aforementioned slogan that my friend disliked, it might be argued that the very fact that she noticed it, even though unfavorably, was a point in its favor. It might be argued that the slogans she didn't notice and the advertisements she didn't remember, either favorably or unfavorably, were the bad advertisements. A famous copywriter once said, "The greatest crime advertising can commit is to remain unnoticed."

The importance of noticeability is illustrated by a story told the editor by Al May, the buyer of children's toys for a major Chicago-area retail chain. When Hahn asked him how he had selected an astonishingly ugly doll that became the year's bestseller, he said:

> When I select dolls for our stores, I find that I can divide them into three classes. First, those that produce a strong favorable impression on me. Second, those that produce a bad effect on me—that seem actually ugly. Third, those that do not affect me much one way or the other.

I always buy the dolls that have a strong effect on me. I buy the dolls that seem to me either beautiful or just the opposite. I have learned over the years that not only the beautiful dolls, but those that seem actually ugly will always be sure to attract both children's and adults' eyes.

The dolls I never buy are the ones that don't affect me one way or the other. I have found that those dolls don't sell.

What is true of dolls is equally true of children's clothing and women's dresses . . . of book covers and breakfast cereal boxes . . . of practically anything and everything from 39¢ stick pens to $39,000 autos. If it isn't noticed, how is it supposed to sell?

THE SPECIFIC APPEAL VERSUS THE GENERAL APPEAL

A dealer in used cars decided to stimulate his business with newspaper advertising. He ran some institutional advertisements with headlines such as:

BETTER AUTOMOBILE VALUES

LONG LIFE AT LOW COST

The advertisements were beautifully laid out, with borders and carefully selected type. But the results were poor. Only a few customers came to the showroom. Said the automobile dealer, "The ads looked like winners, but actually they were flops."

New copy was tried—copy featuring specific car bargains and naming the make, the year, and actual prices. The advertisements were set like the mail order advertisements in successful catalogs. Results were immediate. By actual count, three times as many customers answered the ads.

This experience is typical. It is just one more indication that elegant language and a handsome layout do not, in themselves, make a good advertisement. What you say is more important than how you say it.

In Chapter 18, there are detailed instructions for discovering successful appeals. When, after testing, you have found a successful appeal, you can use many variations of it. For example, a financial advertiser tested a number of appeals and found that an advertisement with this headline brought the best results:

GET RID OF MONEY WORRIES FOR GOOD

Similar advertisements were then prepared with headlines that contained variations of the same basic appeal. Here are the headlines:

HOW TO END MONEY WORRIES

THIS PLAN HAS HELPED THOUSANDS OF PEOPLE TO END MONEY WORRIES

HERE'S A WONDERFUL WAY TO END MONEY WORRIES

YOU CAN LAUGH AT MONEY WORRIES IF YOU FOLLOW THIS PLAN

These similar advertisements all brought excellent results.

The technique of finding and using a successful appeal can be summed up in four basic steps as follows:

1. Have a reason—not just a "feeling"—for choosing the appeals you are going to use.

2. Test a number of different sales appeals.

3. Determine the winning appeal by an analysis of results.

4. Cash in on the winning appeal by featuring it in all your advertising, whether it be space advertising, broadcast commercials, direct mail, or billboards.

This method of finding the best appeal has brought success to the world's greatest advertisers. It can do the same for you.

Let your light so shine that men may know your good works.

The Bible

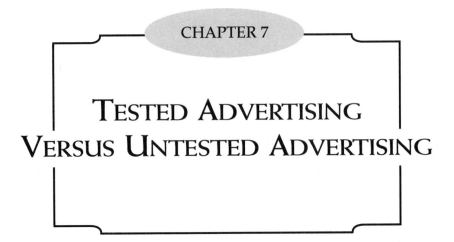

CHAPTER 7

TESTED ADVERTISING VERSUS UNTESTED ADVERTISING

Excluding elected and appointed public office holders from our consideration, three groups of people whose job it is to appeal to the public are: (1) professional entertainers, (2) sales persons, (3) advertising copywriters.

Entertainers have a definite advantage over copywriters. Take the case of a supper club comedienne. She tells a joke to the audience. The audience either laughs or remains silent. If the audience laughs, its laughter can be measured. It is either a perfunctory laugh, or a moderate laugh, or a side-splitting laugh. The point is that the comedienne knows exactly how well her joke has gone across. If she puts on her act a dozen times a week, she gets a dozen chances every week to test the reaction of the public. She can alter the manner in which she tells her jokes. No matter what she does she gets an immediate judgment of her efforts direct from the people she is trying to please.

In the case of the salesman, the prospect he is trying to sell sits or stands a few feet from him. The salesman can study the prospect's facial expression. He can listen carefully to what the prospect says. He can get a good idea of how well his sales effort is going by, noting not only the facial expression, but other body language. He can vary the sales talk at any moment in order to suit a negative reaction or special conditions. The important thing is that he gets an accurate judgment of his selling effort directly from the person he is trying to sell.

Now consider the case of the copywriters working on institutional and much other advertising that has no built-in method of measuring response. They write what they believe to be an excellent advertisement. In many cases it is one of a series. Weeks later, or perhaps months later, the advertisement appears in a publication or in a broadcast commercial.

Depending on what is being advertised, perhaps a few dealers comment on it. Perhaps a few FAXes or e-mail are sent by consumers. Is the advertisement a good one or a bad one? Who knows? The product continues to sell, so evidently the advertisement didn't do any actual harm to the business!

Perhaps sales are up. Did the advertisement cause the increase? Who knows? It is more likely that the entire series of advertisements caused the increase. But who can be sure of even that? Maybe the credit belongs to the sales force. Or maybe it's just a seasonal rise in the business. Or maybe some unknown condition is causing an increased demand. The point is that no matter whether sales are up or sales are down, it is difficult to tell, except in a general way, over a period of years, whether the advertising had much or little effect.

There are many other factors besides the advertising that have a bearing on sales. All we really know definitely is that a number of companies, such as the makers of Wrigley's Gum, Ivory Soap, and Campbell's Soup, who have advertised persistently for years, have built up big businesses.

WHY THE COPYWRITERS' JOB IS DIFFERENT

What has all this to do with the writers of advertising copy? It means that the copywriters' job is different from the jobs of the entertainer and the salesperson. The copywriters lack close and intimate touch with their audience.

This means that the writers of nonresponse advertising have a difficult job or an easy job, depending on their point of view. If they are conscientious workers and want to prepare advertising that will have a definite effect on sales, their job is difficult. They lack the quick reaction of customers to guide their efforts into the proper channels.

If, on the other hand, copywriters are merely interested in preparing some advertising to get an okay from an employer or client, their job may be relatively easy. They can sometimes go on for years writing what may be mediocre copy. The client is never called on by a delegation from the public saying, "We think your ads lack selling power."

COPYWRITERS WHO HAVE TO PRODUCE SALES RESULTS

There are whole classes of copywriters who are not offered the choice of writing either sales-producing copy or mediocre copy. Among these are the writers of department store and mail-order advertisements. These people must write advertisements that sell, or lose their jobs. The result of this situation is shown by the following bit of conversation that took place between a mail-order layout artist and writer:

"I hope we have a rainy Sunday," said the mail order copywriter to the layout artist.

The other laughed. "Why? Do you have a new ad running in a Sunday paper?"

"Yes," was the reply. "We're starting that new encyclopedia campaign, and I want the first ad to bring a lot of inquiries and orders."

Why do mail-order professionals like rainy Sundays? Because they know by past experience that rain increases coupon and 800-number returns. When the weather is rainy, more people stay at home and read the newspapers. They may watch more TV or play more video games, but newspaper and magazines get their share, and naturally they read the advertisements too.

Now consider the case of an institutional, or any other, advertisement on which results can not—or simply are not—checked. Does the writer or artist ever say, "I hope it rains on Sunday! I want a lot of people to read my ad." The chances are that no such remark will be made. Yet their advertisement is affected by the weather just as much as a mail-order advertisement is.

A mail-order advertisement has to do a *complete* selling job. And results can and almost always will be checked. Therefore everybody works hard to make it good. The copywriter works her head off to make the copy pull. The layout man employs every trick he knows to make the advertisement stand out on the page. The account executive or in-house advertising director has a lot to say about how the advertisement should look and how the copy should read. When they've all agreed, the employer or client sees the results and approves or takes a hand—criticizing, making changes, or simply offering suggestions. None of them wants to leave a single stone unturned to make the advertisement sell. No wonder mail-order advertising is so efficient. Everybody works so hard to make it good. They even pray for rain!

Note this: Pay special attention to the word "how" in the sentence above about "how copy should read." Like a classic definition of poetry, "the right words in the right place," advertising, too, is as dependent on where the words go as what they say. For instance, in the following head, would it be equally clear as a single line, or if divided between "advertising" and "disasters"?

------------◆◦◆◦◆------------

HOW NONSCIENTIFIC
ADVERTISING DISASTERS HAPPEN

Consider the attitude of a group of advertising people preparing an institutional campaign. Of course, there is much discussion as to what the advertisements should say and how they will look. But often this discussion is theoretical. It is often based on personal preference rather than on proven research and/or past experience as to what pays and what doesn't pay. The reason is that when advertising results are not tested in some manner, it is difficult to know just what does work best.

Here is a typical example of how the themes of all too many unscientific advertising campaigns are sometimes arrived at. A friend told me that his father was starting a travel agency in Philadelphia. He wanted to know how best he could advertise so that the people of Philadelphia would learn about his travel agency and be persuaded to go there to get information and tickets for travel abroad.

Having worked on several travel accounts, I was able to make a few suggestions. But I noticed that my friend was hardly listening. He was anxious for me to get through talking so that he could tell me his BIG IDEA for advertising the travel agency.

Here's what he said: "Do you remember that Christmas card our class got out during our freshman year at college? It had a beautiful picture of a square-rigged sailing ship on it. I think we could get up a wonderful advertisement built around an illustration like that. We could make it very artistic, very distinctive. We might be able to work in the initial letters P.T.A. (Philadelphia Travel Agency) on one of the sails of the ship."

My friend spent a long time describing just how he thought the advertisement should look and how the picture of the sailing ship should be printed in colors on high-grade paper.

I realized that he didn't want my advice at all. All he wanted me to do was to agree with him and say, "Yes. I'm an advertising professional and I think that's a wonderful idea."

He said he thought that his sailing ship picture would look fine in important national magazines. I told him that since practically everyone flew abroad, they might not connect a vacation to a sailing ship. And if he ran his advertisement in magazines with national circulation, the only readers who would do him any good were the tiny fraction who lived in the Philadelphia area.

My objections seemed to annoy him. All the suggestions I made seemed to annoy him too. He didn't want suggestions or objections. he wanted me to get enthusiastic about his BIG IDEA.

This is undoubtedly an extreme case—though not the only such in my experience. Yet it contains an example of how clients and employers sometimes force their advertising professionals to prepare poor advertising. The client has a pet idea he insists on using. This idea may be based on something no more substantial than a decades-old Christmas card design.

HOW MAIL-ORDER ADVERTISERS ASSURE RESULTS

In certain types of advertising, you can be as absurd as you want to be, and—providing you do not check results—nobody can ever prove that the advertising isn't good. There are no direct returns to indicate the interest or lack of interest on the part of the public.

Now let's look at the mail-order situation again. Suppose the client suggests some ineffective advertising stunt. The advertising-agency account executive will use every possible means to sell the client off the idea. She knows in advance that the advertisements won't pull, and she would rather incur the client's displeasure now than incur it later by running nonpulling advertisements. Experience tells her that once the advertisement flops, the client will forget it was his insistence on using his idea.

In the same way, if either the account executive or the copywriter should suggest an idea that is obviously poor, the client will probably kill it.

This means that every mail-order advertisement has to pass the judgment of three severe critics—the copywriter, the advertising manager or account executive, and the client. If an idea is poor, it will be killed by one of these three. No persuasive flow of theories and arguments can sell it.

What is the result of this situation? Open any publication and you can see it. In 1997, as was true in 1955, there is still an abundance of expensive decorations, the meaningless headlines, the type that is hard to read, the would-be "clever" copy, the big blocks of white space. But in 1997, as in 1955, all these belong to the untested advertisements.

Now look at print media or direct response advertisements such as Figure 7.1. What do you see? Bold-type headlines that stick out. Text set in type that is easy to read. Copy that is full of effective sales points. And no white space, because mail-order advertisers proved many years ago that white space is too often wasted space.

The following quotation, from John W. Blake's booklet "Blind Advertising Expenditure," brings out some important points in regard to tested advertising versus untested advertising:

> General advertising (as distinguished from "mail order") is frequently a structure of opinion and unproven theories. A structure without a

foundation. These theories are so deeply rooted that they have become gospel. The reasoning that brings about the spending of millions sounds logical enough. The selling propaganda that induces this investment is powerfully persuasive, and let us hasten to say, honestly believed in.

If your advertising is answered by the public, you should test not only the media, but also the individual insertions. Then keep a careful record of results. You will soon be convinced. Simple enough, isn't it? But gravely important to your pocketbook. If you have no way of testing your advertising, if your publicity is designed to send the public to retail stores, you owe it to your money, and to your business, to inject if possible some kind of "reply copy" into your advertising: a "send for free circular" appeal. Big money should never be spent on advertising until it has been tested.

Listen to the testimony of another champion of tested advertising:

When an experienced mail order man was called in to help lift the sales curve for a certain soft drink, he announced, after investigation: "The difficulty lies in the fact that the loyal customers are chiefly older people. Old-time products often suffer because friends die. To replace them one must win a new generation of friends. The solution is simple: Sampling . . . New triers . . . New buyers . . . Coupons. Let everything center around coupon costs, and proven ads that pay."

On this basis a complete plan was built and carried out. Coupon costs dropped from $1.20 each to 65¢, then to 55¢ and later to 24¢. The $1.20 coupons offered either a full-size bottle of Soft Drink Extracts at 30¢ or a capping outfit at $2.00. The later coupons offered a free sample, sufficient to make eight bottles of the beverage. The expensive coupons came from full pages in color. The low-cost coupons came largely from quarter-pages. In the year of the expensive coupons the net earnings were $224,854.18. In the year of the 24¢ coupons (three years later) the net earnings were $889,701.60.

All advertisements for this product were tested carefully and then for several seasons subjected to a "breeding" process. Eventually all the high-cost ads were pruned away and good payers were encouraged. Thus the final schedule was built of 15 tested ads. For another example of an effective sampling promotion—and a great two-word headline—see Figure 7.2.

Figure 7.1: *Yes you can*! Yes. You can protect your use of FREE SPEECH as your two-word headline. Just incorporate it into an "SM" (Service Mark) icon design to deliver an attention-grabbing message that makes no attempt to be anything other than hard-sell direct response. Direct mail produced a 10 percent response rate, (four times the sales-per-dollar of TV), an on-line telemarketing follow-up close rate of 87 percent, and transformed a costly promotion fulfillment into a revenue-generating proposition.

Figure 7.2: *If you can write a better headline* . . . The promotion used full-color inserts in scores of the nation's largest circulation newspapers—metropolitan, regional, and suburban . . . billboards in major target markets . . . radio (here left to your imagination) . . . and sampling at major dog and cat shows. Integrated marketing resulted in increased sell through at the store level, as well as customer pull where the product was not in stock. Proof that very clever *can* work very well!

A SIMPLE, INEXPENSIVE PRE-ADVERTISING TEST FOR HIGH-TRAFFIC BUSINESSES

The advertising manager of a large bank described a method of testing bank advertisements. Briefly stated, the method consists of preparing advertisements in poster form and displaying them in bank lobbies and windows. Observers are stationed to keep a record of (1) the number of people who pass the posters and (2) the number of people who are sufficiently attracted by the posters to stop and read them. For lobby posters, flyers can be distributed in pocket-racks to give more information and to help track response. It is an ingenious method of testing that can be applied by almost any high-traffic businesses such as department stores, supermarkets, and so forth.

The accuracy of the tests was indicated by the fact that tests of the same groups of advertisements in four different branches of the bank brought almost identical results.

The bank's advertising manager, reporting on the test in a trade magazine, said:

> The wide difference in the attention-value of various advertising ideas is often surprising. Of two savings advertisements displayed under similar circumstances, one stopped nine persons out of 1,000 and the other thirty-four. Of two proposed trust advertisements, one stopped six persons and the other sixteen. Some advertisements have stopped one person out of every ten. Some have attracted so small a number as to have practically no value from an advertising standpoint. Others, little different in character, have won large audiences.

> One of the lessons we have learned from our display of proposed advertisements is the increased attention-value that a national figure adds to the copy. For a time we tested posters featuring statements of prominent people about thrift and saving. Included in the list were several U.S. presidents and other famous men. All of these attracted attention far above the average. As a test, we removed the name and photograph of one of the famous men from a poster and used only the words he had spoken, not mentioning him as the author. The attention-value dropped 50 percent.

> A question that may be asked regarding all our tests is this: Is attention-value the only test of the effectiveness of the advertisement? Of course not. It is, nevertheless, fundamental.

> If an advertisement fails to attract attention, there is little else that can be said for it. It may be dignified, beautiful, and filled with sales arguments, but if not read, these good qualities cannot redeem it. The sales appeal of an advertisement, its general effectiveness, timeliness, and matters of that sort are qualities to be discussed after the fact has been established that the

advertisement can attract attention. A test of attention-value may show that the advertisement with the best sales copy attracts so few readers as to be almost worthless. Another ad, almost as strong in sales arguments, reaches many. A third, at the top in the number of readers, is weak in its presentation of a product or service. In making a choice between these advertisements, all of the facts that combine to make a successful advertisement must be considered. Attention-value is one of the most important of these factors.

THE PHILOSOPHY OF "AS IF"

One of the popular nineteenth-century German philosophies, "The Philosophy of 'As If,'" can be applied to advertising as well as to metaphysics. Prepare every advertisement "as if" it were a mail-order ad. Apply to your advertisements everything that can be learned about what works best to sell the type of product or service you will advertise. Use a mail-order-type headline, mail-order art, mail-order copy, mail-order typography, and most important, give the readers a personal reason to do what you want them to do. The chances are, more often than not, your "as if" will turn into a reality!

THE LESSONS OF THIS CHAPTER

1. You should find some way to test your advertisements so that you will know for sure which ads are effective and which are not effective. Chapter 18 tells you how to do this.

2. If you are looking for advertising ideas to use in your campaign, don't imitate the fancy art and the fancy language that you will find in the untested ads whose sales results cannot be measured. Instead, emulate and borrow from the ads whose sales are measured daily—namely, the mail-order ads, the direct-response ads, the direct-marketing ads, the department store ads. Give special attention to the tested ads that are repeated again and again. These are the ads that are paying off in sales. These are the ads that contain ideas that will pay off for you.

Advertise, or the chances are that the sheriff will do it for you.

Phineas T. Barnum

CHAPTER 8

How to Put Enthusiasm Into Advertising Copy

One day, the son of a longtime friend came to my office to tell me about a new biomedical stock. He was just an ordinary young man—not much personality. And he was not an experienced salesman. Yet he gave me one of the most compelling sales talks I ever heard.

What made him so compelling? His enthusiasm. He believed in that stock completely and implicitly. He had bought it himself. He had sold it to his friends. He was absolutely convinced that it would double in value in three months.

Later I found out that the founder of the biomedical company had talked to groups of young stockbrokers for hours, telling them what wonderful possibilities the new research had and how they were doing their clients a favor by selling them stock in the start-up company. This process of selling the sales staff was kept up until all the young men and women there were armed with an enthusiasm more compelling than years of training in the techniques of salesmanship.

Enthusiasm is just as vital in advertising as in selling. Perhaps that is the reason that for many copywriters, the toughest part of an advertisement to write is the beginning. It is hard to get started.

An advertising copywriter, working in an agency in which the creative director supplied a headline and layout concept, told me, "When I sit down to write an ad, I find myself doodling on a little pad. I chew the end of my pencil, or I glance at the blank screen. I gaze out of the window. I go to the water cooler for a drink of water.

"Finally I write a few lines of copy. Then I stare at the layout for a long time. I wonder if the headline isn't all wrong. I read over the copy I have written. I cross out a word. I rewrite a sentence.

"Later I change it back to the way it was originally. No way I fix it seems right."

WHY IT'S SO HARD TO GET STARTED

Why do so many copywriters have difficulty in getting started? There are three reasons:

1. The human brain is like an automobile engine. It works best when it is hot. When you sit down to write an advertisement, your brain is cold. This means that sitting down and writing a beginning for an advertisement is like trying to drive an automobile up a steep hill with a cold engine.

2. The experienced copywriter knows that the most important part of an advertisement is the beginning. The opening sentences must be good or readers will lose interest.

3. In agencies in which a proposed headline or layout—or both— come from a creative director, the copywriter may find them a hindrance rather than a help. What she can do about that depends entirely on the agency or in-house department for which she works. Some consider alternative suggestions. Many insist that copywriters use what they are given. The best writers welcome the challenge, waiting for the day when they become creative directors themselves.

HOW TO OVERCOME "COLD BRAIN" STARTUPS

There are several ways to overcome this difficulty. One method is to say to yourself, "I'm going to write some copy about this product, though I'll probably not use the first few paragraphs that I write. But I'll start writing anyway, and before long I'll write some copy that can be used as a beginning."

Another method is to say to yourself, "I'm not going to start writing this advertisement at the beginning. I'll start in the middle. Then, after I've warmed up by writing for a while, I'll read over my copy, pick out the best paragraph, and use it or rework it as my beginning. I'll keep on doing that at least three or four more times as I'm writing and the beginning will take care of itself."

An experienced copywriter revealed, "I don't like to write. But I do like to edit copy and I'm exceptionally good at that, so I write fast and get my thoughts down on paper or on the screen. After that, the job is merely editing."

Do advertising writers ever get "written out"? Of course they do.

One frustrated copywriter said to his new assistant, "We need a Christmas ad for the new Simplex Cellular Phone. I'm sure glad you're here to help me with it. I've been batting out Simplex once a month for the past three years and am just about written out.

"I've written ads about using them for business . . . to impress the bosses . . . and just for pleasure . . . about parents giving them to their kids . . . a wife giving one to her husband or husband to wife . . . kids giving one to Dad . . . brother giving one to sister and vice versa . . . every possible combination. I don't know what else to do and they want an original idea each and every month!"

Imagine writing 36 ads—or six, for that matter—without ever applying the principles of scientific testing to learn what effect your messages have on sales! No wonder the writer was written out.

The problem of what to do when you are written out is a difficult one. Some copywriters solve it by changing jobs every few years.

A less drastic method of getting your mind out of the rut is to forget the "average" customer, that imaginary man or woman to whom you have been writing all these years. Write copy as if you were writing a letter to some friends. Say to yourself, "I've just bought this Widget and it is great. I think Jim and Betty would like to know about it. I'm going to write and tell them about it."

Here is a letter an association president wrote to a friend, then realized it should also go to members of the association. Read it and see if you don't feel the quality of enthusiasm in the letter:

Dear Association Member:

You would have been thrilled to have been with me in Montreal on Friday.

Montreal, as you know, is the site of your convention in September. I was there attending a Board of Governors meeting of your Association.

The Queen Elizabeth Hotel, headquarters for the convention, is something to write home about. It was designed specifically to handle conventions—all of the convention facilities (registration, meeting rooms, exhibits, bar, etc.) are on one floor. The hotel is lovely. Beautiful rooms, excellent elevator service, and probably the best hotel food you'll find anywhere. We had eggs Benedict for the Board breakfast (at 8 a.m.!) and they were wonderful. Rooms are moderately priced, as are valet, laundry, room service, etc.

This Montreal steering committee has really knocked itself out. I'm enclosing a copy of the almost-completed program. Real meat in it for both the little guy and the big guy.

Airline arrivals will get their hotel key at the airport (at least those who have the foresight to make their hotel reservations at the Queen Elizabeth early). Both United and Air Canada have agreed to "Special Delivery Flights" from all main U.S. entry points. Luggage will receive special Queen Elizabeth stickers and be shipped immediately to the hotel. Identification buttons will be supplied immediately. Rail travelers will arrive directly beneath the hotel—and lucky auto travelers will discover something unique—free parking at the QE. Imagine!

Your spouse (and if you don't have one, it would almost be worth it for this trip alone) will get a real treat from the Laurentian Mountain tour including a luncheon and Christian Dior style show. The resort where this activity will take place has a unique feature— a grass roof that is kept "mowed" by two goats. You'd have to see it to believe it. Some of the Board members have actually seen the goats in action!

Chrysler Automotive was staging an exhibit the day we were there and 25,000—count 'em—were accommodated in the exhibit area. The beauty of the exhibit area is its accessibility to the meeting rooms, ball room, and registration. It will be the finest deal our convention exhibitors have ever had. We have also appointed a special broker to lessen the problems of shipping exhibit materials through customs.

The program (as you'll see by the attached) is loaded with talent but will leave enough free time to visit some of Montreal's wonderful French restaurants. Incidentally, the program will be printed in both French and English to give it a truly bilingual flavor. Montreal is second only to Paris for French-speaking inhabitants. This alone adds a flavor you just can't afford to miss.

I was so excited after I left Montreal that I thought I'd best tell you about it immediately. If you miss a reservation at the Queen Elizabeth, you're going to miss some of the enjoyment of the convention. Better make that reservation today—I did.

Sincerely,

Bob

The author of this letter wrote it while he was in an enthusiastic frame of mind. He had experienced something he was excited about and he wrote about it right away. He didn't give his enthusiasm a chance to cool off. That is one secret of enthusiastic writing. If you are excited about something, grab a pencil or sit at your keyboard and get your excitement down on paper immediately.

The same applies in talking. If you have just witnessed an exciting event or experienced an exciting idea and you tell somebody about it that same day, your description is much more effective than if you wait a week and tell about it after the details and the excitement have departed from your mind.

An analogous approach works in preparing a presentation and in public speaking. *Always* carry with you—yes, even to the bathroom—a note pad or small hand-held dictation device. Capture the inspiration that has been working in your subconscious before it can disappear. If you wait, all too often others interrupt with their own enthusiastic ideas and yours is lost, even though you know it was better.

Here are some samples of advertising copy that have the quality of enthusiasm:

1. COPY FOR A RETIREMENT INCOME PLAN

This message is addressed to the man or woman who wants to take things easy some day. It tells how you can provide for yourself in later years a guaranteed income you cannot outlive.

It doesn't matter whether your present income is large or merely average. If you follow this plan you will someday have an income upon which to retire.

The plan calls for the deposit of only a few dollars each month—the exact amount depending on your age. The minute you make your first deposit, your biggest money worries begin to disappear. Even if you should become totally disabled, you would not need to worry. Your payments would be made by us out of a special fund provided for that purpose.

And not only that. We would mail you a check every month during the entire time of your disability, even if that disability should continue for many, many years—the remainder of your natural life.

2. COPY FOR A NEWSPAPER SUBSCRIPTION

"A few years ago I was going broke. High prices and taxes were getting me down. I had to have more money or reduce my standard of living.

"So I sent for a Trial Subscription to the *Wall Street Journal*. I heeded its warnings. I cashed in on the ideas it gave me for increasing my income and cutting expenses. I got the money I needed. And then I began to forge ahead. Last year my income was up 40%. Believe me, reading the *Journal* every day is a wonderful get ahead plan. Now I am really living!"

This experience is typical. The *Journal* is a wonderful aid to the professional man and woman. It is valuable to the owner of a small business. It can be of priceless benefit to the young person who wants to win advancement.

3. Copy for Boxes of Fruit Sent by Express

Right now as I write this, it is late September, and out here in this beautiful valley our Royal Riviera Pears are hanging like great pendants from those 40-year-old trees. We'll have to watch them like new babies from now until picking time—not a leaf must touch them toward the last. Trained men will pick them gently with gloved hands and lay them carefully in padded trays. They'll be individually wrapped in tissue and nestled in cushion packing, and sent in handsome gift boxes lithographed in colors, to reach you—or your friends—firm and beautiful, ready to ripen in your home to their full delicious flavor. I envy you your first taste of Royal Riviera Pears, dripping with sweet liquid sunshine.

4. Copy for a Fat-reducing Remedy

In 10 days I'll reduce your weight 5 to 10 pounds. I don't care how stout you are. I don't care how many times you have tried to reduce and failed. My amazing new method will make your excess fat melt away like magic—give you a normal, youthful figure—make you slim, buoyant, energetic, as Nature intended you to be, or the treatment won't cost you a single penny!

No starving—no exercising—no drugs—no external agencies—no mechanical appliances. You just follow my instructions for a few days until your excess pounds disappear, until the scales tell you that you weigh exactly what you should. This method is so simple that anyone can understand how it works. It is so logical, so sensible that the moment you hear about it you will know instinctively that it works.

Send no money; we will bill you later. Merely send me your name and address and we will send you "How to Reduce" at the special low price. If at the end of ten days you are not completely satisfied—if you do not lose weight rapidly and easily—then simply tell me so on the invoice and you will owe nothing. WRITE TODAY.

HOW TO AVOID MENTAL HAZARDS

One mental hazard that discourages writers is the knowledge that their copy will be judged by a number of critics including:

- The copy chief
- The account executive
- The advertising manager
- The sales manager
- The president

- And—the writer is convinced—several strangers who happen to be passing in the street as the ad is being considered.

Each critic has his or her own idea about copy. Trying to please them all is like trying to hit a dozen different targets with a single arrow. If you want to write enthusiastic copy, you must banish critics from your mind entirely. Ignore them. Forget them. Write the way you want to write . . . the way good advertising must be written.

And write fast. Get steamed up. Make your copy sizzle. Put all the power of a runaway locomotive into it. Later go over it in cold blood and cut out the things your critics will object to. In this way you can produce copy that is both lively and acceptable. If you write with the prejudices and preferences of other people uppermost in your mind, you will produce copy as correct as a school child's essay, but utterly lifeless.

OVERCOMING OTHER MENTAL HAZARDS

Our enthusiastic copy plan helps to overcome two other mental hazards:

1. The things you are not allowed to say about the article you are selling.

2. The things you must say as a matter of advertising policy.

Put these things completely out of your head. Don't sit down to write copy with a string of "musts" and "can'ts" dangling in your mind.

Use a process of self-hypnotism. Say to yourself that Smiths Toothpaste is the best in the world—that there is no other toothpaste like it. It can produce wonderful results in a short time.

Get excited! Get worked up! Tell yourself that you have the biggest piece of news to tell since man walked on the moon. Remember that enthusiasm is as contagious as measles. It spreads from speaker to listener, from writer to reader.

Then start to write. Write fast. Write furiously. Write as if you had to catch a plane. Write as if you had to put all your thoughts on paper in the next five minutes or lose them forever.

Perhaps your first few paragraphs will sound impossible. Never mind. Keep on writing. Somewhere, somehow, you will produce real selling copy. Some of the things you write will work on the emotions of your readers in subtle ways that are perhaps unknown to yourself. Unconsciously you will produce little touches that arouse and stir your readers and listeners to action.

ACTION—that's the vital quality that emotional copy possesses and that "reason why" copy lacks. "Reason why" copy appeals to the readers' intelligence and makes them nod their heads in agreement with you. But emotional copy goes deeper. It gets into those portions of the brain where love and hate and fear and desire are.

Both types of copy are important. Skillfully combine the two and you will make the readers get up out of their chairs and start for the store.

One more word about enthusiastic copy: Everybody knows that you can tame a wild horse and make the animal useful. But it is impossible to put life into a dead horse. The same is true of advertising copy. An advertisement that has been pounded out in the white heat of enthusiasm can be tamed and made effective. But it is impossible to put life into dead copy.

And remember that the polishing and rewriting you do afterwards are extremely important. Anatole France claimed that he rewrote every paragraph five times. The illustrious French author said, "The first four versions of my writing sound as if anybody had written it. Only after a fifth rewriting does it begin to sound like Anatole France."

Advertising is to business what steam is to machinery—the great propelling power.

Thomas Macauley

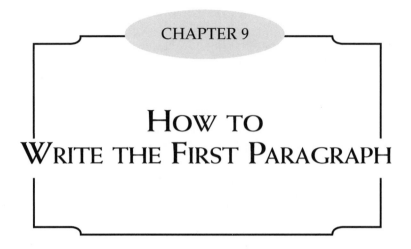

How to
Write the First Paragraph

One of the earliest definitions of writing advertising copy was "Salesmanship in print" (see Figure 9.1). Today, six or seven generations of definitions later, many copywriters forget that "salesmanship" is still the critical element in what they do. Too many miss their chance to make a sale by starting with a few introductory remarks that lose the reader's interest instead of holding it.

Imagine for a moment that you are interested in buying a TV set. You see a good-looking set in a store window. You walk into the store to look at it. Uppermost in your mind are these questions: How many channels will it receive? What is the quality of its reception? Does it have true stereo sound? And, of course, How much does it cost?

Suppose a clerk should walk up to you and say, "This is an age of beauty . . . charm . . . style." Wouldn't you be flabbergasted? Wouldn't you suspect that there was something wrong with him? After all, you're there to see about buying a television set. Yet the statement "This is an age of beauty . . . charm . . . style," are the exact words of the opening paragraph of a $16,000 magazine advertisement for a television set. This sort of copy is not exceptional. You have become accustomed to it because you see so much of it.

Millions of pages have been turned with their millions of ads left unread because of first paragraphs like the following:

> The modern woman demands something more than comfort and utility in the appointments of her home. She is a devotee of style and beauty. She knows color and design. Her taste is cultivated and refined. She is informed, detests spuriousness, and expects authentic value for her money.

Figure 9.1: *Just so they spell the name right*! Since the initiation of this campaign, occupancy rate of the New York Helmsley Hotels went from under 50 percent to over 90 percent in seven months. Say what you will, she inspires a helluva ad campaign!

This bit of philosophy is the first paragraph of a four-color page in a national magazine. Can you guess what product is being advertised? Can you guess what the product will do for you? No. There is no hint, no clue. The copy tells nothing, sells nothing. It is merely a barrier between the readers and what they want to know.

Often a copy chief or advertising manager can improve a writer's copy simply by omitting the opening sentences or opening paragraphs that the writer used in the first draft. "Begin here," says the copy chief, and points to a sentence or paragraph halfway down the page.

Did you ever see a baseball pitcher warming up before he gets into the game? He needs to swing his arms a bit and throw some practice pitches before he is at his best. And he needs an experienced pitching coach to tell him when he's really ready. Some writers are the same way. They need to write a few sentences, few paragraphs, or an entire first draft before they really get hot. A copy chief can help a copywriter by pointing out the exact spot in the copy where the writer begins to say something worthwhile.

If you don't have an advertising manager or a copy chief to guide your efforts, put your copy aside for a day or two and then come back to it with a fresh mind. Perhaps you will find a sentence or a paragraph that will make a more exciting beginning than the one you used originally. More likely you will find that you can simply omit your original beginning without losing any of the essential ideas in your ad. Morton Levin, the advertising director for a successful syndicated book catalog, told his writers to begin every description with "This is a story about" or "This is a book about," then eliminate that phrase from the description. Thus, "This is a book about how to write better advertising copy than you ever thought possible" became "How to write better advertising copy . . . etc." It still works. Every time.

A CLASSIC LESSON FROM READER'S DIGEST

Some years ago I picked up an issue of *Reader's Digest* and copied down the first sentence of every article in the magazine—35 articles in all. I wanted to find out how the editors of the world's largest circulating publication handle the problem of holding the reader's interest after that interest has been sparked by the title of an article. Many article writers as well as ad writers face this same problem, namely how do you hold them after you've stopped them with your headline or picture?

My experiment with a single issue of *Reader's Digest* was so revealing that I went through a number of issues. I found the same successful formulas repeated again and again. Some of these formulas are just as appropriate for ad writing as they are for article writing. Here they are:

1. INTERRUPTING IDEAS

A number of articles begin with a sentence that can be described as an "interrupting idea." What is an interrupting idea? It is a startling statement or a novel twist that breaks through the boredom barrier that often exists in the mind of the reader. For example, an article on deodorizers entitled "It Makes Bad Air Good," began this way:

> The hit of the annual Chemical Show held in New York City a few months ago was a pair of skunks housed in a plastic cage.

Here are the opening sentences of four more articles that use the technique of the interrupting idea:

> As you sit quietly reading these lines, a whirl of activity is taking place in your body.

> While we humans think that penguins look and act like people, there's sobering evidence that they think of us as just big penguins.

> Pleasing your tongue has lately become the chief concern of the world's largest industry.

> Each day hundreds of thousands of harried young mothers thumb nervously through a dog-eared, oatmeal-splattered volume—one of the most extraordinary ever published.

2. THE SHOCKER

Closely related to the interrupting idea is an opening that is even more striking and can be described as "the shocker." Here are examples:

> A Frenchman is rarely seen drunk, but France has the highest rate of alcoholism in the world.

> This morning in the United States 8,000 more mouths demanded to be fed than yesterday morning.

> I used to think that women who did nothing but have babies were stupid creatures.

> There are some crimes a racketeer never commits unless he sees his lawyer first.

3. NEWS

Another type of opening popular with editors is the news opening. Here are four examples:

> There is a new committee in Washington.
>
> In the past two years an exciting era of exploration has opened up.
>
> A billion-dollar in·lustrial empire has sprung suddenly into existence along the banks of the Mississippi River.
>
> Something exciting and heartening is happening on the American college campus these days.

4. PREVIEW

Occasionally used as an article opener is a sentence giving you a brief preview of the article. Examples:

> Port-au-Prince, capital of the Republic of Haiti, is the busiest, noisiest, most colorful city in the Caribbean.
>
> Until about 15 years ago Japanese beetles seemed unstoppable.
>
> Intelligently analyzed, our dreams can give us significant insights into our problems and our relationships with others.

5. QUOTATION

Here is the opening of an article on word power that appeals to everyone who works with words:

> Daniel Webster said: "If all my possessions and powers were taken from me with one exception, I would choose to keep the power of words, because by them I would recover the rest."

6. STORY

I have not yet told you the most interesting discovery of all: Over half of the *Reader's Digest* articles begin with a story. As you know, *Reader's Digest* is not a fiction magazine. It is a nonfiction magazine. Yet more than half of the pieces begin with an anecdote or a narrative of some kind. If you will tie this fact up with the fact that many of the most famous ads ever written are in the form of stories, you will have something for ad writers to ponder.

Below are examples of story openings:

> One night last autumn a visitor in New York noticed lights burning in a church on lower Fifth Avenue.
>
> The time was one A.M., the place a police station on Chicago's South Side.

On a sunny afternoon in Portland, Ore., I was driving my daughter to her weekly swimming lesson.

From the gallery of the Montreal Neurological Institute's main operating room, I recently witnessed a seven-hour brain operation.

At the Eastman Chemical Products laboratories in Kingsport, Tenn., a technician using an eye-dropper placed one drop of a newly developed adhesive on the end of a two-inch steel rod.

Last summer Columbia University student Alexander H. Ladd, a young man from a well-to-do Boston suburb, spent his vacation working as a grease monkey in a Mobil gas station.

When I dropped my letter into the mailbox, I felt exactly as if I'd tossed a bottled note into the ocean.

As dawn broke over Boston Harbor one day last fall, the tugboat Irene-Mae waddled out into the Atlantic on a strange mission.

On a Saturday not long ago, a physician flying in a sport plane over Springfield, Ill., lifted a pocket radio receiver to his ear, pressed a button and in a moment heard a woman say: "One-five-four code three, emergency. Location 20."

For 34 tension-drenched minutes on August 8, nine test-crew airmen expected to die at any instant.

Here are some of the things you should notice about the various *Reader's Digest* openings:

1. They are fact-packed.
2. They are telegraphic.
3. They are specific.
4. They have few adjectives.
5. They arouse curiosity.

The next time you write an opening for an ad, see if you can use an interrupting idea, or a shocker, or a news item, or a story.

ANOTHER FORMULA

If none of the preceding methods fits the ad you are writing—if you can't find an appropriate story or an interrupting idea—you can fall back on the simplest formula of all, namely: You can write a first paragraph that continues the same thought you expressed in your teaser or headline. For a direct mail example of this same technique, see Figure 9.2.

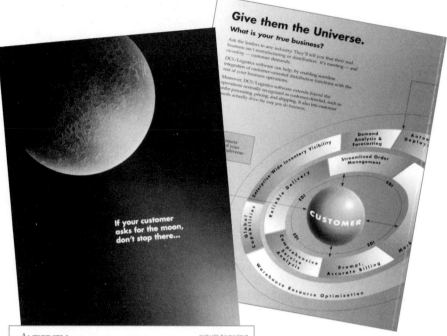

Figure 9.2: *The power of the written word . . . by four to one!* Printing inside the envelope brings home the one/two punch of the message even as the contents are removed. A personalized letter promises answers, with an 800-number to start getting them right now—from the person signing the note. No wonder favorable response to telemarketing follow-up proved four times more likely immediately after the mailing was received than to a telemarketing cold call! *Winner, 1995 CADM Tempo Award.*

For example, if you stop a reader with a headline about house paint, you can be sure of at least one thing about that reader: He wants more information about house paint. You will not lose him as long as you continue to give him what he wants.

If you want proof of the effectiveness of this method, just glance at the opening paragraphs of a few mail order ads. These ads pay for themselves in actual sales.

Here is the first paragraph of a mail order advertisement selling a remedy for a speech defect. The ad has a one-word headline that selects the proper audience. Notice how the first paragraph continues the thought expressed in the headline:

[Headline] STAMMERING

[1st Paragraph] You can be quickly cured if you stammer. Send $2.95 for a 288-page cloth bound book on Stammering and Stuttering. It tells how I cured myself after Stammering and Stuttering for 20 years.

A humble subject. A small advertisement. But the first paragraph contains more real selling punch than many a full-page advertisement.

Notice how this piano school gets down to brass tacks in the following first paragraph:

[Headline] LEARN PIANO

[1st Paragraph] Play popular song hits perfectly. Hum the tune, play it by ear. No teacher—self-instruction. No tedious ding-dong daily practice. Just 20 brief, entertaining lessons, easily mastered.

Read the following telegraphic first paragraph taken from an advertisement for a Civil Service school. In addition to continuing the headline theme, this paragraph gets seven sales arguments into three short sentences.

[Headline] GOV'T JOBS

[1st Paragraph] Why worry about strikes, lay-offs, hard times? Get a Government job. Increased salaries, steady work, travel, good pay.

Now, for the sake of contrast, read the following first paragraph:

The ideal toward which great engineers work is not only mechanical perfection, but automatic maintenance of such perfection. Every great mechanical advance in automobile construction has led us toward a freer enjoyment of automobile convenience.

This is the sort of copy you would engrave on the cornerstone of the Mammoth Motors Building. Or it might do for an epitaph to be chiseled on the tombstone of a deceased manufacturer. But it is neither of these. It is the first paragraph of a full-page advertisement in a national magazine. The product is an automobile oiling system.

Later in the advertisement these excellent arguments appear:

- Each bearing receives only the amount of oil it needs at any given speed.

- No alternate periods of dryness or overflow.

- No waste.

- The System is out of the way, under the dash.

- Needs oil only once in every 12,000 miles.

Why couldn't these facts appear earlier? Thousands more people would have seen them.

Here is an example of correct handling. Notice how the first paragraph of this insurance ad continues the headline theme:

[Headline] HOW TO PROVIDE A
RETIREMENT INCOME
FOR YOURSELF

[1st Paragraph] This new Retirement Income Plan makes it possible for you to retire at any age you wish, 55, 60, or 65. You may provide for yourself a monthly income of $1,500, $2,000, or more.

When you catch readers with a certain idea as expressed in the headline, you may lose them if you introduce a totally different idea in the first paragraph.

Based on mail-order experience, here are three simple rules for writing a good first paragraph.

1. Make it short. A long first paragraph discourages readers before they get started.

2. Continue the thought expressed in the headline.

3. State in a few words the most important benefit or benefits readers derive from buying your product. Benefits! Benefits! Benefits! What do I get? What will it do for me? That's what people want to know. That's what makes them read advertisements.

A READER'S DIGEST LESSON FOR TODAY

The lessons to be learned from the style of *Reader's Digest* are as applicable today as when Caples first taught them. What follows are the titles and opening sentences of the articles in the *Reader's Digest* of July 1995. Note how many reflect one of the six formulas discovered by Caples:

- Interrupting Ideas
- The Shocker
- News
- Preview
- Quotation
- Story

Note, too, how often the first sentence immediately gets to the point with a date . . . a time . . . a fact that expands on the title; that is, on the article "headline." *Reader's Digest* editors, like smart advertisers, do not change what works until they come up with something better. "Humor in Uniform" has appeared monthly since World War II. "It Pays to Enrich Your Word Power" was studied by your editor each month when he was learning English years ago. Nothing is changed by *Reader's Digest* "just because we're tired of it." Everything is subject to change when it no longer works.

25 TITLES AND OPENING SENTENCES FOR TODAY

1. "One Hot Afternoon in July"

    There are certain days when we feel our lives change profoundly, days we remember for a lifetime.

2. "A Toast to Marshmallows"

    It was a touching display of reverence.

3. "Evidence that Does Not Lie"

    Nineteen-year-old Lori Ann Auker was battling her estranged husband, Robert, over custody of their child.

4. "Can You Trust Those Polls?"

This past January, as the new Congress went into session, an opinion poll publicized by the U.S. Agency for International Development (AID) triggered headlines around the country.

5. "Jamel's Way Out"

Three-year-old Jamel Oeser-Sweat sat huddled with his mother, Jeanne, on the tattered sofa.

6. "A Coyote Named Promise"

Early one morning, I awoke to an unearthly cry—like the sobs of a thousand demons.

7. "That's Outrageous"

First-grade public-school teacher [name] has been charged with scamming New York City out of more than $35,000 in welfare benefits.

8. "Encounter with a Great White"

Had I noticed a couple of significant local events, I might not have been so eager to get into the water that day off Cannon Beach, one of Oregon's best surfing spots.

9. "Can Yeltsin Survive?"

With the Russian economy in deep trouble and warfare continuing in the breakaway region of Chechnya, Russian President Boris N. Yeltsin faces political challenges on all sides.

10. "The White Sneakers"

Dr. Beatrice Engstrand burst into the intensive-care unit at New York City Metropolitan Hospital and surveyed the scene.

11. "Where Wealth Begins"

Why do some countries prosper while others remain poor?

12. "Seduced in the Supermarket"

During a typical 30-minute shopping trip down the aisle of an average American supermarket, about 30,000 products vie for your attention.

13. "A Very Tall Tale"

    From time to time people ask if it bothers me that I'm bald, and I can honestly say it does not.

14. "The Recycling Myth"

    One-third of U.S. households make a ritual of sorting their garbage for curb-side-recycling programs.

15. "I'll Blow Your Head Off!"

    At precisely 9:00 A.M., Jason McEnanev sank into a lecture hall seat at the University of New York in Albany ready for his Greek history class.

16. "O Romeo, O, Like, Wow"

    At the end of the school year, my 14-year-old daughter's English class tackled Shakespeare's *Romeo and Juliet* and she had to give an oral report.

17. "Is Your Seafood Safe?"

    Ty Minton's hands were so weak he couldn't even lift a glass of milk to his lips.

18. "Faster than a Speeding Bullet"

    It was a dream assignment—to build a wild stallion of an airplane, so advanced and awesome that it could intimidate America's enemies and maybe even some of our friends.

19. "Ace that Job Interview"

    Job interviewing is a minefield.

20. "The 10 Sexual Senses"

    Because they so keenly want to share everything, lovers imagine that their senses are identical—that they feel the same silk, see the same rainbow, smell the same rose, taste the same wine, hear the same tango.

21. "Take $2000 and Call Me In the Morning"

    A new disease is stalking my home state.

22. "A Boy and His Cat"

I'm not sure how he got to my clinic.

23. "Heroes for Today"

The tiny village of Fishkill, N.Y., has never commemorated the nation's birthday with fireworks or a brassy parade.

24. "Most Important Thing You Can Do for Your Child"

Jim Trelease has devoted the past 16 years to promoting what he considers the best-kept secret in education today.

25. "Deliver Us from Evil"

Daylight was fading in the village when the old woman came to the back door of the house.

With public sentiment nothing can fail, without it nothing can succeed.

Abraham Lincoln

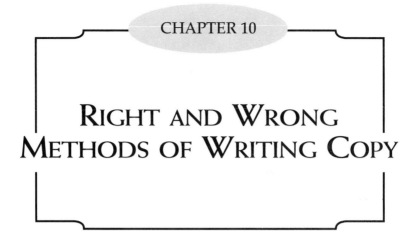

CHAPTER 10

RIGHT AND WRONG METHODS OF WRITING COPY

This chapter discusses 19 different kinds of copy for space ads and direct mail and gives examples of each. Not all of these kinds of copy are recommended. Three are listed as questionable, and three are definitely not recommended.

Let us first discuss some 13 types of copy that are recommended.

1. STRAIGHTFORWARD COPY

This type of copy presents the advertiser's story in a simple, logical manner. It is devoid of style or rhetoric. It merely states the facts in the most understandable way possible. For example:

PERSONALIZED STATIONERY

100-high quality, special-size bond note sheets and 100 envelopes are neatly imprinted with any three-line address you designate. Carefully packed and mailed prepaid to your home for three dollars.

2. STORY COPY

This copy starts off with a human-interest situation. Then comes a story, the moral of which is "Buy the product advertised." While this kind of "story opening" might be considered too old-fashioned to use in print advertising today, notice how closely it matches *in spirit* many health and beauty TV commercials of the 1990s:

"HE TOLD ME I WAS THE GIRL OF HIS DREAMS
AND I THOUGHT HE MEANT IT"

"He said I was wonderful, the one girl he'd been hoping to meet ever since college. And then everything seemed to go wrong.

"My cousin introduced us when we went to our high school reunion. George was wonderful—fun to talk with, good looking, a great education, a great job, even a good dancer."

DIFFERENT AT NOON

"When he asked me to go swimming the next day, it seemed like love at first sight . . . for both of us!

"We talked for a while on the beach. But the more we talked, the less interested he seemed to become in our conversation . . . and in me.

"When he told me he had to leave early, I knew something had changed, but I had no idea what.

"George," I said, "I thought you really liked me. What happened?"

"His answer gave me the shock of my life."

RIGHT IN THE FACE

"Last night, at the dance," he said, "you looked absolutely great. But now, in the sunlight, you have just about the worst complexion I've ever seen! Can't you do *anything* about that?"

Things like this happen all the time. But it does not have to happen to you! True beauty is impossible without a smooth running system, the kind you have with . . .

3. "YOU AND ME" COPY

In the "You and Me" style of copy, the manufacturer speaks directly to the customer, usually in a chatty, friendly way, just as a good salesperson talks to a potential customer. Here is an example taken from a direct mail letter selling mackerel fillets by mail order:

FISH HAS BEEN MY SPECIALTY ALL MY LIFE

In my many years as a fisherman, I've seen a lot of fish. Starting with the days when I used to go "mackerelling" in my father's vessel, I've loved the sea and the good things that come out of it.

I remember how father carefully selected the best fish of the catch to take home. I've never forgotten his "fisherman's test" of mackerel and codfish. We'd pick the plump ones with meat so fat and tender they would break apart at the touch of the fork. They always turned out to be so juicy and sweet—tender as chicken.

The letter continues in this vein for several paragraphs and then closes with this appeal:

Let Me Send You These Fillets Now—On Approval

Just check and sign the enclosed card and mail it, and I'll send you a pail containing 10 Fillets of fat, fall-caught mackerel, each sufficient for two or three persons. Season one of these Fillets and broil to a delicate brown. If you are not fully satisfied that it is the finest mackerel you ever tasted, send the rest back at my expense and the trial costs you nothing.

The chatty "fish has been my specialty" type of approach has proven successful for everything from abalone to yogurt. It is one of the more difficult styles for the sophisticated copywriting professional, yet often the easiest for the do-it-yourself true believer. If you're such a pro, let the client tell you about the product. Tape the conversation, then transcribe it as a first draft. Fix any obvious contradictions, add the selling details, and make it the final draft, too.

4. IMAGINATIVE COPY

In this kind of copy, the copywriter heightens the reader's interest in the product by describing it in imaginative terms. For example, a successful mail order advertisement written by Bruce Barton for a two-year, home-study course in business described the course as follows:

> A WONDERFUL TWO YEARS' TRIP AT FULL PAY—
> ## but only men and women with imagination can take it
>
> About one person in ten will be appealed to by this page. The other nine will be hard workers, earnest, ambitious in their way, but to them a coupon is a coupon; a book is a book; a Course is a Course. The one man or woman in ten has imagination.
>
> And imagination rules the world.
>
> Let us put it this way. An automobile is at your door; you are invited to pack your bag and step in. You will travel to New York. You will go directly to the office of the president of one of the biggest banks. You will spend hours with him, and with other bank presidents. You will not leave these bankers until you have a thorough understanding of our great banking system.
>
> When you have finished with them the car will be waiting. It will take you to the offices of men who direct great selling organizations. Their time will be at your disposal.
>
> Through other days the heads of accounting departments will guide you. On others, men and women who have made their mark in office management . . . [etc. . . . . etc.].
>
> The whole journey will occupy two years. It will cost you nothing in income, for your salary will go right along.

The above is condensed from an ad that brought so many responses that it was repeated again and again for seven years. The complete ad is reproduced in Figure 10.1 selected by Caples as an advertising classic.

Figure 10.1: *An Ad That Ran for Seven Years*: This ad for a two-year correspondence course in business training was written by Bruce Barton, former chairman of BBDO, Inc. The ad brought so many coupon returns that it was run again and again in magazines and newspapers for seven years. The coupons were turned over to representatives. General advertisers sometimes ask, "Is it profitable to repeat a good ad?" Based on the experience of mail order advertisers, the answer is yes.

5. FACTUAL COPY

A large number of successful retail ads were compared with a number of unsuccessful retail ads. The purpose was to discover what kind of retail copy produces the most sales. Conclusion: The ads that tell the largest number of facts about the product are the ads that make the most sales. Stating it briefly: The more you tell, the more you sell.

Here is an example of successful retail copy. Notice how it sells by piling one fact on top of another.

ENGINEERS' BOOTS

For you outdoor men who demand the best in boots. Ease into these comfortable, weather-resistant Wearmasters. Selected grain leather uppers, oil-tanned to repel water . . . stay flexible with repeated exposure to moisture. Leather vamp lining wears longer; gives more comfort across instep. Leather Woodsman's heel, rubber top lift, distributes weight evenly for better balance. Double oak leather soles. Steel shank reinforces leather insole. Outside counter pocket strengthens heel. Top ankle straps adjust. Goodyear welt construction . . . retains original boot-shape . . . easy to resole.

For an example of factual, tested, and proven direct mail selling, see Figure 10.2.

6. FACTS-PLUS-STYLE COPY

Copy that merely imitates the style of some great master of English prose and omits the selling arguments is of little value. On the other hand, copy that has style in addition to selling arguments is acceptable, especially when you are advertising a high-grade product.

Following are paragraphs taken from an advertisement stressing the speed obtainable in a Rolls-Royce automobile. Notice the high speed of the copy. It moves rapidly from sentence to sentence. It has a style all its own, just as a Rolls-Royce has. And every paragraph is packed with facts and selling arguments.

There is not a car made that can measure miles with Rolls-Royce on a cross-country run. And if the run includes every kind of road condition, you only add to Rolls-Royce's advantage. For Rolls-Royce is so vibrationless, so floating-smooth, that it can take rough roads at speeds you would never think of attempting in any other car.

Prove that—at the wheel of a Rolls-Royce! You open the throttle— the scenery takes wings. But where are the rack and rattle that are speed's running mates in most other cars? Absent! You can scarcely hear the motor that is hurrying you on. If you didn't know that the speedometer is as accurate as the finest watch, you wouldn't believe you were going so fast. Rolls-Royce is *so* quiet!

Test package that
beat the control

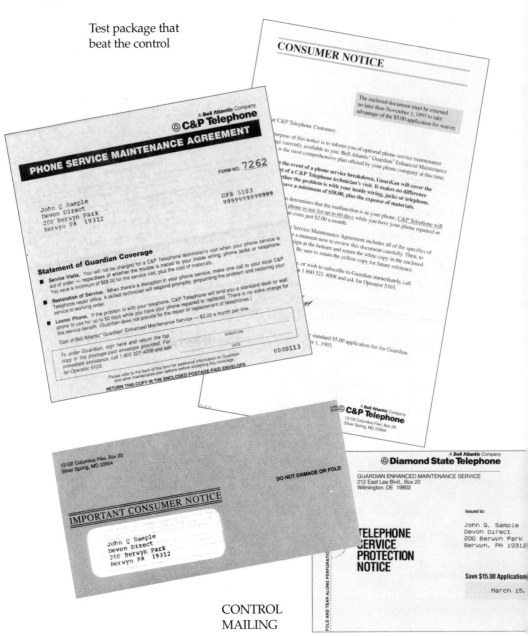

CONTROL
MAILING

Figure 10.2: *The truth . . . the whole truth.* Transforming the FCC full-disclosure rule into a dynamic selling point, Bell Atlantic's simple two-piece-plus-envelopes mailing topped the "control," (the best previous response), to produce a 5 per-

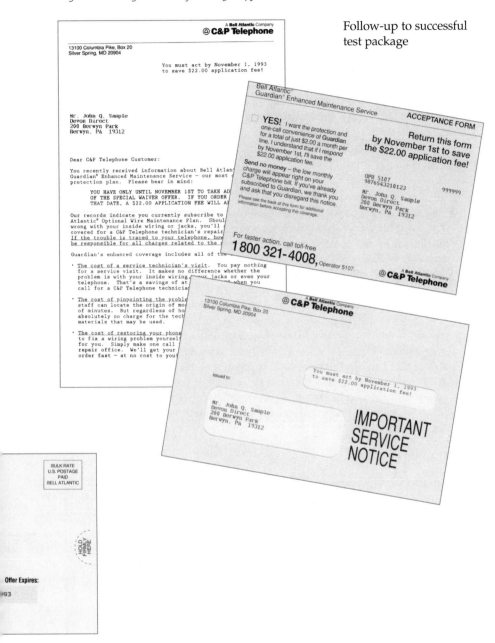

Follow-up to successful test package

cent return. But that's only half the story. An equally basic follow-up, stressing the need to act by a specific date, matched the original for a combined three-year total of four-million sales . . . and still counting!

7. FORTHRIGHT COPY

Sometimes a writer can increase the believability of an ad by admitting that there are some weak points as well as strong points in the proposition she is selling. Here is a classified real-estate ad that uses this method effectively. For this example, from a time when Los Altos real estate was considerably less costly, the author is indebted to advertising consultant Clyde Bedell.

NEGLECTED

JR. ESTATE

$25,000

> Few settings in Los Altos Hills are more beautiful than this full acre. Here you have orchard land and towering shade oaks. The basically charming and comfortable home, however, needs loving attention from a family with the imagination and energy to bring it up to modern standards. There are 3 good-sized bedrooms, nice bath, separate dining room, and huge family kitchen—plus breezeway, garage, and rundown solarium with intriguing possibilities. The Guest House sags at the seams, but perhaps You can make it livable. While you're trying, there IS the reward of a relaxing dip in your 16' x 36' Filtered Paddock Swim Pool. Make no mistake—there's much to be done here. But the potential is great, and the price downright tempting, so maybe you should have a look. If you like what you see, we'll help you to own this picturesque property on terms that suit you. Palo Alto school district. Obey that impulse and call now for an appointment.

8. SUPERLATIVE COPY

In this type of copy you step right out and blow your own horn as loudly as possible. This kind of advertising is effective if you have the facts to back it up. Here are two examples:

Build a library of classics
in replicas of rare bookbindings
decorated in 24 Karat Gold

> Choose any 3 of the masterworks on this page for only $1 with trial membership in the International Collectors Library. We make this extraordinary offer to introduce you to one of the greatest ideas in publishing history.
>
> The private libraries of the past have bequeathed to us rare bookbindings of hand-crafted design. Today these originals are found only in museums and in the home libraries of very wealthy collectors. Now the International Collectors Library brings you the great classics of fiction, history, biography, poetry, drama and adven-

ture—in authentic period bindings—replicas of the designs on the priceless originals.

Yours Free . . . Giant New
Spring Garden Catalog

Over one hundred great garden ideas. Your first chance to see the Rose of the Year, plus the new All-American roses and much, much more.

Golden Gate—brilliant intense yellow, outstanding for cutting. THE yellow rose for arrangements.

Brand New Hybrid Teas—White masterpiece, with 6-inch blooms so perfect you'll have to see them to believe them. Here's Heirloom—pure, clear lilac, one of the rarest colors in the garden world; rich with fragrance like ripe raspberries.

9. SIGNED COPY

Sometimes the manufacturer himself issues a signed statement regarding the product or service he is selling. This method was used by a famous automobile manufacturer to announce a new car. In another case, a watch manufacturer published an advertisement that was written and signed by a well-known author.

Following are quotes from an advertisement for *World Magazine*. The copy is signed by Norman Cousins, who was the publisher.

AN OPEN LETTER TO

THE READERS OF *THE NEW YORK TIMES*

NORMAN COUSINS

TWO DAG HAMMARSKJOLD PLAZA, NEW YORK, NEW YORK 10017

My purpose in writing is to tell you that my colleagues and I have decided to launch a new magazine.

Ever since I resigned from the *Saturday Review*, for reasons you may know about, I have been thinking and dreaming about the possibility of starting a magazine that, quite literally, would belong to its readers and editors.

[There followed 16 paragraphs of description of the forthcoming magazine.]

We ask no money now. That can come later. What we need right now is an expression of your interest.

As I said above, in inviting you to join us in what we hope will be an exciting adventure in ideas, we realize we are asking you to take a chance on us. We have high hopes of justifying that confidence. The process begins with the Charter Subscription form below.

Sincerely,

Norman Cousins

This ad ran three times in *The New York Times* and brought in almost four times the cost of the space. Here are some of the features that made this ad successful: (1) It looks like editorial material. (2) It is signed by a famous editor, Norman Cousins. (3) It is written in the "you and me" style, like a letter to a friend. (4) The name "The New York Times" in the headline gets attention, especially since the ad appeared in *The Times*. For a current example of signed copy, see the long-running campaign shown in Figure 10.3.

10. TITLE COPY

Over a period of years, mail-order book advertisers have discovered by trial and error just what titles are most interesting to magazine and newspaper readers. Titles that do not sell are discarded from the advertising. Titles that sell in large quantities are retained. Here are some titles listed in a typical advertisement. Notice what a world of interest is packed into three or four words. And remember that these titles were not selected at the whim of the copywriter. They are the most popular titles—the titles that produced the most sales.

Take Your Pick of the Books Listed on This Page

What Every Girl Should Know

How to Write Short Stories

Rhyming Dictionary

A Book of Riddle Rimes

Origin of Human Race

How to Argue Logically

Dictionary of U.S. Slang

How to Improve Your Conversation

Physiology of Sex Life

Psychology of Suicide

Common Faults in English

Facts You Should Know About Music

Evolution of Marriage

Art of Being Happy

Manhood Facts of Life

My 12 Years in a Monastery

Hypnotism Explained

Baseball: How to Play

Self-Contradictions of Bible

Evolution Made Plain

How to Love

Develop Sense of Humor

History of World War II

How N.Y. Girls Live

History of Rome

How Not to be a Wall-Flower

Principles of Electricity

Novel Discoveries in Science

Queer Facts About Lost Civilizations

How to Tie All Kinds of Knots

Story of Plato's Philosophy

Short History of Civil War

Evolution of Sex

What Woman Beyond 40 Should Know

A Hindu Book of Love

Hints on Etiquette

Book of Synonyms

Prostitution in the Ancient World

Puzzle of Personality

Do We Need Religion?

Plain Talks with Husbands and Wives

Is Death Inevitable?

Best Jokes About Doctors

Where We Stand

By Albert Shanker, President
American Federation of Teachers

Raising the Bar

Whenever there is a push to raise educational standards, we hear cries from the opposition. What is the point of raising standards when so many students cannot meet the current low standards? Doing that is like raising the bar on the high jump to 6 feet 8 inches when most of the contestants can't even clear the bar at 6 feet. The objection sounds reasonable, but it's wrong.

After *A Nation At Risk* came out in the early 1980s, many states stiffened the requirements for high school graduation. They called for more science and math and English courses, and they refused to accept some of the old, soft courses as fulfillment of graduation requirements. Critics predicted that these reforms would cause students to drop out in droves, but that did not happen. Students took the new and tougher courses, passed them and got their diplomas as before.

Something similar happened in the 1970s and 1980s when more than half the states started requiring high school students to pass minimum competency tests in order to receive a high school diploma. These were not tough tests. Most of the reading and math tests were at a 7th- or 8th-grade level. And when the tests were instituted, half of the kids about to graduate high school flunked.

Opponents of competency tests also predicted that raising the bar would cause a big increase in school dropout rates. After all, how could students be expected to meet 7th- or 8th-grade standards when some of them could not pass 4th- or 5th-grade tests? These critics were surprised when, within a short time, most states reported that 95 percent of their students were passing the new tests. Not only was there no increase in dropout rates, in many states there was a decrease. How can this be explained?

Before the tougher graduation requirements and the minimum competency tests were put into place, students knew that they would get their diplomas even if they did no work. All they had to do was put in the required seat time. Many left school because they were not challenged. Others stayed and learned what they had to: nothing.

The competency tests, like the new graduation requirements, introduced the factor of high stakes. Students realized that if they were not able to pass the courses and the tests, there would be no diploma. They wanted the diploma

States have been satisfied with the same low educational standards that they had twenty years ago.

because they knew that, while future employers do not require transcripts, grades or teacher recommendations, they are interested in whether a prospective employee is a high school graduate or a dropout.

What did the students do? What anyone who wants something that is out of reach does. They *worked* for it. Furthermore, they were no longer bored by sitting around waiting to have the diploma handed to them; they were challenged by the work they had to do to earn one. High stakes turned out to be a great benefit to these students.

So far, I've given you the good news. Now comes the bad news. If you were helping athletes improve their jumping and you got 95 percent of those in your charge to jump 6 feet, what would you do next? You would raise the bar another inch or so, and when most of them were regularly jumping at that height, you'd raise the bar again, and you would keep on going. But not in the world of education!

Some states have had minimum competency testing in place for twenty years. You would expect that when a great majority of students were able to achieve at the minimum competency level, the states would have introduced new and tougher exams that would set the graduation standard at the 8th- to 9th-grade level. Or that if the states continued using the same 7th- and 8th-grade exams, they'd require students to pass them a year or two earlier. Eventually, these exams should have been given as a requirement to *enter* high school rather than to graduate from it. And high school seniors should have been required to take the kinds of exams that students in other industrial nations do. That did not happen. The states just sat back, and they have been satisfied to have the same low standards today that they had twenty years ago.

There is a mood in the country that rejects everything the federal government does and places great faith in the states. Education is and has been a state responsibility, and the states have done some good things in education. But as the minimum competency exams show us, state control is no cure-all. States need prodding from business or outside challenges like the one provided by *A Nation At Risk*. If we are interested in correcting what is wrong with our schools, we'd better not be satisfied with just leaving it to the states.

Figure 10.3: *"Advertising" to think about . . . and with.* Since 1980, the "Where We Stand" column, by the President of the American Federation of Teachers, has appeared in the *Sunday New York Times* (and *The New Republic* since 1991). Why pay advertising rates to run such a column? Because, according to its author, to be effective in educating their students, teachers must also help educate the public about issues in education. Much as Mobil does for a corporate view, Albert Shanker's column not only raises issues, but also urges policies and generates hundreds of weekly responses, pro and con. That's Scientific Advertising responses worth thinking about!

The next time you write a headline, a subhead, or the title of a free booklet, try to put into it the brevity, the simplicity, and the human interest that are contained in the titles of these books.

Compare this 1950s list with today's nonfiction selections from The Book of the Month Club, The Literary Guild, or the bestsellers in *The New York Times, Time* magazine, and so forth. Although the titles have changed, the subject categories remain the same: sex, religion, sports, popular psychology and science, and so on. And just as the appeal of book categories has remained constant, so have the general advertising appeals Caples discovered and taught us in his articles and books. Even the three- and four-word titles still dominate. Of the 30 hardbound bestsellers listed in the September 24, 1995 *New York Times*, 21 have titles of three words or less.

(Incidentally, Hahn discovered the power of brevity when he submitted his own book, cleverly titled *A Handbook for Advertisers Without the Time or Talent to Become Creative Geniuses*, and the publisher said: "That is really clever. We'll call it *Do-It-Yourself Advertising & Promotion.*)

11. Teaser Copy

This copy is a challenge to the reader. Instead of trying to sell him, it apparently tries to discourage him. Perhaps the effectiveness of this method is accounted for by its unusualness. For example, here is the opening of a teaser advertisement for a business-training school.

MEN WHO "KNOW IT ALL"

ARE NOT INVITED

TO READ THIS PAGE

This page is not for the wise young man who is perfectly satisfied with himself and his business equipment.

This page is a personal message to the man who has responsibilities, who feels secretly that he ought to be earning several thousand dollars more a year, but who simply lacks the confidence necessary to lay hold of one of the bigger places in business.

12. News Page Copy

In this kind of copy, the advertiser buys space, usually a page, in newspapers or magazines. The page is made to look like typical editorial matter, with headlines, copy, pictures, and often including a regular small ad. The only difference is that instead of being written by reporters, everything is written by a copywriter with the product sold just as hard in the "news" items as in the regular advertisement.

An advertisement like this, though it must be clearly labeled as advertising, is useful for an occasional variation in a regular promotion campaign. But if used too often, it loses its effectiveness.

A maker of automobile accessories who used coupons in his advertising tried a news page of this type and reported that coupon returns were three times as great as the coupon returns he had previously been receiving from his regular advertisements.

13. COMPETITIVE COPY

Before the 1980s, practically all advertising professionals frowned upon "Competitive Copy." To show how rapidly and dramatically the advertising world has changed, it is the one category that has been moved from "Questionable . . . use with discretion" to "recommended"!

Here is a table of figures and a paragraph of copy taken from an automobile tire advertisement that speaks right out against its competitors, the mail-order houses:

COMPARE
Construction and Quality

	Our Tire	*Special Brand Mail Order Tire
MORE Rubber Volume	172 cu. in.	161 cu. in.
MORE Weight	16.99 pounds	15.73 pounds
MORE Width	4.75 inches	4.74 inches
MORE Thickness	.627 inch	.578 inch
MORE Plies at Tread	6 plies	5 plies
SAME PRICE	(price)	(price)

*A "Special Brand" Tire is made by a manufacturer for distributors such as mail order houses, oil companies, and others under a name that does not identify the tire manufacturer to the public, usually because they build their "first line" tires under their own name. We put our name on *every* tire we make.

THREE KINDS OF COPY TO BE USED WITH CAUTION

Now we come to three kinds of copy that are questionable. These should be used with caution.

14. CARD COPY

Some advertisers use copy so brief that the entire advertisement, although it sometimes occupies full-page space, could easily be printed on a business card. For example, the following full-page magazine advertisement contains only 24 words:

BLANK & CO.

Jewelers   Silversmiths   Stationers
Diamond Jewelry
Noted for Quality
From Generation to Generation
Mail Inquiries Receive Prompt Attention
Fifth Avenue
New York

Other frequent users of card advertising are the financial houses, stock brokers, and so forth, whose advertisements in the financial pages of the daily newspapers consist merely of their name and address and perhaps a slogan, all enclosed in a rectangular box.

This advertising may be heaven for those who work on it. In fact, it should allow its authors practically six months' vacation twice a year. But it goes against the grain of the users of tested advertising who have never been able to get a profitable volume of sales with fewer than 200 words.

15. CLEVER COPY

When copywriters try to be clever, they are likely to produce one of the following results:

1. They may write advertisements that are neither clever nor effective. The headline, in its attempt to be smart, may turn out to be obscure and fail to attract readers. The few readers who do read the copy realize that the copywriter has tried to be funny and has failed. Such an advertisement can actually do harm.

2. They may write an advertisement that seems clever to the people who read it from beginning to end. However, in view of the fact

that the headline is usually tricky, rather than a selling headline, few people actually do read the entire advertisement.

3. They may write the rare advertisement that contains both clever-ness and salesmanship. The following clothing advertising is an example. The element that kept this advertisement from misfiring is the fact that the headline attracted a large number of readers.

[Headline]	THIS IS PROBABLY THE LOWEST PRICED CLOTHING ADVERTISEMENT EVER PRINTED
[Subhead] [Illustration]	This suit $9.79—and very seasonable, indeed [Picture of a man wrapped in a large white cotton sheet]
[Copy]	"THIS SUIT" is really a large white cotton sheet. It covers the body, it launders well—and it costs $9.79
	Like any other low-priced clothing, it has its disadvantages: it doesn't fit, the style isn't so good, and it wouldn't quite pass at a directors' meeting or at the club—but it will keep you out of jail.
	ON THE OTHER HAND, if you do want to look well-dressed and hold the respect of your business associates, and look like success at a time when success never meant more—pay the price of good clothes.

Copywriters should avoid the so-called "clever" type of copy. It is too often a snare and a delusion. To attempt to write it is playing with fire. The chances are a hundred to one against you when you try to be smart in your advertising. Even the men and women who are famous for writing clever advertisements turn out a large number of duds. Why not be on the safe side and stick to selling copy? The chances are a hundred to one in your favor if you stick to a straightforward and simple presentation of the benefits your product will confer on the buyer.

16. HUMOROUS COPY

Humorous copy, like clever copy, should be avoided by 99 copywriters out of 100. Of the millions of people in the United States, less than half have a sense of humor. And those who do appreciate humor are divid-ed and subdivided into at least a dozen different groups. Each group has a sense of humor of a different kind. What is funny to you is likely to be either idiotic or insulting to many others. This means that when you write humorous copy, you limit your audience to perhaps one third or sometimes one tenth of your possible audience.

One of the best-remembered humorous campaigns was published years ago by the makers of Kelly-Springfield Tires. The ads were done in cartoon style with a large picture and a few lines of copy underneath. Example:

[Illustration]	[Picture of minister and layman in conversation]
[Copy]	"Aren't you sometimes tempted to swear a little when you have tire trouble, Parson?"
	"Well, I might be, but you see I avoid temptation by using Kelly-Springfields."

THREE KINDS OF COPY TO AVOID

The following types of copy are definitely not recommended.

17. POETIC COPY

There is a type of copy so poetically worded that the chief impression the reader receives is, "The person who wrote that piece is certainly a master word juggler."

The following advertisement is an example. In this ad a copywriter is attempting to sell his own services.

DRILLING

against granite with a point of putty—that's average advertising.

Aiming to pierce, it only bores. It wallows in a welter of sugary stultiloquence. "Thou say'st an undisputed thing in such a solemn way." The formula of average advertising is as unchanging as the jokes in an after-dinner speech. Advertising must shave off its mustache or grow one. It has looked the same too long. Advertising needs a fresh newpoint and a new penpoint or—LeDéluge . . . Mr. S.Y.Z., declared to be the highest-paid advertising writer, compresses into one luminous sentence what average advertising looks for without seeing. Space is too costly to stop to weigh the fee of supreme ability.

Arrangements for retaining Mr. X.Y.Z. may be initiated through Mr. A.B.C., Director Cliental Relations, 100 Park Avenue, New York.

The above advertisement appeared only once. Perhaps it brought so much business that its author is still busy filling orders. The opposite explanation seems more likely, however, that it brought so little business that it wasn't worth repeating.

Following is an advertisement that was repeated dozens of times in business magazines. It must have pulled or it wouldn't have been repeated so often. It is quoted here not as an example of poor copy, but for the sake of contrast.

SALES PROMOTION

$150 to $50,000 Daily Sales Developed during 28 years for clients by our direct mail campaigns. One product a few years ago was just an idea; this year $100,000 in orders booked. Fifty-year-old concern desired 50 national representatives; we produced 40 in three months. 700 dealers in 10 months at $3 each, for another. Ten years Sales Promotion Manager Larkin Co. Submit Sales problems for free diagnosis. J.C.J., Buffalo.

18. AFFECTED COPY

There is a type of copy that sounds as if it were written by a college sophomore in order to produce an intense effect on the reader. This copy depends on extravagant phrases rather than on real thought or feeling. Here is a sample taken from a jeweler's advertisement for star sapphires.

NOCTURNE

Star Sapphire . . . It is like a cup of night blue, dazed with moonlight and soft shadows, and it bears a promise of the sky. For in its depths stir the six arcs of a veiled silver star . . . eager to fling their beauty to the night.

19. UNBELIEVABLE COPY

Copy that strains the credulity of the intelligent reader is not as effective as it was years ago. Most of the advertisers who procured sales through exaggerated and unbelievable claims have been reduced to using 60-line space in a few of the cheaper publications. or they have gone out of business entirely. Here are the first three paragraphs of a form letter used at one time by a stock promotion advertiser:

Dear Friend:

Thousands of people who have read this letter have QUICKLY BECOME RICH! My sincere wish is that it will produce the same delightful results for YOU.

I'm going to write to you frankly—just as I would to an old friend—and give you some AMAZING FACTS that you can use to your VERY GREAT ADVANTAGE.

You know and I know that the man who can tell what business conditions are going to be six months, a year, or two years, ahead can make a FORTUNE out of this knowledge. That's exactly what I'm going to tell you.

Yours for success,

John Doe

All of us who prepare advertising have a responsibility to the public. The public places a trust in advertising, and those who betray that trust do harm to their own profession as well as to the business of their clients. Following is a story illustrating this point.

A life insurance salesman tried for ten years to sell a man a policy. One day the prospect walked into the insurance man's office with a printed advertisement for that same policy in his hand and wanted to buy it. The advertisement, by means of printed words, sold the same thing that the salesman had for ten years been trying to sell with spoken words. The prospect felt a confidence in the printed message that he did not feel in the sales talk.

This belief in printed words is trained into us from childhood. We learn from printed pages that two plus two equal four and that Columbus discovered America in 1492. These things are facts, and during the most impressionable years of our lives, we are trained to believe what we read.

Advertisers who betray this confidence do harm. For example, let us say that a child aged 12 sees an advertisement with the headline "Free Roller Skates . . . Simply mail coupon." The child fills in and mails the coupon and immediately begins to think about the fun he or she is going to have when he gets the roller skates. Then comes the rude awakening. The youngster receives a letter from the advertiser stating that if the child will sell 30 sets of beautiful colored photographs to friends at a dollar a set and send in the money, the manufacturer will send the roller skates "absolutely free."

Thus is created a skeptic, a doubter. Twenty years later, when this individual is in the market for an automobile, the automobile advertiser may find the selling job has been made more difficult by the misleading advertisement that jarred the prospect's confidence years before.

The pre-eminence of America in industry has come largely through mass production. Mass production is only possible where there is demand. Mass demand has been created almost entirely through the development of advertising.

Calvin Coolidge

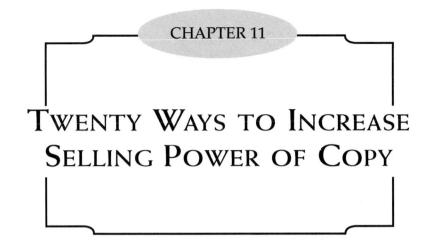

CHAPTER 11

TWENTY WAYS TO INCREASE SELLING POWER OF COPY

This chapter discusses 20 ways to increase the selling power of your advertising. All of these methods have been tested in actual practice and have been found to be effective.

1. USE PRESENT TENSE, SECOND PERSON

Unless there is a definite reason to the contrary, you should write your copy in the present tense, second person. Don't say, "A man will feel well dressed in a Brooks Brothers suit." Say, "*You feel* well dressed in a Brooks Brothers suit."

Don't say, "People will enjoy a sense of security when they use Goodyear Tires." Say, "*You enjoy* a sense of security when *you* use Goodyear Tires."

Keep hammering at the reader with—you—you—you.

2. USE SUBHEADS

Practically all mail order advertisers use three or more subheads in every full-page advertisement. Many general advertisers do the same. There are two key reasons for this:

1. Subheads tell your story in brief form to glancers who don't have time to read your entire advertisement.

2. Subheads get copy read that might otherwise not be read. For example potential customers might be sufficiently attracted by your headline to read a paragraph or two of your copy, and then turn the page. But at that moment an interesting subhead catches their attention, and they read further.

Here are the headline and subheads of a beauty product advertisement. Notice how the subheads tell a brief story as well as arouse interest.

Headline: What Is the Critical Age of a Woman's Skin?

Subhead No. 1:   New York doctor shows how to correct the 4 defects that age your skin.

Subhead No. 2:   Why old-style treatments fail.

Subhead No. 3:   How pore-deep method acts.

Subhead No. 4:   Send $1.00 for booklet, "New Faces for Old."

When setting the price for booklets or similar offers, charge enough to discourage anything-for-free responses, yet not so high it loses your targeted audience. Check for similar offers by analogous advertisers—noting both "similar" and "analogous"—and test . . . Test . . . TEST!

3. PUT CAPTIONS UNDER ILLUSTRATIONS

In newspaper articles, you will always find captions printed under the illustrations. These captions get high readership because they add to the interest of the illustrations and help to explain their meaning. In magazines such as *Time* and *Playboy*, you will also find scores of illustrations with captions under them. These captions, as shown in Figure 11.1 attract and sell to readers.

The point is that people are in the habit of reading the brief messages that are printed under pictures. This habit dates back to the reading of school textbooks, which have always had captions under the illustrations. The advertiser should take advantage of this habit. Don't run pictures without putting captions under them. Put a brief selling message or a human-interest message under every illustration you use. David Ogilvy, in *Ogilvy on Advertising*, tells us: "More people read the captions under illustrations than read the body copy, so never use an illustration without putting a caption under it. Your caption should include the brand name and/or the promise."

4. USE A SIMPLE STYLE OF WRITING

Writing nearly a century apart, the English philosopher Herbert Spencer and the American ad man Roy Durstine give advice every writer of advertising, regardless of medium, should take to heart. Copywriters would do themselves a favor by copying the following passages and keeping them handy. If practical, enlarge them a bit and put them on the bulletin board in front of your desk. Reread their message from time to time until it becomes part of your own mental makeup.

Figure 11.1: *KISS for SUCCESS!* Successful direct-response advertisers practice the KISS principle of "keep it simple, stupid" . . . or find themselves divorced from customers. Lenox Collections embraces this advice in illustration, copy, and response. The free canister is the largest one pictured and shown directly above the coupon. Coupon copy—shown slightly oversize—continues to sell the sets' quality (fine porcelain . . . "crafted") and exclusivity (Not sold in . . . stores). Details of cost and billing conclude with *two* FREE bonuses—both canister and display cabinet. To keep it even simpler, there's no need for credit card information, just a signature. KISS like this to tell about great trips to the bank.

Spencer's *Philosophy of Style* is not the simplest piece of writing in the world. Nevertheless, the idea that you should reduce to a minimum the time it takes the reader to figure out what you are trying to say is absolutely sound.

> Regarding language as an apparatus of symbols for the conveyance of thought, we may say that, as in a mechanical apparatus, the more simple and the better arranged its parts, the greater will be the effect produced.
>
> In either case, whatever force is absorbed by the machine is deducted from the result. A reader or listener has at each moment but a limited amount of mental power available. To recognize and interpret the symbols presented to him requires part of this power; to arrange and combine the images suggested requires a further part; and only that part that remains can be used for realizing the thought conveyed.
>
> Hence, the more time and attention it takes to receive and understand each sentence, the less time and attention can be given to the contained idea; and the less vividly will that idea be conceived.

Roy Durstine in his book, *This Advertising Business*, expressed the same idea, perhaps more potently than Spencer expressed it:

> The most important job of an advertisement is to center all the attention on the merchandise and none on the technique of presenting it.

5. CHOOSE SIMPLE WORDS

Use short simple words to express your meaning. Educated readers understand short words just as well as long words, and everyone else understands short words much better. Even where it is necessary to substitute three or four short words for one long word, it is usually wise to do so.

The following advertisement from BBDO, Inc. makes the point as well today as when it was first run some years ago:

POMPOUS WORDS

> For some years, folks have been finding in the attics of old houses bits of furniture that are priceless. Abandoned farm houses, gaunt and bald, have revealed, with a bit of coaxing, a purity of line and form and a generous sturdiness of build, which are almost lost arts.
>
> When restored, one of these fine old houses stands out from its modern neighbors of Spanish, French, Italian, Tudor, and Mission design, with the calm dignity of a patrician in a rabble.
>
> Since the days of Chaucer and Shakespeare, we have had stored away in the attic a simple, crude language that was made to order

for advertising. It consists mostly of one- and two-syllable words—odd, native, little words that barbarians used to express their uncouth thoughts.

About the time this jargon was in flower, a gang from the Mediterranean muscled in and, with sword and monk, laid the groundwork for modern civilization in England.

Then they began to put together that collection of mongrel words known as the English language. The rude, vulgar, native words had to answer for the masses and so stayed in use, but people with any pretense to culture gradually fixed up a lot of words with fancy Latin fronts, Greek centers and a dash of Turkish in the rear.

For the last thousand years, education in England has consisted chiefly of learning Greek and Latin. We have been about as bad in this country. The result is curiously shown in our writings. Young men who join us each year from big universities for a while find it hard to express themselves in writing with anything less than five-syllable words.

Yet, strange to say, when people are just talking back and forth they still use the old Anglo-Saxon almost entirely.

You see, these built-up words don't, as a rule, mean anything in particular. Take that last word, "particular." That's one of them. It is an adjective or noun and can be made into a verb or adverb. The dictionary gives it something like fifty different meanings. So it really doesn't mean a thing. It is little more than a sound. It started two or three thousand years ago in some wild Latin tribe as "par." The Roman intelligentsia dressed it up into "particula." Then the French made it "particulier." The word has been rolling round for so long that it's all moss and no stone.

Of course, Latin is a beautiful language and has given us a lot of nice little words that are almost Anglo-Saxon in simplicity and clarity. But they are not pompous words.

The reason we use short words to talk with is that they mean exactly the same thing to talker and hearer. When we drag in a lot of jointed words, we forget before the sentence is finished just what it was we were trying to say; and the other fellow never does find out. For the same reason, we use short words to think with.

Now, in advertising, it is vital that the readers shall grasp, in a split second, whatever it is that you want them to know. You can't afford to waste a single syllable just to impress them with your intellectual culture. Broadcasting offers a good example of what we mean. Someone got gorgeous and produced "superheterodyne." One Latin word and two Greek ones. Isn't that a nice word to work into a snappy selling talk? A manufacturer, who likes to have the public know what he is talking about, built his appeal on "Golden Voice."

Short words are easy and pleasant to read. The eye picks up their meaning without conscious effort. But the average reader stumbles over pompous words and loses his mental balance. They annoy and bore him. After about two staggers, his interest wanders and he turns to the next page.

A short word takes up about one third as much room as a pompous word. When you are paying forty dollars a line, that is quite an item. (From an ad by BBDO, Inc.)

6. GIVE FREE INFORMATION

One way to arouse interest is to give free information as well as sales talk in your copy. In doing this, your advertisement should be arranged so that the free information comes first and the sales talk second. If the sales talk is placed first, the reader may never reach the free information section.

Here are the type of headline and opening paragraphs that have proven successful for many a business school advertisement. Notice that the copy starts off, not with a sales talk, but in an editorial style. It might be the beginning of a magazine article:

A WARNING to men and women who would like to be independent in the next five years

You can tell a $200-a-week worker how to make $350 a week.

You can tell a $350-a-week worker how to make $500 a week.

But you can't tell a $25,000 man or woman how to make $50,000. They've got to know.

Between $25,000 and $35,000 a year is where most men and women of talent stop.

Health, youth, good appearance, and brains will carry you far in business.

But you cannot draw forever on that bank account unless you put something else in. Somewhere between $25,000 and $35,000 a year you will stop dead.

Business today is new and complex. The old rules will no longer work. A whole new set of problems is presented by the information explosion. Overseas markets have become a vital issue. An entirely new conception of selling is replacing the old hit-or-miss way.

7. SELLING COPY VERSUS STYLE COPY

Two types of copy in use today are

1. style copy
2. selling copy

Style copy is based on the assumption that customers are swayed by flowery language and elaborate adjectives. Here is an example of style copy taken from a soap advertisement:

> Try this soap for just 7 days and you will be convinced. You will revel in its sculptured smoothness, its deep-piled fragrant lather. How exquisitely soft your skin is after its use—how fresh and clear! Let your mirror show you, a little more clearly each day, the natural charm men love to dream about!

Now read a piece of selling copy taken from another soap advertisement:

> This soap is made of olive and palm oils—no other fats whatever. No artificial coloring. No heavy fragrance to mask other odors. It is a pure soap—with moisturizing lather as pure and wholesome as the complexions it fosters. So pure, in fact, that more than 20,000 beauty experts the world over have united to recommend it.

Notice how style copy consists mainly of unsupported claims, whereas selling copy supports its claims with proof. The first example of soap copy says, "Revel in its sculptured smoothness." The other says, "Made of olive and palm oils—no other fats whatever."

If there is any doubt in your mind as to whether to use style copy or selling copy, remember that advertisers who can trace the sales results from their ads use selling copy.

8. AROUSE CURIOSITY

Curiosity is a powerful selling tool when properly used by the copywriter. On the other hand, the copywriter who satisfies the reader's curiosity, instead of arousing it, is apt to lose customers.

Some time ago I read a review of a new novel. This review aroused my curiosity about the novel and I considered buying it. A few days later I saw an advertisement for the same novel. The advertisement contained several long quotations from the book itself. I read these quotations. They revealed so much of the plot of the story that my curiosity was satisfied and I decided not to buy the book. A book review had practically persuaded me to buy the book. An advertisement lost the sale by satisfying my curiosity.

Here are examples of the proper use of the curiosity appeal. These are taken from copy for mystery and adventure books. Notice how these sentences tell enough of a situation to arouse your curiosity; but they refrain from satisfying your curiosity by telling you the outcome of the situation.

> An intricate tale of big-time mob doings and small-town dirty laundry . . . with a brilliantly staged conclusion at the annual ice festival.

> How could it happen in 1995 . . . a millionaire's yacht stranded helpless on a cannibal island!

Here are some curiosity-arousing paragraphs from a successful advertisement for a book on how to develop a magnetic personality:

> This singular book wields a strange power over its readers by showing them how to develop a magnetic personality almost instantly.

> A strange book! A book that seems to cast a spell over every person who turns its pages!

> A copy of this book was left lying on a hotel table for a few weeks. Nearly 400 people saw the book—read a few pages—and then sent for a copy!

> In another case a physician placed a copy on the table in his waiting room. More than 200 of his patients saw the book—read part of it— and then ordered copies for themselves!

> Why are men and women so profoundly affected by this book—so anxious to get a copy? The answer is simple. The book reveals to them for the first time how any man or woman—old or young— can develop a magnetic personality. It explains how to gain the personal charm that attracts friends—the self-confidence that insures success.

In the preceding paragraphs, notice that the method by which the reader is given a magnetic personality is not explained. You have to buy the book in order to discover that.

The curiosity appeal can be used with free booklets, too, booklets that you want people to send for. Here is an example:

GET THIS FREE BOOK

> A 24-page free booklet tells how you can become financially independent—how you can provide an income to retire on—how you can end money worries—how you can do these things and many other things, no matter whether your present income is large or small.

> This plan . . . is explained in the free book. There's no obligation. Send for your copy now.

Notice that the financial plan is not explained. The reader is merely told that there is such a plan and that it is explained in the free booklet. If the advertisement told what the plan was, the reader might say, "Oh, is that all it is! I've known about that all my life." An advertisement that gives away its secret in advance is like a magician who shows the audience the secret of his tricks before he performs them.

9. MAKE YOUR COPY SPECIFIC

Anybody who works on tested advertising will tell you how important it is to be specific in your copy. For example, the statement that "97,482 people have bought one of these appliances" is stronger than the statement "Nearly 100,000 of these appliances have been sold." The first statement sounds like a fact. It tells the reader that a strict and accurate count has been made of the actual number of customers. The second statement—100,000 have been sold—sounds like a copywriter's claim—and possibly an exaggerated claim.

The reason there are so many general claims used in advertising copy is that it requires time and trouble to collect specific data.

Thus, out of more than 700 large-space ads in the December 1995 issues of 14 of America's most popular consumer magazines, just five ads stood out for their factual approach:

- The California date just might be the perfect snack. It has no fat, no cholesterol, and contains only 23 calories.

- The Cannon Sure Shot 70 Zoom—ultra compact to fit pocket or purse . . . 2x35-70mm zoom lens, fully automatic film handling and exposure, built-in multi-function flash . . . 3-point Smart Autofocus for razor sharp shots over time. [Similar Canon ads appeared in several of the magazines.]

- 5 hours of intensive daily instruction • On court 4:1 student-pro ratio • Video analysis • 45 Grand Slam courts—red clay, Har Tru, Laykold and grass • Fitness Center • Saddlebrook Sport science option.

- 30% more cartilage protein than other premium brands.

- Standard dual air bags • Steel safety cell construction • Side door guard beams • Air conditioning • Electronic AM/FM stereo cassette • Air filtration system • Dual remote heated mirrors • Rear defroster and more. $15,165 [Ford Contour]

Here is a true story that shows the cash value of specific statements. It was so powerful that the industry's association requested that the copy, though true, be toned down.

A national producer of a building material had opened a new mill and began local advertising in this market.

Study of the process of manufacture showed that the product averaged 52.7% higher than the U.S. Government standard of quality, a simple fact that might carry conviction. It was decided to feature this fact and let the readers draw their own conclusions based on this tangible fact.

The 52.7% point was visualized by a simple and easily remembered graphic chart.

Newspaper space in selected cities and towns around the mill was scheduled for a two months' campaign.

Meanwhile the strategy of the plan was developed:

1. Each county was analyzed and assigned a "value" showing annual total consumption of all brands.

2. An unselfish feature was incorporated in each advertisement: space to list in display type, without charge to the dealer, five or six other fast-selling items.

3. The sales staff was instructed to release the newspaper schedule in local papers over the names of local dealers who placed carload orders.

   The sales staff took hold of the plan enthusiastically and within a few weeks booked 150 carload orders, largely from new accounts . . . Soon the newspaper advertisements appeared . . . dealers became actively interested . . . buyers noted the facts presented . . . contractors, engineers, architects and public officials began to talk . . . sales to consumers followed . . . reorders multiplied. Results far exceeded expectations—at a cost of less than half of the budgeted appropriation.

   Then a curious situation arose. The head of the National Association insisted that the copy, though true, be modified. It was feared that new rulings, raising the government standard to an unreasonable level, might result; there were rumors that local mill owners, aroused by the competitive force of the 52.7% copy, might start a vicious price-cutting campaign.

The advertising staff was instructed to "soften" the appeal, remove its sharp selling force. So the figure "52.7%" was changed to "over 50%." Immediately the "kick" was taken out of the advertising. Demand fell off to a fraction of its former strength. Word-of-mouth comment died out. Local competitors and association officials were satisfied.

Note how "52.7%" was accepted as definite proof of quality and value, while "over 50%" was discounted as a mere claim in praise of a product.

10. USE LONG COPY

Whether to use short copy or long copy is a question that is difficult to answer with definite rules. So much depends on your special situation and on what you are trying to accomplish with your advertising.

A. Space Advertising

In general, you can observe the following situation in the advertising in most magazines and newspapers:

1. The short-copy ads, set in poster style and containing only a few words of copy or a slogan, are usually used by advertisers who are unable to trace the direct sales results from their advertisements.

2. Advertisers who can trace the direct sales results from their ads use long copy because it pulls better than short copy. For example, the book club advertisers, the record clubs, and the correspondence school advertisers use ads containing 500 to 1500 words of copy. Also, you will find that real-estate advertisers, patent-medicine advertisers, and classified advertisers put as much selling copy into their ads as the space will allow. These people cannot afford to run so-called "reminder copy." They have to get immediate sales from every ad. (See long copy ad at end of this chapter.)

3. When your picture truly speaks a thousand words, shorter copy is often the right approach to sales success, as shown in the proven Lenox direct response advertisement in Figure 11.1 and in the Guess?, Inc. advertisement in Figure 11.2.

MAN MAG 4/C Los Angeles Sept 95 LH Pg Opp: TOC C/S 98435

Figure 11.2: *How to use a one-word sales talk.* When the right picture does the total selling job in the prospect's imagination, the only word you need is the product name. Of course creating the picture is the key. That's why Guess?, Inc.'s president, Paul Marciano, makes it a major part of his own responsibility. The result, as shown above, speaks for itself.

B. Direct Mail Copy

Advertisers who sell their goods and services by means of direct mail letters have found it profitable to use long copy in their advertising. Long copy is such a tested and proven success that the four-page direct mail letter has become a rule, rather than an option. Where the instruction used to be, "Say whatever you must say, then stop," it now is, "Say it in four pages and make it worth reading."

For example, one of the pioneers in selling seafood by mail—and who made a fortune doing it—started his business with brief letters. Later on he gradually shifted to longer letters because he found that long letters brought in more orders from customers. (See one of his successful letters on pp. 116-117.)

Here is the brief sales letter that he used in the beginning:

Dear Sir:

I wish to call your attention to the "Davis Star Brand" of choice selected Fat Mackerel.

I should be pleased to deliver a package to your address (shipping prepaid by me).

All are of the same quality, differing only in size; are prepared for cooking, and are delivered.

You will find a 20-lb. pail of either Number 1 or Number 1 Extra a desirable size.

Hoping to receive your order, I remain

Yours respectfully,

Frank E. Davis

That is the 75-word letter the seafood seller sent out in his own handwriting when he first started in business. After years of sales testing, he found that he could get more and more sales by adding more and more copy. Eventually, he sent to prospective customers an envelope containing the following:

1. A 750-word letter

2. An order form

3. A four-page folder

The four-page folder contained 14 pictures, four main headlines, 12 subheads, 8 testimonial letters, and approximately 1,600 words of selling copy. In his years of experience in selling by mail, this successful entrepreneur found that long copy pays better than short copy.

This does not mean that long copy should be used merely for the sake of filling space. Long copy should be used in order to crowd in as many sales arguments as possible.

Here are some additional points in regard to length of copy:

1. Advocates of short copy say, "I don't think anybody will read all that small print. Let's cut the copy down to a couple of paragraphs and set it in 18-point type."

   What the advocates of short copy should say, if they want to be accurate, is this: "I don't think everybody will read all that small print." This is perfectly true. Everybody will not read it. But the fact is that the very people you are most interested in will read your ad. These are the prospects who will buy your product or service if you tell them sufficient reasons for doing so.

2. It is entirely unnecessary to set copy in 18-point type. People buy magazines and newspapers to read the stories and articles contained therein. These stories and articles are set in 7-point to 9-point type. The copy you are reading now is set in 10.5-point type.

3. The question arises: Why wouldn't it pay the short-copy users to make their advertising do the utmost selling job by including more sales talk? *Answer*: The chances are that it would pay them.

Here is a solution to the problem of long copy versus short copy that should satisfy the champions of both sides of the question. Put a brief selling message into your headline and subheadings. Put your detailed message into small print. In this way, you accomplish two things: (1) You get a brief message across to glancers with your headline and subheads. (2) You give a complete message in small print to the person who is sufficiently interested in your product to read about it.

11. WRITE MORE COPY THAN IS NECESSARY TO FILL THE SPACE

Said the copy chief of a large advertising agency specializing in testing advertising:

> We find that copy improves in quality when we cut it. That doesn't mean that we favor short copy. It means that the copywriter should write more copy than is necessary to fill a given space and then boil it down.

> For example, we run our new advertisements in full-page size first. If the advertisement is successful, we repeat it as many times as it will pay. When sales fall off to such an extent that it doesn't pay to repeat the advertisement in full-page size, we cut it to half-page size. Usually it can be made to pay for a couple more insertions in this reduced space.

When the advertisement is no longer effective in half-page size, we sometimes reduce it to 60 lines and squeeze out a few more sales.

I have noticed again and again that the quality of the copy improves when we cut it. In the full-page size there are a number of unessential words and phrases. Sometimes there are whole paragraphs that are not essential to the sales story.

When the copy is cut to half-page size, these unessential elements are omitted. This strengthens the copy—gives it greater sales punch.

When the copy is cut to 60 lines, (a single column by five inches), we have to omit everything but the bare essentials. The copy becomes telegraphic. Every paragraph is packed with selling arguments. The 60-line version contains the best copy of all.

As an illustration of this story, look at the headline and opening paragraphs of this sample couponed advertisement. A similar ad was first tested in large space.

RETIRE ON AN INCOME

You don't have to be wealthy to retire on an income. You don't even have to be wealthy to be financially independent and free from money worries for the rest of your life.

This company has perfected a new Retirement Income Plan that enables any person of moderate means to provide a guaranteed income for life.

The income begins at any age you say—55, 60, or 65. It can be any amount you wish—$2,000 a month, $2,500, even $3,000 or more.

The ad brought good results. However, the copy can be cut. In a reduced-size advertisement, the three paragraphs were cut to two paragraphs as follows:

RETIRE ON AN INCOME

This new Retirement Income Plan enables you to provide for yourself a guaranteed income for life.

The income begins at any age you say—55, 60, or 65. It can be any amount you wish—$2,000 a month, $2,500, even $3,000 or more.

Later this copy was put into small space and the message was reduced to a single sentence, as follows:

RETIRE ON AN INCOME

This new Retirement Income Plan enables you to retire at 55, 60, or 65 with a monthly income of $2,000, $2,500, even $3,000 or more, guaranteed for life.

This discussion on cutting copy is not to be considered an argument in favor of short copy. If you have space for long copy, it is advisable to use long copy. The point of this discussion is that copy usually improves when you cut it. Therefore, if you have space for 500 words of copy, don't just write 500 words. Write 1,000 words and boil it down to 500 words. If you have space for only 50 words, write 200 words and boil it down. A piece of copy is like a pot of broth. The more you boil it down, the stronger the flavor gets.

12. AVOID HELPING YOUR COMPETITORS

An advertisement for a large-screen TV set that describes in general terms the enjoyment of television helps to sell not only your own TV sets, but your competitor's sets as well.

Suppose you sell a woman the idea of buying a TV set and she goes to a store where TV sets are displayed. She may buy the type of set you are advertising. But the chances are equally good that she will buy a competitive make. Your advertising will help your sales more if you sell your particular TV set, its tone, its picture quality, its power, or some other special feature.

The same is true in other lines. An automobile advertisement that sells your particular car is better than an advertisement selling the idea of owning an automobile, as no one else has done better than in the Jaguar mailing in Figure 11.3. An advertisement that sells your own special brand of coffee has more effect on your sales than an advertisement describing the pleasures of coffee drinking. Better yet, combine both into the same message. This seems like an elementary rule. Nevertheless, it is often violated.

13. USE MAIL ORDER METHODS IN DIRECT MAIL ADVERTISING

The problems of direct mail advertising are almost identical with the problems of mail order advertising. In each case you are trying to get attention, arouse interest, and induce action. The vehicle carrying your message is the only thing that varies. In direct mail advertising, your message comes to your prospects in envelopes addressed individually, just to them, and, as in Figure 11.4, even hand addressed. In mail order advertising, your message comes to the prospect by means of a page in a magazine or newspaper or via broadcasting.

This means that the rules of mail-order advertising apply with equal force to direct mail. Rules for headlines, first paragraphs, use of subheads, length of copy, type of copy, and so forth, all may be applied to direct mail. In a direct mail letter, however, the first sentence is your headline. Just as the headline of a mail order advertisement decided whether or not the prospect will read the copy, so the first sentence of a direct mail letter usually decides whether or not the prospect will read the letter.

Here are some letter beginnings that were used by successful direct mail advertisers. Computer technology permits cost-effective addressing to individuals by name:

Dear Charles P. Holten:
(Some computer addressing systems must use the entire name.)

Do you know what "The Lost Books of the Bible" are? How they came to be? Why they are attracting such widespread interest?

Dear Mrs. Charters:

I met a woman the other day who, through sheer skill and hard work, has amassed a considerable fortune and has risen far beyond her original associations.

Dear Mr. Mangun:

Here is a letter with a selfish motive. Selfish on my part for I shall gain—and, oddly enough, gain through actually saving money for you.

Dear Friend: (generic, probably noncomputerized letter):

Somehow we failed you.

A few weeks ago, dissatisfied with your personal progress, or ambitious for quicker progress, you wrote us asking whether we could help you.

Dear Friend: [With this first sentence, the salutation hardly matters.]

Enclosed find check for $200.

We all like to get letters that begin that way, don't we?

One advantage you have in direct-mail advertising is that you can enclose a number of different pieces of advertising material in the same envelope.

For example, the mailing may contain the following:

1. An outer envelope, usually with what direct mailers call "a teaser"; that is, a must-open-and-read-more message

2. A personalized letter printed on white stock

3. A four-page folder printed on cream-colored stock

Figure 11.3: *Six questions in search of an answer.* The 14″ × 5-1/2″ envelope, mailed First Class, grabs attention. A personalized letter from the President tells how he fell in love with a car and why you will too. A striking eight-panel flyer unfolds into six questions about your relationship with your present auto, then answers

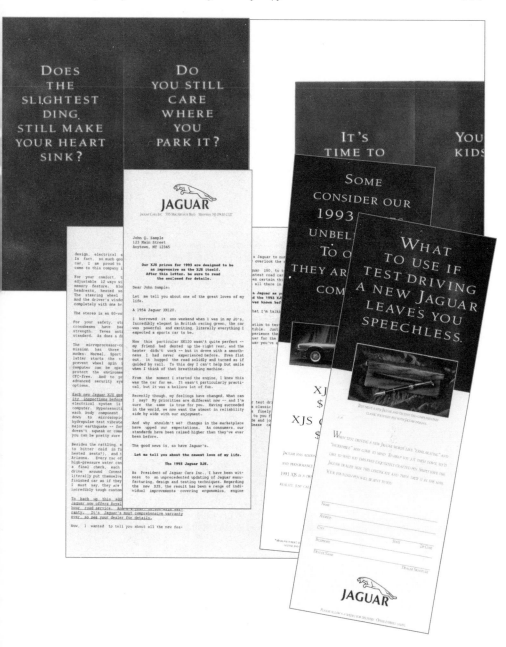

all six . . . with Jaguar. Two full-size inserts tell what it costs and dramatize the premium. No wonder 2,700 cars were taken for a test drive and over $15,000,000 of them were sold. *Winner, ADDY Award Best of Show. Winner, the One Show Gold Pencil First Prize.*

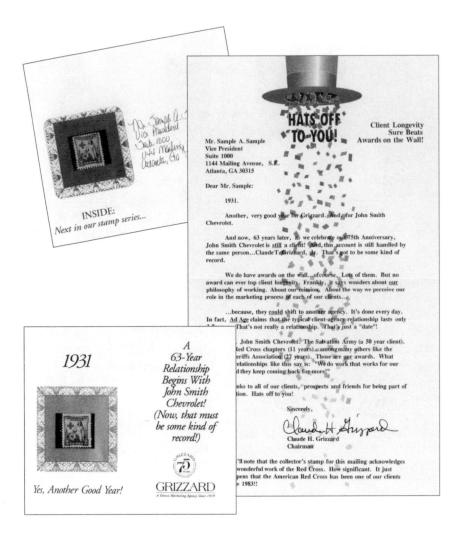

Figure 11.4: *Not your everyday Diamond Jubilee.* As a direct-response agency, Grizzard used the medium it knows best to do more than just brag about its 75th anniversary. At two-week intervals, clients, prospects, vendors, and friends received a personalized letter and a collector-item stamp, valuable in itself, to celebrate an important date in client-agency relationships. Elegant hand-addressed invitation-size envelopes and ample use of gold foil maintained the celebratory feeling . . . and produced a flood of requests for additional copies. *Winner, 1994 John Caples Award.*

4. A leaflet of testimonials printed on green stock

5. A page of newspaper clippings reproduced on newspaper stock

6. An order form, printed on yellow stock

7. A business reply envelope printed on red stock

You may ask, "Why use seven separate and distinct mailing pieces printed on different kinds of stock? Why not incorporate the entire message, testimonials, news clippings, order form, and everything in a 16-page booklet?"

The answer is that all large users of direct mail such as insurance companies, correspondence schools, record clubs, and book publishers have found the other method more effective. The reason is this: Much direct-mail advertising goes directly to the wastebasket. A prospect will rarely throw all of your mailing pieces into the wastebasket, however, without at least glancing at them. If your entire advertising message is contained in a single circular or a single booklet, prospects will devote a few seconds to it and if it doesn't arouse their interest, they will throw it away. On the other hand, if your envelope is stuffed with half a dozen different mailing pieces, prospects will probably glance at each piece before throwing it away. People hate to throw things away without at least glancing at them. They want to avoid disposing of anything valuable. Therefore, your envelope plus six different inserts give you seven opportunities to catch the interest of the prospect instead of only one opportunity. Note that this is an "opportunity," not a guarantee. You must make EVERY SINGLE PIECE of your mailing SELL AT A GLANCE. Put all, or even the major part, of your "sell" into just one piece such as the folder and you have wasted six-sevenths of your selling opportunity.

14. OVERSTATEMENT COPY VERSUS UNDERSTATEMENT

Advertising copy today is showing a trend toward understatement, and in some cases understatement copy has shown greater pulling power than the other kind. Here is an example of the old-style "overstatement" copy:

I WILL TRAIN YOU AT HOME
TO FILL A BIG-INCOME JOB!

Be an Electrical Expert. Learn to earn a big salary. Get in line for a top job by enrolling now for my easily learned, quickly grasped, right-up-to-the-minute, Spare-Time, Home-Study Course in Practical Electricity.

You don't even have to be a High School Graduate. As Chief Engineer of the Engineering Works of a million-plus city, I know exactly the kind of training you need, and I will give you that training. My Course in Electricity is simple, thorough, and complete and offers every person regardless of age, education or previous experience, the chance to become, in a very short time, an "Electrical Expert," able to make big money.

Compare the preceding copy with these more recent conservatively worded and convincing paragraphs taken from a business-school advertisement.

TO THE MAN OR WOMAN WHO IS 35
AND DISSATISFIED

From thirty-five to forty is the critical age for opportunity. In these years a man or woman either marks out the course that leads to promotion or advancement, or settles into permanent unhappiness. There are thousands who see the years passing with a feeling close to desperation.

They say, "I have to make more money." But they have no plan for making more.

They say, "There is no future for me here." But they see no opening anywhere else.

I'm managing to scrape along now," they say. "But how in the world will I ever educate my children?"

To men and women whose minds are constantly—and often almost hopelessly—at work on such thoughts, this page is addressed. It is devoid of rhetoric. It is plain, blunt common sense.

Let us get one thing straight at the very start—
We do not want you unless
You want us

There are the dissatisfied men and women who will do something and the ones who won't. We feel sorry for the latter, but we cannot afford to enroll them. We have a reputation for training those who—as a result of our training—earn large salaries and hold responsible positions. That reputation must be maintained. We can do much, but we cannot make anyone succeed who will not help themselves. So rest assured you will not be unduly urged into anything.

In most advertisements that offer a free booklet, there is a paragraph at the end that urges the reader to send for the booklet. Here is a sample paragraph that is a good example of overstatement copy.

REMARKABLE BOOK, "PRACTICAL SELLING," SENT FREE

With my compliments I want to send you a most remarkable book, "Practical Selling." It will show you how you can easily become a Master Sales Representative—a big money-maker—how our system of Salesmanship Training will give you the equivalent of years of selling experience in a few weeks; how our FREE Employment Service will help you select and secure a good selling position when you are qualified and ready. And it will give you success stories of former routine workers who are now earning amazing salaries as sales representatives. Mail the coupon today. It may be the turning point in your life.

Now read a very different kind of paragraph, also offering a free booklet:

A booklet has been prepared that tells about this new Course and Service. Its title is "What an Executive Should Know." It should be read by all the men and women who face the responsibility of shaping their own future. It is free. We will send you this booklet if you will simply give us your name and address on the coupon below. But we do not urge you to send for it. If you are the type of man or woman for whom the new Course and Service has been constructed, if you are determined to take advantage of the rich opportunities of the next five years, you will send for it without urging.

Even in the selection of testimonials, the copywriter must make up her mind whether overstatement or understatement will be most effective in convincing her particular type of prospect. Here is a typical overstatement testimonial:

PLANT ENGINEER'S PAY RAISED 150%

"I was a dumbbell in electricity until I got in touch with you, but now I have charge of a big plant including 600 motors and I direct a force of 34 skilled workers—electricians, helpers, etc. My salary has gone up more than 150%."

Here is the other type of testimonial, the conservative type. Notice how the copywriter has injected comments that help to sell in parentheses:

We wish you could read the letters that come to us in every mail. Here is one, for example, from John H., of Hagerstown, MD: "I was floundering around without a definite goal," he says, "and was seriously considering a Civil Service appointment."

"The study of your Course and Service was in no way a hardship," he continues, "rather it was a real pleasure, because it is so practical and inspiring throughout." (The method of the Institute makes it practical and inspiring.) "Added self-confidence and increased vision gained from the Institute's work," says Mr. H., "enabled me to accept and discharge added responsibilities successfully."

He is an officer now of the organization in which he was once a dissatisfied "cog."

If it is important to avoid overstatement in copy, it is also important to avoid the appearance of overstatement. When a manufacturer brings out a new product, the best advertisement for it is often a simple news write-up in which the headline clearly states the most important feature, the subhead the next most important feature, and the copy the other features.

Do not try to gild the lily. Do not weaken your entire advertisement by giving the impression that you are trying to make your proposition sound better than it really is.

The news-style copy that follows introduced what has become a standard feature of many alarm clocks:

NEW CLOCK WAKES YOU WITH MUSIC
Tuneful notes replace strident clangor, with loud alarm in reserve

It is no longer necessary to have your morning ripped open with imperious jangling that is little short of cruelty to the sleep-softened nerves. A new Westclox product approaches the subject of awakening, tunefully and softly at first.

Thus amiably roused, you can shut off the alarm and face the day in a pleasant mood. Should this musical awakening go unheeded, the clock waits a few moments and rings again, this time too loud to be ignored.

15. AVOID TRICK SLOGANS

Avoid slogans and catchlines that are obviously untrue. For example, a manufacturer of mint candies used the slogan "On every tongue." This is obviously untrue. Everyone knows that these candies are not on every tongue. It is merely a trick phrase. Some less clever but true selling argument, such as "The flavor lasts," would be more effective.

16. GET HELP FROM OTHERS

It is helpful to take an advertisement or a headline you have just written, show it to others whose opinion you respect, and get their opinion.

But be sure to get a true opinion. Most people don't want to hurt your feelings by telling you that your idea is terrible and should be thrown into the wastebasket. They will be most likely to nod their heads and say, "That's a fine idea." Sometimes you can find a few people who will give you their frank, unvarnished opinion. That is a true find, and useful.

The trouble with most critics is that they are too optimistic. One way to overcome this difficulty is to never show them just one piece of copy or one headline. Show them two pieces of copy or two headlines and ask them which one they like better. Then they will praise one and criticize the other. In this way you can get a true opinion.

It is also helpful for the copywriter to work directly with the client in preparing copy, instead of sending a representative or account executive to sell it to the client. Messages that go back and forth secondhand have four chances to get misunderstood.

17. Do Not Say that Salesperson Will Call

Some advertisers offer a free booklet in their advertising in order to get the names and addresses of people interested in the product. A salesperson delivers the free booklet or, after it has been mailed, telephones or calls on the prospect. If this is your plan of action, do not mention in the advertising that a salesperson will call. To do so will cut down your coupon returns at least 75 percent.

18. Study the Selling Copy in Mail Order Catalogs

The large mail-order houses, such as J. C. Penney, Sears Roebuck, and L. L. Bean, are masters of the art of selling goods by means of printed words and pictures. The next time you are puzzled as to how to sell a product, study a mail-order catalog and see how the mail-order people approach the subject. In the large mail-order catalogs you will find excellent sales talks for almost every product you can think of.

19. Make Every Advertisement a Complete Sales Talk

It is an old rule but a good rule to write every advertisement as if it were the first and the last word to be said on the subject. Do not depend on the reader having read any previous advertisements for the product you are selling. Do not assume that the reader will learn from future advertisements the selling arguments that you fail to include in today's advertisement. Make every advertisement a complete sales talk. Bring in every important sales argument.

Suppose a financial firm is selling an investment plan that enables a man to do any or all of the following:

1. Provide an income for his wife in case of his death.
2. Provide money to send his child to college.
3. Provide money to leave his home clear of debt.

Suppose a sales representative for this financial house has three prospects to call on. She has never seen these prospects before. She knows nothing about them. Suppose the sales representative should plan her calls as follows:

"I will talk to Prospect A about leaving an income for his wife" (regardless of whether Prospect A is married or not).

"I will talk to Prospect B about sending his child to college" (regardless of whether he has a child or not).

"I will talk to Prospect C about leaving his home clear of debt" (regardless of whether or not he lives in a rented apartment).

No sales representative would work under such a disadvantage. Yet every advertisement is a sales representative. Every advertisement is sent out to call on a prospect. Why handicap the advertisement by deciding in advance that it will discuss only a single sales argument? Put every important selling point into every advertisement.

20. URGE THE READER TO ACT

Every mail order advertisement ends with a strong urge to "Act Now." Unless there is a definite reason to the contrary, the general advertisement should end with a similar urge. You have caught the readers with your headline. You have interested them with your copy. Do not leave them hanging in midair. Tell them what to do. If you can give them a definite reason for immediate action, such as "Price is going up" or "Supply will soon be exhausted," so much the better.

Advertising has induced progress in the use by manufacturers of new materials, new tools, and new processes of manufacture by calling their attention to economies which could be achieved and to the new uses to which they could be put. Without such advertising, information of this kind would take years to reach all of those who might benefit by it and progress would be delayed.

Harry S. Truman

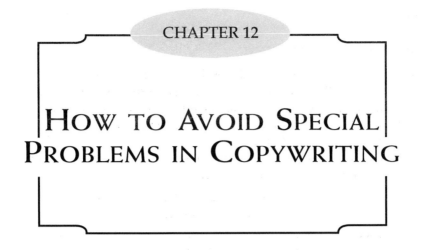

CHAPTER 12

HOW TO AVOID SPECIAL PROBLEMS IN COPYWRITING

DRAMATIZING DULL PRODUCTS

Often the copywriter is handed a tough assignment in the shape of an uninteresting product that must somehow be dramatized in the advertising. A number of instances will be described of how such dull products as cough drops, disinfectants, statistics, sewing machines, and even grave vaults have been made exciting.

ADVERTISING A STATISTICAL SERVICE

Suppose you were asked to prepare an advertising campaign for a statistics company, a company whose business is to furnish statistical analyses to investment houses and other business concerns. Wouldn't you consider it a difficult job? Statistics are so dull—no human interest, no drama.

Yet such a company published a series of advertisements as dramatic as a motion-picture thriller. The series was called, "Famous Wrong Guesses in History."

Here is a sample:

> #### WHEN MILLIONS OF DOLLARS WERE
> #### THROWN INTO THE GUTTER
>
> Forty-five hundred miles of canals costing over $200,000,000. And barely one in ten actually paid. Small wonder men called them "The most expensive gutters in the world"!

The copy tells how the canals of 1830 were doomed by the steam locomotive—how "sure things" fail today just as in 1830—how in the long run, facts and facts alone make for lasting success.

ADVERTISING A DISINFECTANT

A class of products dull in themselves, but sometimes dramatically advertised, are the disinfectants. An example is the campaign that created a nationwide awareness of "bad breath" by equating it with the medically sounding "halitosis" and the practically miraculous curative powers of gargling with Listerine.

Another disinfectant campaign consisted of a series of "horror" advertisements for Lysol. Here is one:

A CROSS ON THE DOOR SEALED THE DOOM
OF ANOTHER HOUSEHOLD

London was a nightmare of horror that summer. The Black Death raged through the city. Victims died so fast that condemned prisoners collected the bodies by the cartload.

In a subsequent paragraph, the product being advertised was introduced:

200 years later the medical world discovered that disease is caused by germs. Today, science wages war upon germs, and one of its weapons is "Lysol" Disinfectant.

A LESSON FROM SHAKESPEARE

In some of his plays, Shakespeare permits the audience to learn, not only what a certain character is saying, but also what he or she is thinking. This is done by letting the actor make a remark directly to the audience. The remark is labeled an "aside." Eugene O'Neill, among other contemporary playwrights, also used this method in some of his plays.

This same trick has enabled copywriters to inject drama into dull products in the form of "hidden thoughts" copy. For example, a cough drop is not an exciting article, yet cough drops were dramatically brought to the reader's attention in a Luden's series called, "If he said what he thought." A typical advertisement pictured a salesman coughing across the desk of a purchasing agent. The purchasing agent flies into a rage and orders the salesman out. Underneath the picture is this headline:

If he said what he thought:
"Get out . . . I'm tired of you salesmen giving me colds!"

ADVERTISING PAPER TOWELS

Paper towels are another product that, at first glance, seems to lack dramatic possibilities. What can you say about them? Softness? Smoothness? Absorbency? These are the things everybody expects you to say and are consequently commonplace.

Here is how a paper towel manufacturer put human interest into his copy:

HE NEVER KNEW UNTIL HE

OVERHEARD THEM

[Illustration:]   Office Manager overhearing talk in employees' washroom.

"Plenty of hot water, good soap—but these things they give us for towels—"

"Second the motion—we ought to be paid to use 'em."

A HAND LOTION CAMPAIGN

The makers of a hand lotion decided to tell the world that their product was good for chapped hands. But a dozen manufacturers of skin lotions have claimed the same thing. This advertiser wanted to be different. A dramatic "Shame on You" campaign did the trick. Typical headlines:

She hid her hands in her lap . . . shocked at their rough, chapped redness against the snowy cloth.

She sat out every dance . . . ashamed of her chapped hands.

ADVERTISING CELLOPHANE

Another product that seemed to offer little drama was cellophane, the first transparent film used to wrap candy, cake, and at-home leftovers. What could be said about cellophane? That it kept products clean and safe from handling? Or that customers could see what they bought, even though it was wrapped? That might be copy material, but it's far from dramatic.

The makers of cellophane boldly compared their man-made wrappers with the protective wrappers produced by nature—and to nature's disadvantage! For example:

Corn hides behind its husk . . . but nothing is hidden when wrapped in transparent cellophane.

The coconut's wrapper calls for X-ray eyes . . . but anyone can see what's wrapped in cellophane.

Nature shows her onions . . . She gives them a protective, transparent skin almost as good as cellophane itself!

GRAVE VAULT COPY

Perhaps the most difficult product in the world to dramatize is a grave vault. Try to think of some dramatic treatment yourself. Then read how the Clark Grave Vault Company handled the problem.

THE TREMENDOUS POWER OF STEAM . . .

BUT METAL CONTROLS IT!

[Illustration:]   Steam locomotive rushing head-on toward reader

Rails sing as the railroad train hurls its thousand-ton weight across the continent. Steam rages to be free from the monster's belly, but steel confines it.

Wherever there must be imperviousness to water in any form—metal never fails. Naturally the Clark Grave Vault is made of metal—12-gauge copper steel.

BEVERAGE COPY

At one time the makers of a chocolate flavoring powder used four-color full-page ads to tell people that their product was nourishing—that it contained Vitamin D—that children loved it. Sales were falling off. Then the makers of this product started using dramatic situations to bring their chocolate milk drink to the attention of the public. Sales increased. Here is a typical advertisement:

HELEN DISLIKED THE VERY SIGHT

OF MILK . . . NOW I GIVE IT TO

HER A NEW WAY AND SHE LOVES IT

[Illustration:]   Angry mother exclaiming to child, "Drink that
                       milk or go straight to bed!"

"My little girl was underweight. Then my sister suggested this chocolate flavoring for the milk. How glad I am! Helen loves it . . . put eight pounds on her already . . ."

SEWING MACHINES

Sewing machines were used by our grandmothers. One would think that all the possibilities of advertising them dramatically would be exhausted by now. Not so. There is drama that will appeal to any woman in the series published by a popular sewing machine company. For example:

YOU REALLY LOOK GREAT TONIGHT"

It was like old times to hear her friends say it. Not in months had they said one word about her clothes . . .

Are you, too, dreaming of the clothes you want, but can't afford? . . . Our modern sewing machine will make sewing a joyous adventure. . . .

COURSE IN ENGLISH

How can a copywriter put drama into a correspondence course in English grammar—a subject often considered dull? A dramatic campaign for a correspondence course in English showed the way. The headline of a typical advertisement said, "What are your mistakes in English?" The illustration showed a young lady talking to her boyfriend. Mistakes in English were popping out of their mouths: "I ain't . . . You was . . . Can't hardly."

Proof of the effectiveness of this advertising was found in the fact that although comparatively little money was spent for space in magazines, many people became familiar with the campaign. Each advertisement got as much attention as three or four ordinary advertisements.

OFFICE STATIONERY

A maker of writing paper, sold a lightweight paper for office use. *Questions*: How do you dramatize it? How do you impress office managers with the fact that this paper lets them send multipage letters and documents at low cost? The following headline accomplishes this purpose:

NOW YOU CAN SEND A 12-PAGE LETTER FOR A SINGLE
FIRST CLASS STAMP

The copy makes this offer: "Just by way of proof—ask your secretary to write for a sample and we shall send 12 letterhead sheets by First Class mail."

SEA CRUISE

For years the ship companies—sellers of travel—have been singing the same song with headlines like these:

An ideal winter cruise
follow the sun to South America
come with us to Mexico
Live where winter's smile is sunniest

One line added a dramatic touch by advertising to women using copy like this:

WATCH YOUR HUSBAND . . .

IS HE A DRAWING-ROOM SPHINX?

Conversation is a lost art with many a successful businessman, unless the talk turns to business.

The unfailing remedy is a winter cruise. Sea travel takes a man's mind completely off his business concerns . . .

The copy sold sea voyages to entirely new prospects. It caught the attention of people who never before had considered an ocean trip.

SUMMING UP THE VALUE OF DRAMA

What can drama do for advertising? By its attention value it can make a small advertising appropriation do the work of a large appropriation. It can attract new customers—people who would not normally be customers. It can give emphasis to some particular feature of your product or service. It can put new life into a worn-out theme.

One of the most popular of the dramatic methods seems to be the "domestic drama"—little dramas involving husbands and wives, girlfriends and boyfriends, and, in select media, same-sex couples. The "hidden thought" type of copy and the "Shame on You" theme are also popular.

The next time you write an advertisement for a dull product, try to dramatize it. And remember, many products are dull until some copywriter puts life into them.

PROBLEMS WITH HEADLINES

How can a life insurance company explain in a few words the fact that a small down payment on a life insurance policy can immediately increase the size of a man's estate? Here is a headline that does this:

TODAY . . . ADD $10,000 TO YOUR ESTATE—
FOR THE PRICE OF A NEW SHIRT

How can an automobile brake relining service emphasize the high value and the relatively low cost of its service in terms of accidents avoided and lives saved? The following headline puts the story into a few words:

Is the life of a child worth $99 to you?

A correspondence school selling a mail order course in business training had this problem:

1. Experience showed that the ads that pulled best were those that featured salary increases as a result of taking the course.

2. It was not possible to make a specific promise in the ads such as "You can add $5,000 to your income" because some of the students who took the course did not receive salary increases.

The advertising manager said: "Our problem is—how can we talk about salary increases in the headlines of our ads without making a specific promise?" The following headline was devised to accomplish the desired purpose:

TO A TEN-THOUSAND-DOLLAR EMPLOYEE
WHO WOULD LIKE TO BE MAKING $25,000

Notice that the headline skillfully implies the possibility of a raise in pay without making a definite promise. Depending on the target audience and with an appropriate adjustment of the dollar amounts, the same approach works today, 20 years after this headline first ran.

Here is another successful device:

[Illustration:]   Photograph of an executive in a handsome
                   office.

[Headline]:   This private office with salary to match may be
                   waiting for you.

The suggestion of a benefit without actually making a specific promise can also be accomplished by putting your headline into the form of a question.

For example, a beauty-product manufacturer was so excited about a new item that they wanted to claim that they had discovered the fountain of youth. But a specific claim to this effect would have been refused by almost all publications and disbelieved by readers. A successful ad was prepared, however, with a headline in the form of a question, as follows:

HAS THE SECRET OF ETERNAL YOUTH BEEN DISCOVERED AT LAST?

A medical advertiser wanted to tell people how they could cure nervous disorders. However, the promise of definite cures is not permitted. So this advertiser prepared a successful ad with a headline in the form of a question:

DO YOU HAVE THESE SYMPTOMS OF NERVOUS EXHAUSTION?

The advertisers of a stock market guide wanted to say "How you can make money in the stock market." A toned-down headline was used, however, that was more believable and therefore more effective:

WHY SOME PEOPLE ALMOST ALWAYS MAKE MONEY IN THE STOCK MARKET

Providing a testimonial is true and can be documented, you can prepare a qualified but effective ad by writing testimonial style headlines as follows:

HOW A NEW KIND OF CLAY IMPROVED MY COMPLEXION IN 30 MINUTES

HOW I IMPROVED MY MEMORY IN ONE EVENING

These headlines cause readers to say to themselves: "Maybe I can get the same results." Though the headlines do not specifically promise that everybody will get these results, you must be ready to prove that the person quoted got them!

Another way to qualify a promise is to include a money-back guarantee in your headline as follows:

GET RID OF DANDRUFF IN 10 DAYS OR THERE'S NO COST!

HANDS THAT LOOK LOVELIER IN 24 HOURS OR YOUR MONEY BACK

USING COUPON OFFERS TO ATTRACT STORE CUSTOMERS

Practically every day, retail stores advertise special offers to induce customers, old and new, to come to the store.

For example, in one city, a department store ran a small newspaper ad offering a ten-speed bicycle at a reduced price. The ad contained a coupon that the reader was instructed to bring to the store. Printed in the coupon was a picture of the bicycle, and the following copy:

$68.88—Reg. $89.95.
Coupon good Washington's Birthday only.
Limit 1 per customer.

All the bicycles on hand were sold out the first afternoon. More than 200 coupons were redeemed, with total sales in excess of $14,000. Yet the ad cost only $480!

An increasing number of merchants are successfully using the same device, namely, a small newspaper ad containing a coupon to be clipped out and brought to the store. An attractive offer is printed in the coupon. So common has this become that many everyday consumers, as well as professional commercial buyers, will no longer buy at full price. They know that a special offer is likely to appear if only they can wait. Here are some typical offers, together with the sales results obtained:

Sam's Restaurant: 2 chicken dinners for the price of one. Over 750 returns. Sales: approximately $2,900.

Checker Auto Parts: Oil filter $3.99. Over 4,000 returns. Sales: over $5,000.

Kennedy's Firestone: Service offer: (1) Complete lubrication. (2) Oil change. (3) New oil filter. (4) Rotate tires. (5) Adjust brakes. (6) Repack outer front wheel bearings. (7) Check wheel alignment. (8) Complete safety inspection . . . All for $55.88. Six stores booked solid. Sales: over $11,000.

Robo Car Wash: One free car wash. Over 2,000 returns. Sales: approximately $4,500.

Antoine's Sheik Restaurant: $5 off on each $16.95 combination dinner. Over 150 returns. Sales over $2,500.

Vaughn's Clothing Store: 10% off on all suits, coats, slacks, shirts, sweaters, pants, etc. Sales: over $4,600.

A.N.A. Photo and Appliance Center: FM/AM Radio $16.95, reg. $37.95 . . . Minolta Camera $169, Reg. $265. Over 70 returns. Sales: approximately $5,500.

Worth's Clothing Store: Wet-Look Coats $23, Reg. $60. Over 100 returns. Sales: over $3,300.

Pizza Palace: $1 off any large pizza. Over 1,200 returns. Sales: over $9,600.

Fish Monger—Food to go. 1¢ Special. Buy one at reg. price and pay 1¢ for the 2nd order (fish & chips $5.35; Swordfish steak $7.75; Halibut steak $7.45.) Over 1,100 returns. Sales: over $8,200.

HOW TO MAKE STORE COUPONS EFFECTIVE

Here are some points to notice regarding coupon promotions:

Many advertisers set time limits. Examples: "Coupon good thru [date] . . ." "Offer expires [date] . . ." "Coupon good 1-day only [date]."

Some stores set restrictions. Examples: "Limit 2 items per coupon" . . . "Limit 1 per customer" . . . "Not valid for take-out orders."

Some stores specify that the customer must bring the coupon. Examples: "$5.88 with this coupon" . . . "This coupon entitles, [etc.]" . . . "Come clip us—with coupon."

Some stores include items like these: "Please phone for appointment" . . . "Supply limited" . . . "First come! First served" . . . "Free pony ride for the kids."

A big advantage of a coupon is that it becomes a *reminder* to the customers after they have torn it out and put it into a pocket or purse. They can't forget it because it is right there staring at them.

Another advantage is that customers need to do little or no talking when they approach the dealer. Many people are not articulate. They don't like to walk up to a proprietor and say: "I understand that you are offering a complete lubrication, oil change, new oil filter, brake adjustment, wheel alignment, etc., all for $55.88." The coupon does the customers' talking for them. They don't have to say a word if they do not want to.

> *QUESTION*: Briefly stated, how can you use special coupon offers to induce customers to take the first important step, namely, to step into the store?
>
> *ANSWER*: Make an irresistible offer. Print the offer on a coupon. Put the coupon into the hands of as many prospects as possible, and at the lowest possible cost.

American advertising has learned to tell the truth attractively about American products. When the product is good, and the truth is told, we have the appealing combination that secures sales and keeps the wheels of industry turning.

Norman Vincent Peale

Thirty-two Ways to Get More Inquiries from Your Advertising

Sometimes in advertising it becomes advisable to secure as many inquiries as possible. For the sake of ready reference and at the risk of repetition, 32 effective methods for increasing ad replies follow.

These methods may be divided into two general classes:

1. The methods that increase inquiries by increasing the total effectiveness of your advertising. For example, the use of long copy plus an interesting headline increases the total effectiveness of an advertisement, and the increase in replies is merely a by-product of a better advertisement.

2. The methods that increase ad replies but do not increase the total effectiveness of your advertising. For example, a picture of a free booklet with the subcaption "Get This Free Book" will get more inquiries, but it does not make your advertisement any better.

The methods are explained in detail on the following pages and summarized at the end of this chapter.

1. Mention the Offer in the Headline

Suppose your headline is "How to retire on an income." You can increase response by changing it to read "Free booklet tells how to retire on an income."

Suppose your headline is "Overweight Men and Women." You can increase response by changing it to read "Free to Overweight Men and Women."

Here are other examples:

YOURS FOR ONLY $1.00—This Lovely Box of Greeting Cards
FREE SALES KIT—Make Up to $200 a Day
GIVEN TO YOU—The Oxford Dictionary
Free Ski Guide
Home Repair Book—Read It for 7 Days Free

2. EMPHASIZE THE WORD "FREE"

You can increase replies by putting the word "Free" in big print or in capital letters. In broadcast advertising and in printed advertising, you can repeat the word "free" several times. Or you can frequently repeat phrases that mean essentially the same thing, such as "Send no money," "Don't pay a penny," or "Yours without cost." However, "FREE" means exactly what it says. The FTC requires that any and all conditions be *conspicuously* disclosed in immediate conjunction with the offer.

3. MENTION THE OFFER IN A SUBHEAD

The subhead may follow immediately after the main headline like this:

[Main headline]   New electronic calculator
[Subhead]   Free 10 day trial

Or the subhead may be placed in the middle of the ad or near the end. Here are typical subheads:

SEND FOR LIBERAL SUPPLY

THE FACTS ARE FREE

WRITE FOR BOOKLET

SPECIAL $1 OFFER

FREE TALENT TEST

4. SHOW A PICTURE OF THE BOOKLET OR SAMPLE

If you have lots of room, you can show the booklet or sample package in large size. Your layout can include eye-catching devices such as an arrow or a hand pointing at the booklet.

The speed with which an offer registers on the eye of the reader is important. Therefore, one of the best inquiry-getting layouts is a picture of the booklet with the word "Free" printed alongside it or under it, as shown in Figure 13.1.

Profitable Businesses You Start For Under $50.00

...And Foley-Belsaw helps you every step of the way. In business since 1926 Foley-Belsaw has helped more people start their own successful business than any other company of its kind. Pick one of the opportunities listed below and we'll send you a **FREE INFORMATION PACKET.**

No need to leave your present job — ✓ Only One ☐ Below Please

☐ **Locksmith** - A high demand business where you earn $40.00/hour. D0389
☐ **Small Engine Repair** - $45 in 1/2 hour for a tune-up, even more on easy repairs. D0390
☐ **Professional Saw & Tool Sharpening** - Make $18 to $25 by running simple machines that do the work for you. D0391
☐ **Gunsmithing** - Turn your hobby into a profitable career. D0392
☐ **Upholstery** - Learn Upholstery to make profits in commercial and consumer markets. D0393
☐ **Woodworking** - Build over $3,000 worth of woodworking products while you learn. D0394
☐ **VCR Repair** - No electronics experience is necessary to make $50.00 an hour. D0395
☐ **Computer Repair** - A high paying occupation of your own with an unlimited future. D0396
☐ **TV/Satellite Dish Repair** - Learn to repair the entertainment system of the 21st century. D0397
☐ **Computer Programming** - A shortage of programmers can mean big earnings for you. D0398
☐ **Vinyl Repair** - A business that will lead you to a career repairing vinyl and similar materials. D0399

Name _____

Address _____

City _____

State _____ Zip _____ + _____

Figure 13.1: *How to make small-space promotions work harder.* Direct response card packs have reached the consumer market. There is no other promotion in which every single element means so much, and this one does them all right. All seven headline words work hard at grabbing attention. The first three products tell of excellent hourly rates. Eleven career opportunities are described and a Free Information Kit offered. The prospect doesn't even need a stamp; the card is returned postage free. Despite the tiny type and jam-packed format, testing showed that switching from single to multi-product cards and ads reduced per-inquiry cost by 50 percent.

In small ads you can save space by reducing the picture of the booklet down to the size of a postage stamp. You can even cut it in half and show only the top half of the booklet. If your booklet title is hard to read in reduced size, you can reset the title on the ad artwork in readable type before you make your reduced-size print. If you control the design, have a legible title created for the original booklet and for everything else that is likely to be shown in reduced size. If only the top half of the cover is seen in advertisements or "take-one" displays, put the title on the top half only. Not only will this reproduce better without costly reworking, but the stronger title will be more effective as a selling tool when it is received by the customer. This may sound obvious, but you will be astonished at how often it is contradicted by artists more interested in show than in sell.

In TV commercials, you can have the actors or actresses hold up the booklet or gift and show it to the audience. Or else they can hold up the gift all wrapped and ready to mail, point to the address label and say: "Send me your name and address so I can put it right here and mail this free gift to you."

Incidentally, the phrase "free gift" is especially good in both printed and broadcast advertising because this phrase says free twice in just two short words.

5. MENTION THE OFFER IN THE FIRST PARAGRAPH

Most copywriters remember to include a description of the free booklet at the end of the ad. But many forget to include a brief mention of the booklet at the beginning of the ad. Some of the best-pulling ads mention the free booklet twice: (1) A brief mention early in the ad; and (2) a complete description at the end of the ad.

In broadcast advertising, you can use this same technique by saying at the beginning of the commercial: "Get pencil and paper ready. In a few seconds I am going to offer you a free gift."

6. USE AN ATTRACTIVE BOOKLET TITLE

Just as ad headlines are often the deciding factor in getting people to read ads, so are booklet titles often the deciding factor in getting people to send for booklets. Here are some attractive booklet titles:

ACCOUNTANCY—THE PROFESSION THAT PAYS

NEW BEAUTY FOR YOU

HOW TO PROTECT YOUR INVENTION

YOUR FUTURE IN COMPUTER PROGRAMMING

HOW TO GET A GOVERNMENT JOB

NEW YORK VACATION GUIDE

HOW TO CARE FOR YOUR DOG

7. INCLUDE AN ATTRACTIVE DESCRIPTION OF THE OFFER

In writing a description of a booklet, you should sit down with the booklet in front of you and turn the pages and write down every good thing you can say about it. Then take your list of items and condense it into a paragraph. For example:

Booklet contains 32 pages, 14 illustrations (5 in color), 9 sketches, 4 diagrams, 7 case histories, 2 maps, a list of do's and don'ts, 5 chapters (including complete instructions), a chart for predicting results, and an appendix containing scores of useful items.

The "table of contents" technique is also effective. You can include a panel of copy like this:

AUTO MECHANIC'S BOOK TELLS

How to fit pistons	Page 3
How to locate engine knocks	Page 7
How to service main bearings	Page 12
How to recondition valves	Page 14
How to adjust fan belts	Page 20
How to rebuild a clutch	Page 22
How to service brakes	Page 25
How to adjust steering gear	Page 27
How to time ignition	Page 29
How to tune up an engine	Page 31

In radio advertising, you can use the "table of contents" technique by having the script say "On Page 3 you will find instructions on how to fit pistons. On Page 7 you will find out how to locate engine knocks. On Page 12, how to service main bearings," and so on. For television, you can use essentially the same script for voice-over while the pages appear on the screen.

Hint: Some booklets are difficult to describe attractively because they contain only sales talk. In these cases, it may be worthwhile to revise your booklet and include some information of a helpful nature. A garden-seed advertiser made his seed catalogue ads pull better by putting in a chapter of gardening advice.

8. INCLUDE A BOOKLET FOREWORD BY A FAMOUS PERSON

A booklet on hearing aids was made more attractive by including an introduction by a popular author who used a hearing aid himself. A music-school booklet contained a foreword by a well-known conductor. A booklet on beauty care had a chapter written by a movie star. A recipe booklet featured favorite recipes of famous chefs. And the book you're holding in your hands was undoubtedly helped by the Foreword by David Ogilvy.

9. INCLUDE TESTIMONIALS

An ad for an income tax guide included testimonials from a homeowner, a sales representative, a professional, a working parent, and so forth. For example:

> Sales representative: "I use my car for selling and do a lot of entertaining. I thought I had deducted everything until your Income Tax Guide showed me 18 deductions I never thought were allowable."

> Working parent: "Saving on even our combined salaries isn't easy. I thought tax returns were an impossible job until your Income Tax Guide showed me how many of our expenses are deductible—like the clothes we donate to the Salvation Army."

10. SWEETEN YOUR OFFER

The ad for the income tax guide mentioned earlier contained this paragraph:

> Special Free Bonus: Filled-in Tax Forms . . . To give you every possible tax saving—and to save you time and trouble you will also receive a 16-page booklet of sample tax forms, completely filled in for your guidance. This is yours to keep, even if you return the Income Tax Guide for refund.

A series of ads for G.E. light bulbs offered "a booklet about light and seeing." When it was desired to increase replies, a free gift was offered in addition to the free booklet.

An airline wanted to increase replies from ads about flights to Bermuda so that sales literature could be mailed to as many prospects as possible. A free booklet offer did not pull sufficient replies, so the following offer was used and brought excellent results.

> Absolutely free—a Bermuda Vacation Kit. The kit contains detailed map of Bermuda and photographs and descriptions of the big, new luxury Air Liners. Included in the free Kit are a pair of Bermuda sunglasses.

If you have been charging for your booklet, you can probably increase replies by reducing the price. If you want to charge for your booklet and at the same time feature the word "free," you can use the following wording, *providing it is true*: "Free booklet. Enclose [amount] to help cover cost of handling and mailing." Beware, however, of making your offer so appealing and at such a low price that you will attract premium hunters rather than prospects. Here, as elsewhere, testing and careful record-keeping is the key to profitable success.

11. INCLUDE A COUPON

A coupon printed in an ad helps increase returns in several ways. It draws attention to the offer. It makes the offer clear and simple. It indicates to the readers that you really want them to write and that they are fully entitled to receive your booklet or sample. It gives the readers a convenient form in which to write their name and address. When torn out of the ad, the coupon serves as a continuing reminder until it is mailed.

In a small ad, where space is limited, you can gain some of the advantages of a coupon without using one. You can say, "Tear out this ad and send it with your name and address to:"

Caution: If your coupon leads are followed by in-person sales calls, "qualify" each response by a *professional* telemarketing person or service. If you do not, you may find that your sales staff is wasting valuable time following up prospects who are primarily interested in getting a booklet or a sample rather than in buying your product.

On the other hand, if you are actually selling your goods by mail, and if the customer has to charge to a credit card or send payment with the coupon, you can put as much emphasis on the coupon as you wish.

12. PRINT THE VALUE ON THE COUPON

Some advertisers print "Value 10¢ or "Worth 50¢" or some other value on the coupons in their ads. An ad published by a greeting card manufacturer had this headline: "This giant $2.75 greeting card assortment yours to keep for 25¢." Printed across the top of the coupon was the line, "This coupon worth $2.50."

13. INCLUDE SOME SELLING COPY IN THE COUPON

Examples:

BOOK LEAGUE OF AMERICA

Please send me—FREE—the brand-new giant Webster's New World Dictionary of the American Language, over 2,000 pages, weighing 10 lbs., containing over 140,000 definitions, 1,400 illustrations, maps, etc., and enroll me as a member.

American Technical Society (Publishers since 1898)

Please rush me the following books I'm checking below to examine at home. If I'm not convinced these books will help me save thousands of dollars by doing my own building and planning, I may return the books and owe nothing.

14. PRINT YOUR ADDRESS TWICE IN EACH AD

Did you ever pick up a magazine in a doctor's or dentist's waiting room and find a coupon missing from one of the ads? Suppose you wanted to answer that ad? You wouldn't know where to address your reply if the only address in the ad was contained in the missing coupon. To guard against loss of replies, some advertisers include their address twice— once in the coupon and once elsewhere in the ad. For example, in a full-page ad for the Coyne School, the address and key number appeared in a coupon in the lower righthand corner of the ad as follows:

Coyne School, 500 S. Paulina St.
Dept. 62-73H, Chicago, Illinois 60612

In the lower left-hand corner of the ad, the address and key number were repeated in the form of a logotype as follows:

Coyne School
500 S. Paulina St. Dept. 62-73H
Chicago, Illinois 60612

15. INCLUDE A TELEPHONE NUMBER—ESPECIALLY A TOLL FREE NUMBER

Some people like to act fast, and they like to make inquiries and order by telephone. If you are advertising in newspapers or using local broadcasting, you can limit yourself to a local telephone number. However, even local response is increased greatly by emphasizing the free-to-the-caller 800 option. Since many of us expect 800 (or the new 888) service to be limited to long-distance calls, use a bold-type statement such as **Free 800 service for local calls too!** An adult education school advertiser found that putting a telephone number in their ads not only increased inquiries but also improved the quality of the inquiries. They found they could sell only one out of five people who wrote for a school catalog, but they could sell one out of two people who telephoned. By asking discreet questions they could find out the special problems of people who telephoned and offer to solve their problems. They could say, "We have many students who have the same problems that you have. We are starting a new class next Tuesday night at 8 P.M. You are invited to sit in and listen. If you will tell me where you are located, I will tell you the easiest way to reach the school."

Do you use national advertising in newspapers, magazines, or broadcasting and have a network of local dealers or use a national Yellow Pages program? You can say, "See the Yellow Pages in your telephone book." Or you can use a toll-free 800 number. For example, an Air Force recruiting ad said: "Send in the postcard or call toll-free 800-447-[number]."

16. Spotlight FAX for Ordering—Make It Toll-free

Put your FAX number where it can't be missed. Place it directly above the coupon in newspaper and magazine ads and right on the reply card or order form. Make it toll-free too. If you think you can't afford your own 800 number, use a nearby answering service for a test.

17. Emphasize "No Obligation"

Here are sample phrases you can use in copy or in coupons:

> No obligation
>
> Send me without obligation
>
> I understand that this does not obligate me
>
> I am under no obligation, now or ever
>
> I understand this book is mine to keep, and sending for it does not obligate me in any way
>
> No salesman will call

18. Offer Certain Information in a Plain Envelope

Here are examples of the type of information people prefer to receive in an envelope that does not identify the product:

1. Hearing aid booklet
2. Data on personal loans
3. Personal hygiene booklet
4. Maternity booklet

19. Urge Immediate Action

Some advertisers increase inquiries by offering a reward for immediate action. For example:

> Fill in the coupon below and mail it for your free copy of 32-page information Booklet. If you act at once, we will include Success Booklet and Chart, which supply additional information you should have. All will be sent postage paid.

Other action-promoting devices are sentences such as "Supply is limited," or "For a short time only." Or you can use simple urges to action such as the following:

> Mail coupon today
>
> Act now—offer expires April 30th
>
> Rush your name for free outfit
>
> Get free book by sending coupon NOW

John Stern, the Hahn agency's top copy consultant, had extraordinary success because of a "computer error" in such an action-promoting device. A single line of the letter, seen in an envelope window, should have said: RESPOND BY THURSDAY, MAY 19. Instead, it said: RESPOND BY THURSDAY. And indeed they did . . . 39% more than a mailing without the "mistake."

20. INCLUDE A BUSINESS-REPLY POSTCARD

A number of advertisers include in their ads a business-reply postcard that requires no postage stamp. Examples of these may be found in *Reader's Digest, TV Guide,* and to a lesser extent, in hundreds of other publications. A reply card adjacent to the ad usually brings dramatic increases in response. It also gives you dramatic increases in cost. Testing will show the *cost effective* use.

21. INCLUDE A FOLD-OVER COUPON

A less expensive way to get some of the effectiveness of a business-reply postcard without paying the premium rate for it is to include a preaddressed business-reply coupon that is double the size of the normal coupon. Providing the paper meets postal regulations, the prospect can simply cut out this double coupon, fold it over, seal it, and mail it with no postage stamp. In effect, this is a do-it-yourself business-reply card. Be sure to check with the post office on *current* rules for size and paper thickness ("weight").

22. USE A FREE-STANDING INSERT

What is it that catches your eye and falls into your hands when you open your Sunday newspaper? A free-standing insert. This device is made to order for a mail-order advertiser. If you have an extra-long message, your free-standing insert can be a multipage booklet or even a complete mail-order catalog. If your message is not so long, you can use a single-sheet insert of stiff paper and print your message on two sides, front and back. The insert can contain a business-reply postcard or order form. Free-standing inserts cost more than ordinary ads, but they bring more response. They combine important elements such as attention value, long copy, and an easy-to-mail order form that requires no postage stamp. In many larger communities, free-standing newspaper inserts can even be designated for delivery to specific neighborhoods or ZIP codes.

23. TEST SEVERAL DIFFERENT OFFERS

One way to step up returns is to test the pulling power of two or more different offers in one publication and then run the best-pulling offer in your entire list of publications. To get the most accurate test, you should use the facilities of some publications offering "split-run" copy testing whereby one offer appears in half the circulation and the other offer appears in the other half of the circulation on the same day and in the same position. More than 1,000 newspapers offer split-run copy testing; so do hundreds of magazines.

As a rule, you will find that offers of food samples and soap samples pull well, whereas offers of patent-medicine samples, such as cold remedies and headache remedies, pull poorly.

Another way to test offers is to make two or more different offers in your coupon and say, for example:

Check the offer you want

___Sample can of floor wax

___Sample polishing cloth

If you are selling insurance, for example, you can test offers by listing several different pamphlets in your coupon, as follows:

Check the pamphlet you want

___How to provide money to send a child to college

___How to provide money to pay off a mortgage

___How to provide an income in case of disability

After you have found out which offer pulls best, feature that offer in future advertising and subordinate the others as "also available." Just because an offer didn't "win" does not mean you can afford to ignore its particular audience.

24. TEST SEVERAL DIFFERENT ADS

After you have discovered the best-pulling offer, you can test several different ads containing the offer. In a series of ads containing the same offer, you will often find one ad that due to a better headline or better picture will pull twice as many inquiries as the other ads.

You can test your advertisements in inexpensive space before you run them in expensive space. For example, you can get a quick, low-cost test in a daily newspaper. After you have found your best-pulling ad, you can run it in your entire list of newspapers and magazines and adapt it for use in radio and TV commercials.

25. USE THE MOST EFFECTIVE MEDIA

In some cases, publication ads will bring inquiries at lower cost than will broadcast commercials. In other cases, broadcasting will do better than publications. Your judgment and experience will often enable you to select the best medium. If you are not a media expert and do not have one on staff, however, contact several media services to learn how they can help in media selection and evaluation. In either case, sometimes you will have to run actual tests of media.

After you have found out whether broadcast advertising or publication advertising is best for your proposition, you can further refine your testing and find out which broadcasting stations or which publications, are most efficient. And what is true of testing publications and broadcast, is equally true for direct mail, telemarketing, the internet, and media yet to be discovered.

26. SKIM THE CREAM FROM VARIOUS MARKETS

After a few ads have run in a certain publication or on a certain broadcasting station, you may find that your cost per inquiry is rising because you have skimmed the cream off that particular market. If you are using broadcast commercials, you can try shifting to a different time of day in order to reach a different group of listeners or viewers. Or you can try different channels or stations. If you are using publication advertising, you can try different publications.

Mail order advertisers find that readers of certain magazines are so responsive that it is profitable to run an ad every month. On the other hand, certain magazines can be used only once or twice a year if inquiry costs are to be kept down. This system of shifting media is something like fishing. The experienced fisherman shifts from one location to another in order to catch more fish.

27. USE THE MOST EFFECTIVE SPACE SIZE

Certain propositions, such as book clubs, get the most sales per dollar of space cost by using full-page ads, whereas other propositions, such as vacation guide books, do best with ads measuring one-half column or smaller. Apparently, it takes long copy to sell the idea of a book club, whereas a small ad is sufficient to induce people to send for a free vacation-guide booklet. What size space is most efficient for your proposition? You can determine this by testing ads in several different sizes.

28. Use long Copy

After you have found your most efficient size ad, you should jam your space full of copy, no matter whether it is a one-inch ad or a full-page ad.

Brief, reminder-style copy consisting of a few words or a slogan does not pull inquiries as well as long copy packed with facts and reader benefits about your product or service.

If you want to see efficient use of space, look at mail order catalogs or at the mail-order ads in magazines or in your Sunday newspaper. Some of the strongest-pulling mail-order ads have contained as many as 1,200 words of copy set in small print. Don't be afraid to use long copy or small print. Just be sure that your copy is interesting. Remember the saying, "The more you tell, the more you sell," as dramatically demonstrated in Figure 13.2.

29. Use the Best Season

During certain seasons, people read publications, listen to radio, and watch television more often than during other seasons. Good months for high mail-order returns are September through Christmas and January, February, and March. The summer months are not as good. One test of couponed ads in which the same ad appeared in January and in August showed that January pulled twice as many replies as August.

The day of the week makes a difference in newspaper advertising. One test showed that Sunday newspaper ads pulled 40 percent more replies than did daily newspaper ads. Of course, the Sunday editions, depending on circulation, cost proportionately more too!

30. Use the Best-pulling Positions in Publications

In checking ad returns, you will find that there is a logical relationship between position and pulling power. The financial page in newspapers pulls best for financial and business items. The women's page is usually best for household items. Position alongside food articles is good for food ads. Pages 2 and 3 and the back page are good in newspapers. The top of the page is better than the bottom of the page. The magazine sections of Sunday newspapers usually have good pulling power. In national magazines, pages 1, 3, and 5 are usually excellent.

31. Study the Offerings of Your Competitors

If you are just starting out and have no experience in a particular line, it is important to study the keyed ads of other advertisers—especially mail-order advertisers. No mail-order secret can long be kept secret from

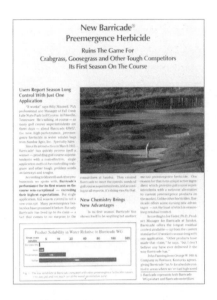

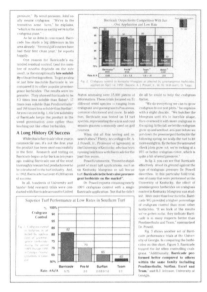

Figure 13.2: *Sixteen times better than a news-style page*! What's 16 times better than a news-style ad page? A 16-page news-style insert! Ads from "business partners" lend authenticity to this advertorial targeted at golf course superintendents. Preadvertising research had shown this audience to be information hungry. Post-publication research showed a 20 percent jump in product awareness. The resulting sales leads and sales catapulted Sandoz's new fungacide brand to #3 in a mature market.

the eyes of an observant student of advertising. The reason is because the survival of a mail-order business depends on repeating the best-pulling ads over and over in the best-pulling media. Therefore, if you want to know which is the most resultful ad of certain mail-order advertisers, all you have to do is to look in the back files of publications and see which ads they have run most often. If you want to know which publications are best, for them, just make a note of the publications in which they spend the most money. Information of this sort gives you a head start in placing inquiry-getting ads for your own proposition.

32. KEEP RECORDS OF YOUR RESULTS

Of course, you should key all of your ads and keep careful records of results. You can key your ads by saying in the address "Write to Dept. 1" or "Write to Dept. 2," and so on. Or you can print in the coupon a tiny key number such as RD-5, which would mean *Reader's Digest*, May issue.

In addition to your computer records, it is good to use a card file system of small filing cards for each type of sales effort—print, direct mail, and so forth. For instant accessibility, print the computer data or make a separate card for each ad. Include the essential facts about each ad, namely, headline, size of ad, cost of ad, publication, date, position, and number of inquiries and/or sales. Divide the cost of the ad by the number of inquiries or sales and enter the cost for each at the top of each card. File the cards according to cost per response, beginning with the lowest cost. Keep analogous records for telemarketing, direct mail, and radio and TV. Then review your card file at regular intervals and determine which ads and which media are doing best for your proposition. In this way, you will be able to plan your future efforts to avoid failures and repeat your successes.

SUMMARY OF 32 WAYS TO GET MORE INQUIRIES FROM YOUR ADVERTISING

For your convenience, the thirty-two ways to increase ad inquiries are summarized here.

1. Mention the offer in the headline
2. Emphasize the word "Free"
3. Mention the offer in a subhead
4. Show a picture of the booklet or sample
5. Mention the offer in the first paragraph

6. Use an attractive booklet title
7. Include an attractive description of the offer
8. Include a booklet foreword by a famous person
9. Include testimonials
10. Sweeten your offer
11. Include a coupon
12. Print the value on the coupon
13. Include some selling copy in the coupon
14. Print your address twice in each ad
15. Include a telephone number
16. Spotlight FAX for ordering
17. Emphasize "No obligation"
18. Offer certain information in a plain envelope
19. Urge immediate action
20. Include a business-reply postcard
21. Include a fold-over coupon
22. Use a free-standing insert
23. Test several different offers
24. Test several different ads
25. Use the most effective media
26. Skim the cream from various markets
27. Use the most effective space size
28. Use long copy
29. Use the best season
30. Use the best-pulling positions in publications
31. Study the offerings of your competitors
32. Keep records of your results

The advertising profession is an integral part of the life of a free nation. It has helped create markets where markets did not previously exist. It has not merely sold products which the public wanted. It has sold products which the public did not know it wanted. More important still, it has made possible the only free method for the large scale manufacture of goods on a mass basis.

Thomas E. Dewey

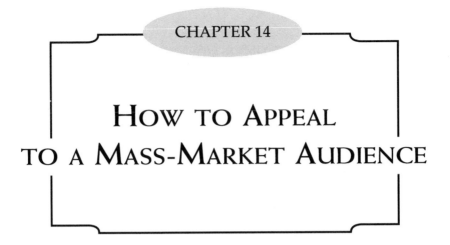

HOW TO APPEAL
TO A MASS-MARKET AUDIENCE

One of my earliest advertising assignments was to prepare an advertisement for Mr. Blank's Hair Growing Treatment. In attacking this problem, I reasoned thus: If everyone realized that this treatment actually grows hair, we would make thousands of sales. Therefore, our problem is to prove that the treatment works. Why not let the public know that if the treatment does not grow hair, Mr. Blank, the manufacturer, would be criminally liable for fraudulent advertising?

With this idea in mind I produced this headline:

I WOULD BE IN JAIL IF MY TREATMENT DIDN'T GROW HAIR

To add a dramatic touch, I illustrated the advertisement with a picture of Mr. Blank actually behind prison bars.

The advertisement produced loud laughs from a fellow copywriter. "So that's the way you spend your time" she exclaimed, "making fun of our clients!"

I concluded that if my advertisement were misunderstood by one of our own copywriters, it would certainly be misunderstood by the public.

> The average reader makes a snap judgment in interpreting an advertisement. Therefore, for the sake of clarity, the headline and the illustration of an advertisement should tell the same story.

In this case, the headline said, "I would be in jail," but the picture said. "I am in jail." My copywriter friend reacted to the picture before she read the headline. Pictures convey their message faster than print.

Here is an example of a mail-order book ad in which the headline and the picture do tell the same story:

[Headline]:   This is Marie Antoinette riding to her death.

[Illustration:]   Picture of Marie Antoinette riding to her death.

This ad dramatized a scene described in a set of literary classics. The ad drew eight times as many coupon results as any previous ad for this set of books.

THREE AIDS TO PULLING POWER

Three well-known and often neglected aids to pulling power are

1. Short paragraphs

2. Short sentences

3. Short words

There is nothing more discouraging to the eye than a block of solid type. Break up your long paragraphs into short ones. Short paragraphs invite the eye. A long sentence forces readers to do tiresome mental gymnastics. It forces them to keep your opening thought in mind while they absorb half a dozen other thoughts.

As for short words, the following story illustrates their value. A publisher of children's books wanted to know the secret of the popularity among children of a certain history book. Children preferred this particular history book to any other. Some even read it in their spare time when lessons did not require it.

The publisher questioned the author of the book. The author replied, "When the manuscript was finished, I gave it to a ten-year-old child and asked him to cross out all the words he didn't understand. I then substituted simpler words."

OTHER WAYS TO MAKE COPY EASY TO READ

Do not clutter up your copy with too many contractions such as "We're" instead of "We are," "We'll" instead of "We will," "He'll" instead of "He will."

Contractions tire the eye. They force the eye to take the tiny apostrophes into consideration. To the careless reader, "We're" looks like "Were." "We'll" looks like "Well." "He'll" looks like "Hell."

Other contractions such as "Shan't," "He's," "It's," "You'll," "They'll," and so on, may not look like other words, but they tire the eye just the same. In the following columns, you will notice that it is just a bit easier to read the words in the right-hand column:

Shan't	Shall not
He's	He is
It's	It is
You'll	You will
They'll	They will

Do not use too many exclamation marks. An exclamation mark looks like the letter "l." Consider this headline for a popular beverage:

HERE'S HOW!

The word "how" with the exclamation mark coming immediately after it looks like the word "howl."

Consider this headline:

How to get Your name on Uncle Sam's payroll!

To the careless eye, the word "payroll" looks as if it were spelled with three "l's." Result: slight confusion.

A PLAN FOR AVOIDING DIFFICULT SENTENCES

When you have finished writing a piece of copy, give it to someone to read aloud. An agency executive received a mailing from a magazine. Here is the opening paragraph:

> The purpose of this letter is to demonstrate the market an analysis of *Blank Monthly* readers presents to advertisers.

The chances are that you stumbled just a little in reading that paragraph. If the writer of the letter had given it to someone to read aloud, that person would have stumbled, too. The paragraph could then have been changed to read like this:

> The purpose of this letter is to show you the type of readers you can reach by advertising in *Blank Monthly*.

A piece of advertising writing should be not only grammatically correct and properly punctuated, but it must read smoothly—swiftly. There must be no need to go back and read certain portions again. The reader should not be forced to keep an eagle eye out for commas and apostrophes. Avoid sentences that require complicated punctuation.

Small irregularities in your copy may confuse the reader for only a second. But a second's confusion multiplied by a million readers is a lot of confusion.

STYLE-CONSCIOUS COPY

Read this paragraph taken from an advertisement:

> You haven't tried Blank's Biscuits? . . . Try them, like them—and thereafter you'll find them always the same, all around the world, unchanging and good.

This is a mild example of style copy—the kind of copy that pays more attention to how a thing is said than to what is said. Consider the first sentence. You do not know it is a question until you come to the question mark. Up to that time you have been reading the sentence as a simple statement. Result: slight confusion.

The last sentence of the copy says: "You'll find them always the same, all around the world, unchanging and good." Does this mean that you can buy Blank's Biscuits anywhere in the world? Or does it mean that if you take a package of Blank's Biscuits around the world with you they will not spoil in any climate?

There is much of this style copy being written. It gives the reader the impression that something brilliant has been said, but just exactly what has been said the reader cannot remember.

The weakness of style-conscious copy can be seen in the following headlines. Each headline expresses the same thought. But the thought comes out strongest in the third headline, which contains no style, just plain English.

1. TO THE $25,000 MAN OR WOMAN WITH $50,000 POTENTIALITIES.

2. WHEN YOU REACH IT, $25,000 IS JUST ANOTHER MILESTONE.

3. TO THE $25,000 MAN OR WOMAN WHO WOULD LIKE TO MAKE $50,000.

Here is a sentence that conveys an idea in a rather complicated style: "It is unlawful to appropriate, for your personal use, any property that rightfully belongs to other individuals."

Here is how the same idea is expressed in simple language: "Thou shalt not steal."

The simplicity of the latter wording is not offensive to sophisticated readers, no matter how many college degrees they have. And the simple wording is clear to readers who have little schooling.

> In order to increase the pulling power of your advertising, your copy should be simple, not subtle. You will not offend educated readers by making your advertisements understandable to all readers.

WORDS THAT NEED EXPLAINING

The manager of a department store prepared an advertisement for some household articles. Before publishing the ad, he handed it to an experienced copywriter for suggestions.

At the beginning of the copy, this sentence occurred:

> Most of these articles are exclusive with this store.

The copywriter added four words to the sentence, making it read:

> Most of these articles are exclusive with this store—
> Cannot be obtained elsewhere.

Further on in the copy, this sentence occurred:

> Every one of these articles is guaranteed.

The copywriter expressed the sentence in fuller detail as follows:

> Every one of these articles is guaranteed. If any trouble develops
> within a year, we will replace the article with a new one. Or,
> if you prefer, your money will be cheerfully refunded.

The copywriter said: "Words like `exclusive' and `guaranteed' have appeared in advertisements so often that they have lost their original force. Furthermore, there are plenty of people who never did know the real meaning of the words. Therefore, it is wise to explain them."

PRESENTING THOUGHTS SIMPLY

Here is a plan that can be used effectively in writing advertising copy. Read the following paragraph:

> This chapter tells some methods for making advertisements simple.
> The average reader understands only simple advertisements.

Now read a slight rearrangement of the same paragraph.

> This chapter tells some methods for making advertisements simple.
> Simple advertisements are the only kind that the average reader
> understands.

The difference between the two arrangements is this: In the first arrangement the second sentence begins with the words. "The average reader." In the second arrangement the second sentence begins with the words. "Simple advertisements."

Arrangement number two is slightly easier to understand. Here is why: The first sentence ends by leaving the thought "simple advertisements" in the reader's mind. The second sentence begins with the same thought.

PROOF THAT SIMPLICITY IS VITAL

The necessity for simplicity in appealing to a mass audience is proved by the experience of other businesses besides the advertising business.

Consider the motion picture business. It is well known that the sophisticated motion pictures are, more often than not, box-office failures.

Compare the circulations of the great national magazines. Those that reach large audiences are not the sophisticated magazines. For example, the circulation of the *Atlantic Monthly* is only a fraction of the circulation of *Reader's Digest*.

Take the case of the tabloid newspapers. These journals have gone the limit in simplicity by telling the news primarily in pictures instead of words. What has been the result? Until it lost much of its audience to the even more pictorial medium of television, The New York *Daily News*, a picture newspaper, had the largest circulation in America. It still ranks among the top three, if we exclude the nationally circulated *The Wall Street Journal, U.S.A. Today*, and *The New York Times*.

MORE PROOF

There are a number of people in the advertising business who are not sold on the value of simplicity. These people continue to write *New Yorker* copy for *Reader's Digest*.

There are other writers who admit that simplicity is valuable. Yet they continue to write difficult copy because it is easier to write. They are like the man who at the end of a long-winded letter added this P.S.: "Please pardon this long letter. I didn't have time to write a short one."

In spite of the sales advantage of simplicity, scores of advertisers continue to print advertisements that are over the heads of readers. Here are some ad headlines that were published in magazines:

For a Discriminating Clientele
The Giant and the Pygmy
Give Your Toothpaste Proxy to Her

Does the average citizen know the meaning of clientele, pygmy, or proxy?

Modern advertising copy is full of words such as these: fastidious, distinctive, exhilaration, virtual, veritable, heritage. It is full of phrases such as: Sophisticated cuisine . . . Beautifully appointed interiors . . . Craftsmanship in volume production. Is this the language of the mass audience?

What advertising man or woman has not read (or perhaps written) a paragraph like the following, which appeared in an ad:

> In the big centers where a multiplicity of power broadcasting stations embarrasses less selective receivers, the full range selectivity of the Excelsior Receiver simplifies reception by banishing overlapping.

The next time you write a paragraph like this one, or the next time you write a clever advertisement, give it to a few people of average education and see what they get out of it. Their reaction will tell you more clearly than words why it is not clever to write clever advertisements.

When young writers first enter the advertising business they often rebel at the advice: "Write simply. Use short words and short sentences." There is a temptation to write clever advertising that brings praise from fellow copywriters, from account executives, and from clients. In fact, some writers never recover from this temptation.

In the mid-1930s, I once made a marketing investigation in several small cities in Ohio. The job consisted of going from house to house and asking housewives if they used a washing machine, and if not, why not.

One night, while at a hotel in the city of Ashtabula, I received this telegram from the advertising agency that employed me: "Ask one hundred women if they know what a Pianola is." I smiled to myself. What a silly question? Of course, the women would know. Everybody then knew that a Pianola is an old-style mechanical piano. I recalled a popular song—vintage of high school days:

And we'll tickle a tune
upon the Pianola

The next morning, when I had finished asking the first housewife her opinion of washing machines, I grinned a bit sheepishly and said, "Do you know what a Pianola is?" She looked at me blankly—as if I had asked her to explain Einstein's Theory of Relativity. I looked back at her blankly. I could scarcely believe that she did not know. Finally I managed to smile and say, "I guess you never heard of it. They are not very well known. Thank you. Good day."

The second housewife I spoke to also looked blank and could give no answer. The third asked if a Pianola was a new kind of washing machine. The final tally showed that only one woman out of ten knew the meaning of Pianola.

In writing advertising copy, use words you would expect to find in a sixth-grade reader.

A MISUNDERSTOOD ADVERTISEMENT

A manufacturer of Hi-Fi radio receivers prepared a billboard poster featuring the fact that his particular set had power. The poster consisted of the following elements:

1. The name of the radio. Let us call it the Acme Radio.

2. A picture of a powerful speedboat traveling at such high speed that the bow of the boat was lifted out of the water.

3. The single word "Power."

This diagram shows how the poster looked.

```
+---------------------------------------+
|                                       |
|           ACME HI-FI RADIOS           |
|        [picture of motorboat]         |
|                POWER                  |
|                                       |
+---------------------------------------+
```

The poster caused advertising professionals, including myself, to say "Wonderful."

One day while riding in a bus I passed one of these posters. I heard this conversation behind me:

"What kind of motorboat is that Acme Motorboat?"

"I don't know. She sure cuts through the water."

Always remember that you are writing for people like that. To them a picture of a motorboat is an advertisement for a motorboat. And nothing on earth—not even the word "Radio" in huge letters—can make it an advertisement for a radio.

> When you are advertising motorboats, show pictures of motorboats. But when you are advertising radios, no matter how powerful, show pictures of radios.

Here is another incident. One evening while riding in a bus along Riverside Drive, New York City, I heard a woman behind me read an advertisement aloud to her companion. The advertisement consisted of three sentences flashed from a Mazola Oil electric sign facing the drive. One of the sentences was, "You will like its smooth, bl— flavor." She started to pronounce the word "bland," hesitated and gave it up. What a pity it is that we copywriters are not more frequently brought into contact with the literary limitations of our readers.

A LAWYER'S SECRET

A successful lawyer discovered by experience the value of simplicity in winning lawsuits. He said, "Half the cases that go to court today are not presented to a jury. Instead, each lawyer presents his or her side of the case directly to the judge in the form of a written brief. I am always glad to work on this type of case because I have learned how to write a more effective brief than many of my opponents.

"The way I accomplish this is to make my brief very simple. I omit all legal language such as 'the party of the first part,' and 'the party of the second part' etc. I write my brief as if I were writing a letter to a friend who did not understand legal terms. I have considerably increased my percentage of successes in this manner."

A MISUNDERSTOOD HEADLINE

I once wrote an advertisement for a book called *Courage*. The book told how to banish fear and develop self-confidence. In searching for a striking headline, I reasoned thus: One of the best-known examples of courage is the bulldog. And one of the most striking words for expressing the idea of courage is the word "grit." I put these two ideas together and produced this headline:

I will give you Bulldog Grit

In preparing the layout, a picture of the author of the book was placed above the headline like this:

[Picture of Author]
I will give you
Bulldog Grit

[copy]

This arrangement gave the impression, so desirable in mail order advertisements, that the author of the book was speaking directly to the reader.

I showed the advertisement to a friend. "How does this ad appeal to you?" I asked.

My friend nodded approvingly. "It sure would stop me if I owned a bulldog."

I stared at him. "What has owning a bulldog got to do with it?"

"Well, isn't that Bulldog Grit a brand of dog food?"

I went back to my desk and changed the headline to "I will give you Bulldog Courage."

HOW TO MAKE A GOOD HEADLINE BETTER

Often the more direct the approach, the bigger the difference. Take two ads for a gasoline additive. The first ad had the headline: "Save one gallon of gas in every ten." It pulled a large number of requests for a sample of the product.

It was then decided to try a more selective approach. The two words "Car owners" were inserted at the beginning of the headline as follows:

"Car owners! Save one gallon of gas in every ten"

There was no other change. The copy in both ads remained the same.

The two versions of the ad were split-run tested in a daily newspaper. The second version, beginning with the words "Car owners" pulled 20 percent more sample requests than the first version.

This test is just one of many experiments that have been tried over the years involving changes in headlines. In a number of cases, these headline changes have resulted in appreciable improvements in results. The following are examples of these successful changes.

HEADLINE: "HAY FEVER"

A maker of a hay fever remedy got good response from a sample offer contained in a small ad headlined "Hay Fever." This advertiser then tested other ads containing the same copy, but with different headlines. One of the new headlines was "Dry Up Hay Fever."

Here are the results of a newspaper split-run test: The ad with the headline "Hay Fever" pulled 297 sample requests. The ad with the headline "Dry Up Hay Fever" pulled 380 sample requests. This is a 27 percent increase obtained by merely adding two words. These two words "Dry Up" added a promise of a benefit to the purely selective headline "Hay Fever."

HEADLINE: "RETIRE IN 15 YEARS"

A retirement income advertiser seeking leads for sales representatives got good response from an ad headline "Retire in 15 Years." This ad ran successfully for several years. Then the advertiser changed the headline to "How a Man of 40 Can Retire in 15 Years." The response was increased. And equally important, the quality of the leads was improved. The replies came from men ages 35 to 45—just the age group that insurance sales reps like to call on. Many men and women in this age bracket have both the desire to start saving for retirement and the means to do it.

HEADLINE: "HOW TO HAVE A COOL, QUIET BEDROOM"

A manufacturer of portable air conditioners ran ads with the headline "How to Have a Cool, Quiet Bedroom." The ads contained a telephone number and offered further information. The telephone replies were switched to the sales staff who invited prospects to come to the manufacturer's showroom. Later on, four words were added to the headline of the ad as follows: "How to Have a Cool, Quiet Bedroom— Even on Hot Nights." This change made the headline more dramatic and strengthened the promise of a benefit. Replies and sales increased.

HEADLINE: "HOW TO REPAIR CARS—QUICKLY, EASILY, RIGHT"

At an advertising conference, a mail-order copywriter told this case history. An ad with the headline: "How to Repair Cars—quickly, easily, right" was successful in getting orders. Then the word "Repair" was changed to "Fix." The new headline was "How to Fix Cars—quickly, easily, right." Orders increased 20 percent. Apparently, the word "Repair" sounded like hard work, whereas the word "Fix" sounded quick and easy.

HEADLINE: "FIVE ACRES AND INDEPENDENCE"

A book publisher planned to bring out a book on country-home ownership entitled *Five Acres*. The publisher tested two titles as follows:

1. *Five Acres*
2. *Five Acres and Independence*

The latter title *Five Acres and Independence* was the winner by a wide margin. The book was published and it sold well.

HEADLINE: "HOW I RAISED MYSELF FROM FAILURE TO SUCCESS IN SELLING"

Here are two more book titles that were tested:

1. *How I Raised Myself to Success in Selling*
2. *How I Raised Myself from Failure to Success in Selling*

The latter title containing the words *from Failure* was the winner. This book became a best seller.

A LESSON FROM MAGAZINE PUBLISHERS

The next time you buy a magazine that has a paper sticker attached to the front cover, read the article titles printed on the sticker and then open the magazine and read the actual article titles. Sometimes the wording is different. For example:

"How to Beat Insomnia Without Sleeping Pills," was the title of a magazine article. "How to Sleep Without Pills" was the shorter and simpler title printed on the front cover sticker.

It is the job of the circulation department of a magazine to sell as many copies as possible, and so they sometimes simplify, modify or reconstruct the titles of articles in order to give them more sales punch. In doing this, the men and women in the circulation department are, in effect, working with headlines. They try to make a good headline better. Sometimes they do this by shortening an article title, as in the above example. Sometimes they do it by lengthening a title. Sometimes they change only a word or two. Sometimes they reconstruct the entire title.

Here are some magazine article titles that were given more impact by being shortened.

(Original title)	Hot Tips on Heating Your Home
(Revised title on cover sticker)	How to Cut Fuel Bills
(Original title)	A Smart Shopper's Guide to Bargains
(Revised title)	Shopper's Guide to Bargains
(Original title)	Three Ways to Mothproof a Marriage
(Revised title)	3 Ways to Save a Marriage

(Original title)	How to Understand the Perplexing Teen-Ager
(Revised title)	How to Understand Your Teen-Ager
(Original title)	Which Diet Tips Pay Off?
(Revised title)	Diet Tips That Pay Off

Here are some article titles that were given more sales appeal by being lengthened:

(Original title)	When Your Husband's Affection Cools
(Revised title)	When Your Husband's Affection Cools—and what to do about it
(Original title)	Birth Control for Men
(Revised title)	Now—Safe, Simple Birth Control for Men
(Original title)	You Can Read Faster
(Revised title)	Read Faster—a 20-Day Plan
(Original title)	Key to Fitness at Any Age
(Revised title)	Key to Fitness at Any Age for Men and Women

Here are some article titles that were given greater interest by reconstructing:

(Original title)	The Smugglers of Misery
(Revised title)	Where All the Drugs Come From
(Original title)	Building on the Positives in Marriage
(Revised title)	4 Ways to Keep Your Marriage Young
(Original title)	High Blood Pressure—New Light on a Hidden Killer
(Revised title)	New Protection Against Heart Attack
(Original title)	Backyard Gardens Are Back in Style
(Revised title)	How to Start a Backyard Garden
(Original title)	What You Can Do to Combat Inflation
(Revised title)	10 Ways to Beat the High Cost of Living

SUMMING UP

The next time you write a headline, don't be satisfied with your first draft. Put it aside overnight and then read it again. See if you can make it better by shortening it or by lengthening it or by reconstructing it.

Advertising is your means of public approach. If you make a product good enough, even though you live in the depths of the forest, the public will make a path to your door, says the philosopher. But if you want the public in sufficient numbers, you would better construct a highway. Advertising is that highway.

William Randolph Hearst

CHAPTER 15

LAYOUTS AND ILLUSTRATIONS THAT ATTRACT THE MOST READERS

It has been said that the greatest crime an advertisement can commit is to remain unnoticed. Getting advertisements to be noticed is the job of the layout artist and the art director. But just as the copywriters who hope to write the Great American Novel must put away "fine writing" when they are writing copy, so must the art directors put away "fine art" when they are producing an advertisement. At least, fine art must be made a secondary consideration. The principal job of an advertisement is to sell goods. Therefore, you should use layouts and illustrations in which salesmanship comes first and art second.

An art director described the mental development she went through in trying to produce advertisements that sold goods. When she first started in the advertising business, she tried to apply the things she learned in art school. Her first consideration in making an ad layout was good taste and good design. Her first consideration in selecting an illustration was that it should be as similar as possible to the painting of the old masters. The result was that her advertisements brought "Ooo's!" and "Ah's!" of delight from other art directors. Her advertisements were the kind that won prizes at commercial art exhibitions.

Being practical and knowing that the principal job of an advertisement is to sell merchandise to a mass audience, this art director showed her creations to taxi drivers, stenographers, clerks, and others not directly interested in art. She showed each of these people a group of advertisements and asked which attracted them the most. When the first man showed preference for the most inartistic advertisement, the art director laughed the matter off. When a female clerk did the same thing, it seemed like a coincidence.

But when dozens of people passed over the artistic creations and selected something that looked like a typical Sears Roebuck ad, the art director began to see a great light. Since then she has conducted hundreds of tests. She has found that the artistic qualities of an advertisement are not nearly as important as the ability of the advertisement to get attention and to drive home a selling point. Sometimes the rules of fine art must be completely reversed in producing an effective advertisement.

FINE ART VERSUS COMMERCIAL ART

Many advertising artists are still in the mental stage that this art director was in before she started showing advertisements to average people. The trouble with applying the rules of fine art to advertising is that fine art seeks to please the senses and to tone in with surroundings. Why are park benches usually painted green instead of orange? Because green is more artistic. Because green tones in with the surroundings. But do advertisers want to tone in with their surroundings? Do manufacturers want to pay $40,000 for a color page in a magazine just to soothe the artistic senses of the readers? No. They want to jar the readers and stop them on the spot—to rouse them and stir them to action.

HOW TO MAKE TYPE WORK FOR YOU

The principal consideration in selecting the style of type for your headline is that it should be big enough and powerful enough to seize the attention of the reader.

The principal consideration in selecting type for your copy is that it should be easy to read. The easiest type for people to read is the type they read most often. Therefore, set your copy in the customary, everyday styles of type used in newspaper articles and magazine articles. Avoid fancy type. Avoid script. Avoid too many italics. Avoid type that is too faint or too bold. Avoid any style of type that calls attention to the type itself rather than to the message. Do not try to create atmosphere with type.

Some art directors use type merely as a decoration. They force the type into neat squares or oblongs or other shapes. They arrange it so that all the lines will come out to equal length, like the inscription on a memorial tablet. Sometimes they use an unusually light (thin)-face type or a script so that the block of copy will not interfere with the illustration. Sometimes they use the type as part of the design by setting it in long, hard-to-read lines of fancy type with wide white spaces between the lines. Devices of this kind may make an advertisement more artistic, but they do not invite the eye to read. Remember that people buy magazines and newspapers to read stories and articles. Therefore, if you want your copy to be read, set the text like a story or an article.

In selecting type for your advertisements, you would do well to take a look at the typical mail-order ads that are repeated again and again, such as figures 1.2 and 11.1. Note the strong, black, readable type in which the headlines are set. Note the clear-cut type in which the copy is set. If you do not know the names of the various styles of type, you will not go wrong if you tear a good mail-order ad out of a magazine or newspaper and say to your typesetter: "Please set my ad like this."

In preparing your ad layout, make your headline large enough and bold enough so that even the most careless glancer cannot help but catch your message. If your headline is a long one, set some of the more important words in capitals or extra-large type, or both, as seen in Figure 4.2.

Large type in a headline has strong attention value. It also gives force to your message. Consider this headline in ordinary size type:

ANNOUNCING NEW MODELS

Now see how much more emphatic the headline looks in larger type:

ANNOUNCING NEW MODELS

The big type adds strength and force to your announcement. It makes big news out of it instead of little news. It gives the impression that you are speaking in a strong voice instead of in a whisper. An announcement in small type suggests that you yourself do not think that the announcement is important.

Even when you have no news—no announcement to make, you can give your headline a news flavor by putting it in big type. Consider this headline in ordinary size type:

TO MEN AND WOMEN WHO WANT TO GET AHEAD

This is an interesting headline, but consider how much more important it becomes when it is spread clear across the page in large type:

TO MEN AND WOMEN WHO WANT TO GET AHEAD

The big type seems to add an announcement quality, a news quality, even though the headline contains no news at all. Do not, however, use capitals for more than six or seven words in a row. For almost all adults, "All-Caps" becomes harder to read easily beyond that point. Set the above headline as:

To men and women
who want to get ahead

FEATURING IMPORTANT WORDS IN HEADLINES

When you are dealing with a lengthy headline, you may not have room to set all the words in large type. In that case, you can set part of the headline in large type. For example, here is a long headline in which none of the words have been featured:

YOU CAN LAUGH AT MONEY WORRIES

IF YOU FOLLOW THIS SIMPLE FINANCIAL PLAN

Here is the same headline with certain words featured in large type. In setting up an ad, these featured words can be made to stand out on the page and stop readers. Note that the featured words convey a complete message in themselves. This is important. Do not feature words that are meaningless by themselves.

YOU CAN LAUGH

AT MONEY WORRIES

if you follow this simple
financial plan

Here are four more headlines that have been given the same treatment. In the first version of each, no words have been featured. In the second version certain meaningful words have been set in large type:

(1) To men and women who want to
     quit work some day

(2) To men and women who want to
     QUIT WORK some day

(1) Break up a cold
     this quick way

(2) BREAK UP A COLD
     this quick way

(1) Thousands now play who
     never thought they could

(2) THOUSANDS NOW PLAY
who never thought they could

(1) Who else wants a whiter wash
with no hard work

(2) WHO ELSE WANTS
A WHITER WASH
with no hard work

When you hand your ad copy to your layout artist or to your art director, they will appreciate it if you will indicate which, if any, important words in your headline should be emphasized or set in larger type than the rest of the headline.

If you write a long headline, it is wise to include a meaningful phrase that can be set in extra bold or extra-large type. If you can do so, it is especially good to arrange your thoughts so that the meaningful phrase occurs at the beginning of your headline. This arrangement is used in three out of four of the headlines listed above. It is not used in the headline "To men and women who want to QUIT WORK some day."

PICTURES THAT GET ATTENTION

Hundreds of readership surveys have been conducted in which people have been asked which ads they noticed in various publications. As a result, it is possible to list certain types of pictures that are especially effective in getting attention. For example:

- Pictures of brides

- Pictures of babies

- Pictures of animals

- Pictures of famous people

- Pictures of people in odd costumes, such as might be worn at a masquerade

- Pictures of people in odd situations, such as a man wearing an eye patch

- Pictures that tell a story, such as a little girl trying on her mother's hat

- Romantic pictures, such as a man carrying a girl across a rushing brook

- Catastrophe pictures, such as car accidents
- News pictures, such as the launching of a space vehicle
- Timely pictures, such as pictures of Santa Claus at Christmas time and pictures of Abraham Lincoln on Lincoln's birthday

One interesting observation that has come out of readership surveys is, for most products, men tend to look at ads containing pictures of men and that women tend to look at ads containing pictures of women. Apparently, the pictures act as labels. A man figures that an ad containing a picture of a man is likely to be an ad for a man's product and that an ad containing a picture of a woman is likely to be an ad for a woman's product.

Before the widespread use of readership surveys, some advertisers believed that the way to stop a male reader was to show a picture of a bathing beauty. Apparently this technique stops the wrong readers or it stops them in the wrong mood. This type of picture may create desire for the girl, but it does not seem to create desire for the product being advertised. There was a story from the early days of direct mail about the man who sent $29.95 in response to a mail-order catalog ad for a woman's dress. When the dress was delivered, the man complained. For $29.95 he had expected to get the woman model who had been shown wearing the dress in the catalog illustration!

PICTURES THAT SELL

In using information gained from readership surveys, it is wise to remember that the high attention value of a picture does not necessarily mean high sales value. In order to have sales value, the picture should be related to the product.

Some advertisers have wrongly used readership survey results by illustrating ads with pictures of high attention value but without relation to the product. For example, if you use a picture of a bride or a baby in order to get high attention value for an automobile ad, you will stop the wrong people in the wrong mood. On the other hand, a picture of a bride is fine for selling wedding gifts such as silverware. And a picture of a baby is fine for selling baby powder.

Based on sales tests of advertisements, following are typical examples of pictures that have sales value:

1. Picture of the product. For example, in an automobile ad, show a picture of the automobile.

2. Picture of product in use. For example, a woman using a new garden tool she just bought.

3. Picture of reward of using the product. For example, a woman admiring a cake she baked, or eating a pudding she prepared, or wearing the better coat she's always wanted, as in Figure 15.1.

4. Picture of attainment of ambition. For example, a boy receiving a diploma. Another example: A correspondence school ad showing a smiling man handing his wife some money. Headline: "Here's an extra $50, Grace—I'm making real money now." (*See Caples' classic ad in Figure 15.2.*)

5. Picture of an enlarged detail. For example, a magnifying glass showing an enlargement of a new kind of pen point.

6. Dramatic pictures. For example, an ad for a memory course showed a picture of a blindfolded man. Headline: "A startling memory feat you can do."

An error to avoid in the choice of pictures is the use of pictures that are too far-fetched or too clever. Here is what sometimes happens. An agency works for years preparing ads for seagoing cruises. They get tired of pictures of happy people embarking on a ship or pictures of joyful groups playing shuffleboard on the deck of a ship. They crave something different. And so they prepare a cruise ad that features a picture of a ship's compass or a picture of a ship captain's hat. This is clever, but too far-fetched. This agency has forgotten two important truths, namely:

1. To the average person who is glancing rapidly through a publication, a picture of a compass is an ad for a compass. A picture of a hat is an ad for a hat.

2. The persons who have finally saved up enough money to take a cruise are delighted with pictures of people embarking or pictures of groups playing games aboard ship. This is just what they are looking for. So don't lose them or confuse them with pictures of hats or compasses.

Figure 15.1: *Turning on the off-season.* The need to generate fur sales in warm weather spurred this promotion. THE AD: Picture and words combine to make every element sell. "First time" creates news value. "Thursday through Saturday" emphasizes action. Add a "TRADE-IN" possibility, then reinforce and expand in just three copy lines. THE RESULT: A promotion so different it raised customers' curiosity, developed a new awareness of Evans . . . and brought fur sales not normally made during summer.

Figure 15.2: *One of the All-time Greats.* This ad first appeared in 1919. It is typical of a famous series that built the International Correspondence Schools into the largest in the world. The appeal is as valid today as ever. For example, the copy says: "The cost of living is mounting month by month. You can't get along on what you have been making. Somehow you've simply got to increase your earnings."

When you are looking for an idea for an ad illustration, you will often find that a picture of the product will produce the most sales. For example, the Book-of-the-Month Club shows pictures of books. If you look through a mail order catalogue you will find the following:

- Pictures of sewing machines in sewing machine ads.
- Pictures of vacuum cleaners in vacuum cleaner ads.
- Pictures of dresses in ads for dresses.
- Pictures of shoes in ads for shoes.

The preceding examples are not intended to rule out the use of dramatic and exciting illustrations. Exciting pictures are fine if you can think up a picture in which the excitement in the picture is related to the product.

WHY PHOTOGRAPHS MAKE GOOD ILLUSTRATIONS

After you have selected the subject matter for your illustration, it is usually better to use a photograph of the subject instead of a drawing. For believability, there is nothing as effective as a photograph. If you do use a drawing or a painting, let your drawing be as lifelike as possible—as photographic in style as possible.

The effectiveness of photographs can be illustrated by a few personal experiences. A woman friend of mine spent half an hour telling me about her little nephew, whom she adored. I didn't learn much about the child from what she said. Her description was too idealized. Then she showed me a large crayon portrait of a beautiful boy. I looked at the drawing, but there wasn't enough reality in it for me to tell what he was really like. Finally, she showed me a snapshot of the youngster on roller skates. This tiny photograph told me what the boy was really like. He looked like a real boy with a character of his own and a nice smile. I could have recognized him. But I could never have recognized him from the crayon portrait. The portrait was unreal and unconvincing.

Another time, I was looking through a summer resort catalog. The advertisements of two resorts attracted me. But one advertisement had a distinct advantage over the other. It showed photographs of the resort and the surrounding country. These photographs told me exactly what the resort was like. They offered the next best thing to an actual visit of inspection. The other advertisement showed an idealized drawing of the hotel and surrounding grounds. It pictured flags flying, fountains playing, and artistic sailboats on the lake nearby. The drawing didn't prove a thing. It gave no real information. It failed to convince. It was plainly just an artist's ideal conception of a summer hotel.

At another time, I wanted to buy airplane luggage. I searched through newspapers and magazines for advertisements. Some of the ads showed drawings of luggage, some showed paintings, others showed photographs. The ads with the photographs interested me most. I knew that if I went to look at that luggage, I would not be disappointed. The actual luggage would look like the photographs. On the other hand, if I went looking for luggage of which I had seen only a drawing or an idealized painting, I might be disappointed. The actual article might not look anything like its portrait.

A photograph adds real information to an advertisement. Photographs convince. Photographs are proof. Everybody knows that when you look at a photograph of a person or a piece of merchandise or a summer resort, you are looking at a real likeness. There are little details in photographs that tell so much—little details of expression or surrounding atmosphere. A glance at a photograph is the next best thing to seeing the actual object.

An old Chinese proverb, often misquoted, says, "A *good* picture is worth a thousand words." If this is true, then a good photograph is worth two thousand words.

USING HEADS OF PEOPLE IN ADVERTISEMENTS

Why do mail-order advertisers so often use men's heads and women's heads as illustrations for advertisements? The answer is that this type of illustration often brings more sales than other types.

Pictures of people's heads are good attention-getters. This is especially true when the model is looking directly at you and is related to the product or service, for example, a photo of a user of the product or a graduate of a mail order correspondence course. A photograph of a person looking you square in the eye will stop you quicker than a picture of a cake of soap or a landscape.

Pictures of people's heads are economical in the matter of space. All you need to show is the face. This means that if you have a large space reserved for your illustration, you can enlarge the face until it fills the space, thus making an illustration that simply cannot be missed.

If you are using long copy and have only a small space left for the illustration, there is nothing you can put in that space that is more eye-catching than a person's head. Many 60-line mail-order advertisements are so crowded with copy that the space left for the illustration is no larger than a postage stamp. Yet this small space is big enough to carry an effective picture of a man's or woman's head.

What are the other types of illustrations used in advertisements? Outdoor scenes, groups of people, office scenes, home scenes, and landscapes are some. Illustrations of this kind are all right if you have plenty of space in which to put them. But they cannot be used to good advantage where you are using quarter-pages or where your copy is long.

Take the case of the landscape picture. You cannot crowd an effective landscape into a small space. If you show a miniature of the entire landscape, the details of the picture become unrecognizable. If you try to cut off parts of the landscape, you are likely to spoil it.

But suppose you are using a man's head. You can omit his shoulders and his collar. You can even cut off the top of his head, leaving only his face, and still have a good illustration. A person's head, especially if he is looking at you, is one of the most effective illustrations you can use in small space. It is also extremely effective when enlarged to fill a larger space.

There are other strong reasons for using people's heads as advertising illustrations. Take the case of a testimonial advertisement. If you show a photograph of the person who wrote the testimonial, the readers will feel more confidence in the message. They will feel that it must be true, or else the testimonial givers would not dare to allow their photograph to be used. Furthermore, as the readers read the testimonial, they can glance every now and then at the person who wrote it. They can see what that person looks like. This increases reader interest and gives a more intimate touch to the message.

THE ADVERTISER'S LOGOTYPE

An important part of many advertisements is the advertiser's logotype or name of the advertiser, which is featured in large type, usually at the bottom of the ad, as in the Mobil editorial-style ad shown in Figure 15.3.

THE GLOBAL ECONOMY #3

Time to move forward

In late July, there will be a welcoming ceremony in Asia. Vietnam will be formally welcomed into the group of nations that constitutes the Association of Southeast Asian Nations (ASEAN). It marks the first time Vietnam has joined an organization whose aims are peaceful adjudication of disputes and the promotion of trade among its members.

It demonstrates that Vietnam's neighbors see it as ready to take its rightful place in the region and to participate in the area's economic growth.

It's an important first. The next step should be for the U.S. to normalize relations with Vietnam. The Senate will soon be considering whether the president should establish full diplomatic relations with Vietnam.

A non-partisan effort to support full diplomatic relations is being spearheaded in the Senate by several members, including highly respected and decorated Vietnam veterans. And their efforts are being backed by the Veterans of Foreign Wars, AMVETS, the U.S. Chamber of Commerce and more than 110 members of the Coalition for U.S.-Vietnam Trade.

Full recognition, of course, raises concerns about American prisoners of war (POWs) and those missing in action (MIAs). The goal hasn't changed. All Americans want reconciliation of the POW/MIA issue. It's a concern

Mobil respects and shares as many of our employees and shareholders are Vietnam veterans. The best way, in our view, to resolve these issues is through constructive engagement. As diplomatic and commercial ties strengthen, progress on outstanding issues between our two countries will be enhanced.

Mobil's experience in Vietnam dates back to 1974–75 when we made the first oil discovery. Since the president lifted the trade embargo against Vietnam in early 1994, American companies have been competing with foreign companies for a wide range of business opportunities. But we haven't been able to compete on an equal basis. That's because the governments of those foreign companies already have established relations with Vietnam and provide them with a full range of commercial services and programs. Normalization would help make American companies more competitive. Moreover, normalization will increase export opportunities in this fast-growing market for American companies, which will result in more jobs here at home.

Lifting the trade embargo was a big first step. Now is the time to move ahead and complete normalization of relations between our two countries. We need to accomplish it before the politics of an election year muddies the issue. America will not forget its history, but it's now time to move forward.

Mobil®

Our Internet address is:
http://www.mobil.com.

©1995 Mobil Corporation

Figure 15.3: *A public voice for a public corporation.* Since 1970, the Mobil Corporation has appeared on the Op-Ed page of *The New York Times.* In an instantly recognizable format, Mobil's Public Affairs Department expresses its views on business, economic, and public issues. Although many corporations and individuals use the Op-Ed space, no other uses this advertising format so consistently—and few use it so well—to contribute to the debate about topics of importance to us all.

Sometimes the logotype is the name of the manufacturer and sometimes it is the name of the product. For example, here are some manufacturers' names that are often used as logotypes:

- General Electric
- General Motors
- IBM
- Kodak

Here are some product names that have frequently been used as logotypes:

- Tide
- Nike
- Chanel
- Cadillac

The manufacturer repeats the logotype over and over again in the hope that you will remember it and be favorably inclined toward that brand when you buy. This is long-haul advertising as distinguished from short-haul advertising for immediate sales.

In radio advertising, the manufacturers cannot feature a logotype in big print and so they often compensate for this by repeating the name or the name of the product over and over again. For example, in a one-minute radio commercial for Colgate Toothpaste, the name Colgate may be repeated many times.

In TV advertising, the manufacturers can get name publicity in two ways if they desire, namely, by flashing the product name in big print on the screen and by having the name frequently repeated by the announcer.

The effect of the logotype on the consumer is difficult to measure because it takes months and sometimes years to produce a measurable result. Yet the effect is known to exist because tests have shown that people will buy a familiar product in preference to one that is unfamiliar. They will buy from a known manufacturer more readily than from an unknown manufacturer. Therefore, the advertiser's logotype should not be omitted from an ad except under special conditions such as the following:

1. If the name of the product is mentioned in the headline of an ad, it need not be mentioned again in the logotype.

2. Sometimes a picture of the product with the name printed on the package takes the place of the logotype.

3. Some mail order advertisers omit the logotype because they are selling an item or service that is bought only once in a lifetime, for example, a book or a correspondence course. These advertisers are advertising for an immediate sale instead of building up name publicity over the years. By omitting the logotype, these concerns reduce their space cost.

4. Readership surveys are mixed about whether editorial items get higher reading than ads. Much, obviously, depends on the specific headline or illustration for each. Nevertheless, some advertisers omit the logotype in order to produce ads that don't look like ads. For example, ads that look like cartoons, or ads that look like news items, articles, as in Figure 10.3, or stories. These ads sacrifice the advantage of a logotype in order to gain the advantage of increased readership of their complete text set in small print.

ADS WITHOUT PICTURES

Some of the best pulling mail order ads have been all-type ads with no pictures. For example, the ad for the Roth Memory Course with the headline: "How I Improved My Memory in One Evening." This ad pulled so well that it ran for years. An all-type ad for Tecla Pearls was also run for years and became famous. (See Caples' classic ad in Figure 15.4.)

An all-type ad selling subscriptions to a well-known newspaper was the best puller of a number of ads tested, some with illustrations, some without illustrations. The headline of this ad was: "How to Get the *Times* Delivered to Your Home." At the present writing, this ad has been running for 14 years. No other ad has equalled it in pulling power.

These examples are not intended to sell you off the idea of using pictures, but to point out that a picture is not a must in every ad. Pictures cost money, and the space they occupy costs money. Every illustration should be tested with this question: Does it add sufficient sales value to warrant its cost?

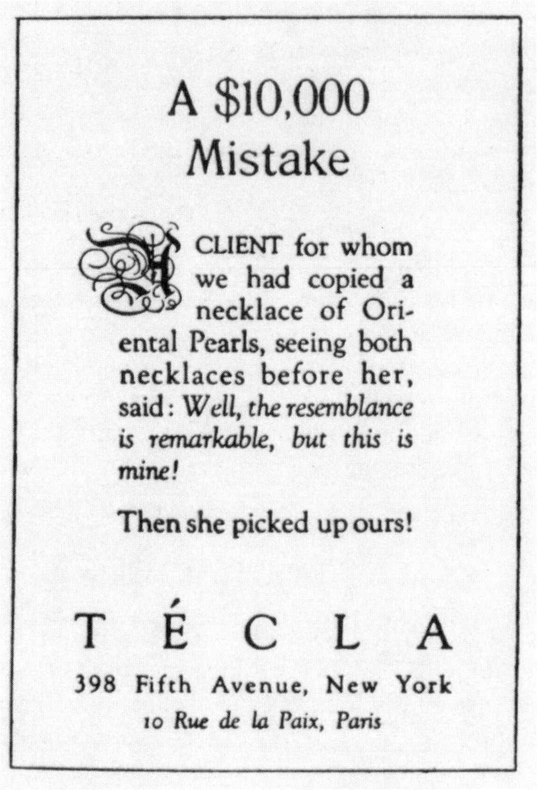

A $10,000 Mistake

 CLIENT for whom we had copied a necklace of Oriental Pearls, seeing both necklaces before her, said: *Well, the resemblance is remarkable, but this is mine!*

Then she picked up ours!

TÉCLA

398 Fifth Avenue, New York

10 *Rue de la Paix, Paris*

Figure 15.4: *Written by the World's Highest Paid Copywriter.* Frank Irving Fletcher, the highest-paid ad writer of his time, was famous for his ability to tell a story in a few words. This is an example. "But brevity is not desirable in all cases," he said. "If a man is interested in buying what you have to sell, you can't tell him too much."

SUMMING UP

In choosing illustrations for your ads, you will usually get more sales if you cash in on the experience of mail-order advertisers and department stores whose existence depends on ads that produce direct, traceable sales.

Avoid weird, outlandish, or far-fetched pictures that have nothing to do with the product or service you are selling. Use pictures that attract buyers, not curiosity seekers. Here are some safe bets:

1. Pictures of the product.

2. Pictures of the product in use.

3. Pictures of people who use the product.

4. Pictures showing the reward of using the product.

The American standard of living is due in no small measure to the imaginative genius of advertising, which not only creates and sharpens demand, but also, by its impact upon the competitive process, stimulates the never-ceasing quest of improvement in quality of the product.

Adlai E. Stevenson

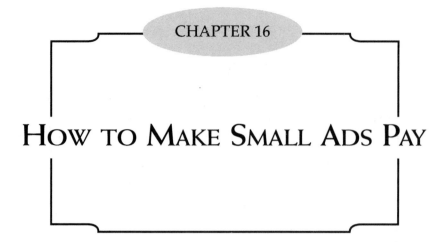

HOW TO MAKE SMALL ADS PAY

One of my earliest discoveries in mail order advertising was that different products have different space size requirements.

For example, a reducing belt was sold at a profit by using small, 60-line, single column mail-order ads (in newspaper measurement, there are 14 "lines" per inch) with the headline FAT MEN. The illustration showed a fat man being pulled in at the midsection by a broad belt around his waist. When full-page ads were used to advertise this product, the per-belt selling cost was increased. In other words, the full-page ads did not bring in enough extra orders to pay for the extra space.

On the other hand, a treatment for growing hair was sold profitably by mail-order by using full-page magazine ads. We tested some 60-line ads for this product, but these small ads failed to bring in enough mail-order sales to make a profit.

What is the reason for this situation? The copy chief of the agency that handled this advertising said:

> The small ads worked well in the case of the reducing belt because a reducing belt is easy to explain. A picture of a man being pulled in at the waistline and a few lines of copy are all that is needed to make clear how the product works. On the other hand, there is a lot of skepticism in men's minds regarding hair-growing treatments. It requires a long, scientific explanation to make clear how the product works and a lot of testimonials from satisfied customers to prove that the treatment really does work. Therefore, full-page ads are required. A small ad does not give you enough room to do a convincing selling job for a hair-growing treatment.

A third class of products are those that can be sold profitably in both small- and large-size ads. For example, in writing mail-order ads for the U.S. School of Music Correspondence Course, we found that various sizes of space were profitable, from full pages down to one-inch, single-column ads.

In considering the question of whether to use small ads or large ads, there are arguments for and against both. There are limitations of small ads and there are also advantages. You should bear in mind the limitations and advantages listed below:

TEN LIMITATIONS OF SMALL ADS

1. Small ads don't impress your dealers as much as large ads.

2. You can't include a long list of names and addresses of your dealers.

3. You can't use color in small ads. It would be too expensive.

4. You can't show an appetite-arousing picture of a lemon pie or a chocolate cake.

5. You can't, in most instances, create a large volume of sales quickly.

6. You can't create the impression of importance or bigness as well as you can with large ads.

7. You can't show a landscape picture or a family group admiring the new living room furniture.

8. You can't show an effective picture of your new model car or refrigerator.

9. You can't use certain effective editorial techniques, such as comic strips or ads that look like magazine articles.

10. You can't get the best positions for your small ads in magazines or in newspapers.

TEN ADVANTAGES OF SMALL ADS

1. You can run a whole series of small ads for the price of a single full page. Thus, small ads enable you to advertise frequently at low cost. Note, however, that smaller space costs proportionately more per inch. Thus a 1/6-page ad (1/2 of a magazine column) may cost the equivalent of 1/4 of a full page space charge.

2. If you make a variety of products, you can feature a different product in each ad in a series of small ads.

3. If your product has a variety of uses, you can feature different uses in different ads.

4. Instead of running a series of pages in a single publication, you can advertise in six or more publications by using small ads.

5. You can gain flexibility by putting part of your appropriation into big ads and part into small ads.

6. You can offer free booklets, literature, samples, and catalogs. You can make mail-order sales.

7. You can get leads for the sales staff.

8. In newspapers, you can get special paid position, such as running your wedding-ring ad alongside the engagement notices, your baby-carriage ad alongside the birth notices.

9. You can get high readership by using such editorial techniques as small cartoons, news items, and picture-caption ads.

10. You can profitably advertise so-called limited-market products or services as illustrated by headlines such as these: Accounting, Corns, Drafting, False Teeth, Feet Hurt, Hearing Aids, Kill Rats, Loans, Maternity Dresses, Shorthand, Stenotype, Toothache. The reason is this: There is not enough profit in corn remedies, for example, to support full-page ads. Furthermore, if the reader of a publication does not have a corn, your full-page ad, no matter how attractive, will not sell him a corn remedy. On the other hand, if the reader does have a corn that is bothering him, he will be stopped by the one-word headline, "CORNS," in a small ad. Since you cannot predict when the reader's corns will be troublesome, you are better off with a small ad in every issue of a publication than with a big ad once in a while.

SUGGESTIONS FOR MAKING SMALL ADS PAY

Use telegraphic language, as if you were sending a cable and you had to pay $5 a word. For example, the sentence, "We will be glad to mail you a copy of our free booklet on request," can be condensed to two words, "Free Booklet." Sometimes a single word "Booklet" is used. A classified ad describing farms for sale ended with the terse offer, "Bklt."

One way to produce a good small ad is to take a big ad and boil down the copy. Cut out the introduction. Cut out the sentences with the least selling power. Omit all unnecessary words. Use short words in place of long words. This is often done with mail-order ads. By the time a page ad is cut down to a half-column there is not an ounce of fat left in the ad. It is all bone and muscle, and it frequently pulls several times its weight in sales.

But suppose you don't have a big ad to cut down. Then write a long piece of copy today and cut it down tomorrow.

HEADLINES OF SMALL ADS

If you can find a one-word headline that will attract the right prospects, such as "Accounting," "Deaf," or "Loans," it will probably be your best headline. The reason is because it can be set in big type without taking up much room. However, never feature a meaningless word such as "If" or "Because" just to get a one-word headline. It is more important for your headline to mean something than it is for it to be brief. If your product doesn't lend itself to a one-word stopper headline, try to write a headline in two, three, or five words.

Good phrases to use in small ad copy are those that condense a lot of meaning into brief space. Examples:

$250 a Week	Anybody Can Learn
Learn in 6 Weeks	Amaze Your Friends
Our 36th Year	Money Back if Not Delighted
Since 1893	Equipment Included
New	100,000 Users
Fun-packed	Trial Plan
Now You Can	Test Yourself
15 Minutes a Day	Free 48-page Book
Mrs. E. C. Made $65	No Obligation
No Special Talent Needed	Send No Money
Age No Obstacle	Write TODAY

ILLUSTRATIONS FOR SMALL ADS

Question: Should you use an illustration? If you are using a line drawing or a picture-caption ad, your ad will be mostly illustration. In the standard type of ad, however, you should evaluate the illustration carefully before using. *Reason:* You can put a lot of selling copy into the space usually occupied by an illustration. If a picture is needed to show the product or to make clear the use of the product, put it in. If the illustration is appropriate and compact, such as the head of a nurse for a course in nursing, put it in. Otherwise, omit the illustration to make the ad smaller or to allow more room for copy.

AD STYLE VERSUS EDITORIAL STYLE

There are two opposite techniques you can use to prepare small ads. You can use either one, but not both at the same time. Technique Number One is to make your ad look like an ad. Use all the ad pro's tricks—stopper headline, long copy, small print, jam-packed layout. But use these tricks so effectively that prospects will be stopped and sold in spite of the fact it is obviously an ad.

Technique Number Two is to make your ad look like editorial material, such as a cartoon or a picture-caption item, or like a news item. This technique will get you a higher readership rating. But you have to omit all your standard ad tricks such as one-word headlines or coupons. If you use ad tricks in an editorial ad, you will simply be telling people, "This is an ad." You will let the cat out of the bag before the cat is in the bag.

CHECKING RESULTS FROM SMALL ADS

Key your ads by telling readers to write a certain department number to obtain a booklet or sample, or offer to sell the product by mail at full price. By keying your ads, you can tell which ads, which publications, and which seasons of the year are more resultful for you. Then after a while you can stop spending money on the less successful ads and spend that money running your best ads in the most responsive publications.

TEST YOUR ADS

Prepare several different ads and run them with a keyed offer in one of the publications on your list in order to find out which ad brings the most replies. Better still, do a split-run test so that two ads can be tested on the same day, under identical conditions. Newspapers in many cities offer split-run testing. Many magazines also offer split-run testing, though some of them limit split runs to full-page ads only. See Chapter 18 for a detailed explanation of split-run testing.

One final word: Publications and agencies should not fear that the use of small ads will reduce advertising appropriations. You can spend just as much on small ads as on large ads. You simply run the small ads more often and in more publications. One advertiser who recently shifted to small ads said, "These little ads are making our sales go up faster than the big ads did. If this continues, we will be able to spend more money on advertising."

Small ads enable small concerns to advertise who otherwise could not afford to advertise at all. These small advertisers often become big advertisers!

So do not underestimate the power of small ads. Remember that David slew Goliath with a small pebble. Two speeches were made at Gettysburg, but the short one was remembered longer.

GETTING RESULTS FROM CLASSIFIED ADS

All over the United States in the classified ad departments of newspapers, men and women ad takers sit at telephones and write insertion orders for ads that come in by phone. Sometimes an advertiser will specify that the ad is to run three times or five times, thereby earning a lower rate. And sometimes an advertiser will telephone and cancel the ad after one or two appearances because the merchandise, or whatever, has been sold. It is then that the ad takers get stories of the results produced by classified ads. These result stories are often published in the papers.

For example, here is a classified ad that ran in *The New York Times*:

PARTNER WANTED

I have just obtained the exciting MRS. AMERICA FRANCHISE for N.J. Already showing extraordinary potential income. My partner could not raise his $10,000. Can YOU? Mr. Richard Stockton at Mrs. America Headquarters will handle interviews. Phone NYC 212 MU 2-XXXX

Regarding this ad *The Times* reported the results as follows:

The advertisement for Mrs. America Productions, Inc.—a firm that produces pageants and license rights to the Mrs. America name in each state—appeared in the "Business Opportunities" columns of *The New York Times*. Only two days after it ran—even before a contract was signed—the advertiser had the $10,000 he had asked for.

Here are stories that were published by newspapers:

A family that ran a "House for Sale" ad in Baltimore said: "We had a full house. Over 40 prospects called."

A sailboat owner ran this ad in the *Philadelphia Bulletin*: "PENGUIN with trailer. Exc. cond. $500." . . . "I was swamped with offers," he said.

A Norfolk woman ran this ad in the *Virginian-Pilot*: "Seven months old male, half German Shepherd, all shots, Va. license, rabies tag, $150." . . . "Sold my dog to the first person who came by," she said.

A Montana rancher ran this ad in the *Rapid City, S.D., Journal*: "Married man for year 'round job on southeastern Montana cattle ranch." The rancher said, "We had very good results—six or seven responses."

A coffee shop owner said he got 60 calls from this ad in the *Washington, D.C. Post*: "COOK—For a small downtown cafeteria, 5 days a wk., gd salary & benefits for the right man or woman."

To promote the use of classified advertising the *Buffalo Courier Express* reprints successful ads and tells readers the results obtained and the low cost of the advertising. Examples:

"SNOW TIRES, 2 Atlas Weatherguard 815x15 on Ford wheels, used 1 season, $80 pair." . . . 5 calls first day. Ad cost $11.10.

"FRANCISCAN china, Desert Rose pattern, matching crystal, service for 8. Bargain price." . . . 22 calls first day. Ad cost $9.35.

"RUGS, 1 each: 14x12 and 9x15. Reasonable" . . . 15 calls first day. Ad cost $7.60.

The Baltimore News American promoted the use of tiny classified ads using abbreviated copy and occupying only a single line of space in the newspaper. The paper reported that all of the following ads were successful.

BIKE—Boys, 24" $20.
PIANO—Upright. rea.
WIG—Champagne beige, $25.
14' Boat, trailer. $50.

Classified advertising has a long history of success. Today, this form of communication is bigger than ever. The daily *New York Times* often carries more than a dozen pages of classified ads; and on Sunday up to 100 pages. Another stronghold of classified ads is the *Los Angeles Times*. A newspaper sales representative figured that it would take an average reader more than 24 hours to read all the classified ads in a single daily issue of that paper.

Classified advertising offers the advantage of low cost, flexibility, and selectivity. You can run your ad in the city where your prospects are located and you can run it under the classified heading that selects the buyers of your product or service.

The prosperity of every country in the world is directly in relation to the amount of advertising.

Col. Robert R. McCormick

CHAPTER 17

TEN BRAIN TEASERS

Twenty tested advertisements are described in this chapter. Ten were successful in getting sales. Ten were unsuccessful. See if you can pick the successes. Correct answers, with the lessons we can learn from their success, can be found on pages 231–233.

Imagine for the next ten minutes that you are the creative director of an advertising agency specializing in tested advertising. Your agency has ten accounts, and each account needs new copy. You have called your copy staff into conference and you have asked them to submit ideas. You have received 20 advertising suggestions—two on each account. It is now up to you to decide which ideas you will use and which you will discard.

The 20 suggestions are arranged in pairs below. Each pair consists of a success and a failure. Headline, illustration, and offer are included in every case. Where it is not obvious, the copy plot is explained.

Out of each pair of suggestions, as you go along, you are to check on page 225 (or on a copy) the one suggestion you believe would bring the best results. Then turn to pages 231–233 where the headlines of the successful advertisements are listed, and see how many you got right.

There are no catch questions in this "test"—no large displays of the word "Free." No extra prominence has been given to the offer in one advertisement and not to the other. Each pair of advertisements was tested in magazines or newspapers under conditions as nearly similar as possible. The inquiries were followed up by direct mail or by a sales representative's call. The pulling power or lack of pulling power of each advertisement rests mainly on its headline and illustration.

Bear in mind also that in every case the pulling power of the two advertisements differed, not by a narrow margin, but by a wide margin. The advertisements that failed were bad failures. They were used only once. The advertisements that were successful were highly successful. They were repeated again and again before their effectiveness wore out.

Probable Ad Test Winners

☐ 1A	☐ 1B
☐ 2A	☐ 2B
☐ 3A	☐ 3B
☐ 4A	☐ 4B
☐ 5A	☐ 5B
☐ 6A	☐ 6B
☐ 7A	☐ 7B
☐ 8A	☐ 8B
☐ 9A	☐ 9B
☐ 10A	☐ 10B

If you "flunk" this test, you are in good company. Some of America's most successful—and highest paid—copywriters wrote the losing ads. Of course many of them wrote the winning ads too! As always, the real winners are the ones who test . . . Test . . . TEST.

(1) Suggestions for Advertising a Home-study Course in Business

1A: Suggestion Number One

Illustration:	[No illustration]
Headline:	To a $25,000 man or woman who would like to be making $50,000
Offer:	Free booklet: "What an Executive Should Know."

IB: Suggestion Number Two

Illustration:

> Picture of man reading booklet

Headline:	Here's proof that this training pays financially
Offer:	Free booklet: "What an Executive Should Know."

(2) Suggestions for Advertising a Hair-growing Remedy

2A: Suggestion Number One

Illustration:

> Man pointing his finger at another man's bald head

Headline:	"60 days ago they called *me* 'Baldy'"
Copy Plot:	The copy tells the story of a man who got excellent results from the hair-growing remedy.
Offer:	Free book, "The New Way to Grow Hair."

2B: Suggestion Number Two

Illustration:

> Hair specialist offering a bank check to the reader

Headline:	If I can't grow hair for you in 30 days you get this check
Copy Plot:	The copy explains that the check you get is your money back refund in case you are not satisfied with the results from the hair-growing treatments.
Offer:	Free book, "The New Way to Grow Hair."

(3) SUGGESTIONS FOR ADVERTISING LIFE INSURANCE

3A: Suggestion Number One

Illustration:

> Picture of man and wife

Headline: Here's one question you shouldn't ask your wife

Copy Plot: "I want to talk it over with my wife," is what some men say when a salesman urges them to buy life insurance. This is wrong. A husband should buy life insurance without asking his wife.

Offer: Free book: "How to Get the Things You Want."

3B: Suggestion Number Two

Illustration:

> Miniature picture of family standing at one end of a life insurance policy; miniature picture of home at other end of policy

Headline: Get rid of money worries for good

Copy Plot: This life insurance plan can provide money to take care of a man's family, pay off a mortgage, and pay a disability income if needed.

Offer: Free book: "How to Get the Things You Want."

(4) SUGGESTIONS FOR ADVERTISING A COURSE IN PIANO INSTRUCTION

4A: Suggestion Number One

Illustration:

> Picture a man playing piano

Headline: "A few months ago I couldn't play a note"

Offer: Free book: "Music Lessons in Your Own Home."

4B: Suggestion Number Two

Illustration:

> Picture of group of people playing musical
> instruments. Panel shows method of instruc-
> tion and displays the words "Easy as A B C"

Headline: Here's a strange way to learn music
Offer: Free book: "Music Lessons in Your Own Home."

(5) SUGGESTIONS FOR ADVERTISING A RETIREMENT INCOME PLAN

5A: Suggestion Number One

Illustration:

> Picture of happy couple starting on an
> automobile trip

Headline: A vacation that lasts the rest of your life
Offer: Free booklet: "Retirement Income Plan."

5B: Suggestion Number Two

Illustration: [No illustration]
Headline: How you can retire on a guaranteed income for life
Offer: Free booklet: "Retirement Income Plan."

(6) SUGGESTIONS FOR ADVERTISING THE *WALL STREET JOURNAL*

6A: Suggestion Number One

Illustration: [No illustration]
Headline: "How $27 started me on the road to $75,000 a year"
Copy Plot: The story of a man who sent $27 for a trial
                 subscription to *The Wall Street Journal*. Later he
                 became a regular subscriber. Reading the *Journal*
                 helped him get an income of $75,000.
Offer: Send $27 for a trial subscription.

6B: Suggestion Number Two

Illustration: [No illustration]

Headline:	Some $75,000 jobs are looking for applicants
Copy Plot:	There are a number of jobs paying $75,000 or more that are available to trained men and women. Reading *The Wall Street Journal* will help you train for one of these jobs.
Offer:	Send $27 for a trial subscription.

(7) SUGGESTIONS FOR ADVERTISING A WEEKLY BOOK REVIEW MAGAZINE

7A: Suggestion Number One

| Illustration: | Group of men and women chatting in living room |

Headline:	This fascinating literary circle now open to you
Copy Plot:	This magazine keeps you up to date on the latest books
Offer:	Send for a free copy of the magazine.

7B: Suggestion Number Two

| Illustration: | Photograph of famous contributor to the Book Review Magazine |

Headline:	Can you talk about books with the rest of them?
Copy Plot:	This magazine keeps you up to date on the latest books.
Offer:	Send for a free copy of the magazine.

(8) SUGGESTIONS FOR ADVERTISING A COURSE IN DANCING

8A: Suggestion Number One

| Illustration: | Picture of dancing instructor dancing with young lady |

| Headline: | Why good dancers are more popular than "Walk-Arounds" |

Offer: Free Test Lesson and beautifully illustrated 32-page
                    book that tells all about Arthur Murray's course in
                    dancing.

8B: Suggestion Number Two

Illustration:
┌───┐
│   Picture of couple dancing with masks   │
│   on at a masquerade   │
└───┘

Headline: "How a *faux pas* made me popular"

Copy Plot: A story about a young man who is embarrassed by
                    his poor dancing. He takes the course in dancing
                    and soon becomes popular.

Offer: Free Test Lesson and beautifully illustrated 32-page
                    book that tells all about Arthur Murray's course in
                    dancing.

(9) SUGGESTIONS FOR ADVERTISING A COURSE OF TREATMENTS FOR PEOPLE WITH NERVOUS AILMENTS

9A: Suggestion Number One

Illustration:
┌───┐
│   Panel containing list of symptoms of   │
│   nervous troubles   │
└───┘

Headline: Thousands suffer from sick nerves and don't know
                    it

Offer: Please send me a copy of your book, "New Nerves
                    for Old." I am enclosing 50 cents in coin or stamps.

9B: Suggestion Number Two

Illustration:
┌───┐
│   Photograph of nerve specialist   │
└───┘

Headline: Have you these symptoms of nerve exhaustion?

Offer: Please send me a copy of your book, "New Nerves
                    for Old." I am enclosing 50 cents in coin or stamps.

(10) SUGGESTIONS FOR ADVERTISING A SET OF BOOKS CONTAINING THE WORLD'S GREAT LITERATURE

10A: Suggestion Number One

Illustration:

Picture of set of books

Headline: How to Get Rid of an "Inferiority Complex"

Copy Plot: Reading this set of books will improve your education, and your conversation and help you in business and in social life.

Offer: Free "Guide Book" to books

10B: Suggestion Number Two

Illustration:

Picture of Joan of Arc at the siege of a walled city

Headline: The writings in these immortal books are as stirring as the mightiest deeds of history

Offer: Free "Guide Book" to books

ANSWERS TO BRAIN TEASERS

Below are the headlines of the 20 keyed advertisements that were tested by actual sales response. Each headline is marked successful or unsuccessful. See how many you guessed right.

(1) (a) To a $25,000 man or woman who would like to be making $50,000 [successful]

(b) Here's proof that this training pays financially [unsuccessful]

The headline of the successful ad is specific, mentions money twice, and contains a strong indication of increased earnings. The headline of the losing ad features the word "financially," which is not as effective as specific dollar figures.

(2) (a) "60 days ago they called *me* `Baldy'" [successful]

(b) If I can't grow hair for you in 30 days you get this check [unsuccessful]

In the successful ad, the picture of the bald-headed man and the word "Baldy" selected the right audience at a glance. The copy contains evidence of results. In the losing ad, the picture does not select the audience and the headline suggests that the remedy may not work.

(3) (a) Here's one question you shouldn't ask your wife [unsuccessful]

(b) Get rid of money worries for good [successful]

The headline of the successful ad contains a promise of a benefit. The other headline is purely a curiosity headline and fails to promise a benefit.

(4) (a) "A few months ago I couldn't play a note" [unsuccessful]

(b) Here's a strange way to learn music [successful]

The successful headline promises a benefit ("learn music") and arouses curiosity with the words "strange way."

(5) (a) A vacation that lasts the rest of your life [unsuccessful]

(b) How you can retire on a guaranteed income for life [successful]

The successful headline selects the right audience and promises a benefit. The other headline lacks clarity and is misleading. It attempts to be clever by describing retirement as a vacation that lasts the rest of your life.

(6) (a) "How $27 started me on the road to $75,000" [successful]

(b) Some $75,000 jobs are looking for applicants [unsuccessful]

The successful headline selects the right audience and offers a specific benefit. The other headline reads like a help-wanted ad and selects the wrong audience.

(7) (a) This fascinating literary circle now open to you [unsuccessful]

(b) Can you talk about books with the rest of them? [successful]

The successful headline selects the right audience for a book-review magazine and implies a promise—namely, that you will be able to talk about books if you read the magazine. The other headline is not entirely clear and is misleading. It suggests that you are being invited to join a literary club.

(8) (a) Why good dancers are more popular than "Walk-Arounds" [unsuccessful]

(b) "How a *faux pas* made me popular" [successful]

The words "made me popular" imply a promise of a benefit. The French phrase, *faux pas*, arouses curiosity, which is increased by the picture of the masked couple. The unsuccessful headline does not promise a benefit.

(9) (a) Thousands suffer from sick nerves and don't know it [unsuccessful]

(b) Have you these symptoms of nerve exhaustion? [successful]

The successful headline contains the word "you," and arouses curiosity. It also implies the promise of a remedy for nervous ailments. The other headline is simply a statement of a fact.

(10) (a) How to Get Rid of an "Inferiority Complex" [successful]

(b) The writings in these immortal books are as stirring as the mightiest deeds of history [unsuccessful]

The successful headline contains a specific promise of a personal benefit.

Perhaps you scored 100 percent correct answers on this test. If so, you are to be congratulated. You are a better judge of pulling power than some copywriters who have spent years in advertising. Perhaps you scored 50 percent or less. If so, don't be discouraged, because all ten of the advertisements that failed were considered good enough to test by the agencies and clients working on these accounts. If the advertisements had not been considered good, no money would have been spent to test them. It is this difficulty of judging results in advance that makes advertising, as one advertising professional said, "The hardest, most interesting, most exasperating, satisfying, worthwhile, and exciting business that ever engaged the talents of a group of people."

Advertising can never be an exact science, like mathematics or chemistry, but it can become more accurate and more scientific than it is today. The purpose of this book is to help make advertising more scientific. Advertising can never become completely accurate, however, because of the human element involved—in advertising you are dealing with the minds and the emotions of human beings, and these will always be, to a certain extent, unstable and unmeasurable. That is why it is necessary to test, test, test—to test copy, media, position in publications, seasonal variation, and time of day in broadcast advertising. Test everything on a small scale before you spend money on a large scale.

Mail-order advertisers have learned this lesson over and over again. For example, a new mail-order advertisement is prepared. The copywriter is enthusiastic about it, the copy chief thinks it is good, the account executive is sure it will pull, and the client rubs her hands in expectation of the orders she is going to get. The advertisement runs. The orders fail to come in. The experts were wrong—all wrong. Yet they have been working on mail-order copy for years. They are close students of what pays and what does not pay. If anybody should be able to judge in advance the pulling power of a piece of copy, mail-order advertisers should. Yet they were all completely mistaken. It is experiences like this that teach scientific-minded advertisers to beware of limiting themselves to theories and stick to facts.

The reverse of the above experience sometimes happens. A new advertisement runs in which few have confidence. And the orders pour in. That's what makes tested advertising one of the most exciting and challenging fields in this exciting business. The rules are hard to learn. Sometimes it seems as if there are no rules. But at least there is this one great rule:

> Test everything. Doubt everything. Be interested in theories, but don't spend a large sum of money on a theory without spending a little money to test it first.

I know that half of my advertising is wasted but I do not know which half.

John Wanamaker

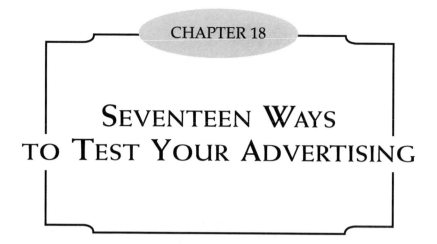

SEVENTEEN WAYS TO TEST YOUR ADVERTISING

What kind of headlines attract the most readers? What kind of pictures get the most attention? What sales appeals sell the most merchandise? What kind of copy will be most successful in persuading people to buy your product or service? You'll see an example that tested all of these to produce the successful ad in Figure 18.1.

This book has given you the findings of years of experience and the results of millions of dollars spent in discovering answers to these questions. But there will always be new questions coming up. You will write new headlines and new copy. You will think up new sales appeal and new illustration ideas.

Which of your new ideas will be the most effective? There will be times when you will want to subject your ideas to some sort of testing, in order to make sure that the dollars you spend in advertising will bring the best possible results.

On the following pages there are described 17 different kinds of advertising tests you can use. Included are detailed descriptions of certain tests that have been briefly mentioned before. Which—and how many—of these tests you should select will depend on the nature of your problem and the amount of time and money you can afford to devote to testing.

1. PUT YOUR NEWLY WRITTEN AD ASIDE UNTIL THE NEXT DAY

The simplest way to test a piece of advertising copy you have just written is to put it aside and read it the next day. In rereading your own copy a day later, you can approach it with a cold, analytical mind, almost as if you were an outsider reading somebody else's copy. Certain errors that were not apparent to you when you were writing with speed and enthusiasm may become clear to you as you read calmly and objectively.

Figure 18.1: *Being different isn't enough, but it can help.* You'd never suspect from the headline and picture that Canyon Ranch has a plot to make you healthier. But it has! And in the highly competitive "health ranch" market, this deliberately "different," curiosity-raising campaign is a rousing success. Tested throughout 1994 against another version with the headline "New life form discovered in Massachusetts" and a picture of a face wearing swimming goggles, "Feel pleasure" proved 97.4 percent better in generating inquiries and 50 percent better in conversion to sales.

Also, you may be able to improve the style of the piece you have written. You may think of short words that can replace long words. You may find unnecessary phrases that can be omitted. You may find long sentences that can be broken up into short sentences. You may find that your message can be speeded up by omitting the first paragraph. You may discover that your copy should have an action paragraph added at the end.

Your chances of producing a good ad will be improved if you will write several ads instead of just one. Your chances of finding a good headline will be increased if you will write many headlines. Then you can select the best copy and the best headline.

2. ASK SOMEBODY TO READ YOUR AD COPY ALOUD TO YOU

Some writers test their copy by reading it aloud to another person. This method has advantages, but it is not as good a test as having another person read your copy aloud to you.

The trouble with reading your own copy to another person is that you know in advance what message you want to convey. You know what words to emphasize in order to bring out your meaning. You know how to make a long sentence sound simple by pausing at the proper places. Other readers do not know these things. They approach your copy with a cold mind. It is up to your copy to warm them up. You can tell by their tone whether your copy has interest or emotion or humor. You can tell by the smoothness of their reading whether your copy is clear.

While other persons are reading your copy aloud, you should sit with pad and pencil and make notes. If they stumble over a sentence, you should assume that this is your fault, not theirs. You should rewrite the sentence. If an idea is not clear to them, you should assume that it will not be clear to other people. You should make your idea clear or omit it.

By asking somebody else to read your copy aloud, you can get a quicker reaction to it than by putting it aside to reveal yourself the next day. The reader you choose can be your boss, your spouse, your associate, your assistant, or the person in the next office.

3. OPINION TEST BY INTERVIEW

An opinion test consists of showing another person some ad layouts or a list of headlines or some samples of copy and saying, "Which do you like best?" or "Which ad would you be most likely to read?" Experiments have shown that it doesn't matter how you phrase the question.

The important thing is to give your respondent at least two things to choose from. The reason is that since most people want to please, they are likely to respond favorably to the ad. If you show just one ad and say, "Here is an ad I wrote . . . please tell me what you think of it," most people will reply, "I think it's good." This gets you nowhere. You should hand your respondent two or more ads and say, "Which do you like best?"

If you are testing a list of headlines on several people, it is good to hand each person a clean copy of the headlines and say, "Please check with pencil the headlines you like best." Don't let one person see the check marks made by another person. Their judgment may be swayed in favor of a headline that other people have previously checked.

Where possible, opinion tests are refined by talking only to prospects. Show food ads to housewives, pipe-tobacco ads to pipe smokers, dog-food ads to dog owners.

Opinion tests can be extended to any degree you choose. You can interview five, ten, or 20 people. You can hire focus groups and other survey reporters who will show your ad layouts to 100 people. You can conduct opinion tests in several cities.

IMPORTANCE OF SALES TESTS

No matter how much you refine an opinion test, you should remember that it is subject to error because it is based on opinions. It is not a sales test. In those cases where it has been possible to apply both opinion testing and sales testing to the same set of ads, it has been found that the two methods do not always obtain the same results. Here are some of the reasons for this:

1. People avoid voting for an ad that reflects discredit on themselves. For example, suppose you want to test the following appeals for toothpaste:

   a) How to avoid tooth decay

   b) How to get rid of bad breath

   The appeal "bad breath" will not win in an opinion test, but it might win in a sales test.

2. Most people believe that an ad has to have a picture in it in order to be a good ad. Therefore an all-type ad will not win in an opinion test. An all-type ad will, however, sometimes beat an illustrated ad in a sales test.

3. People tend to vote for so-called "clever" ads in an opinion test. However, simple ads usually beat "clever" ads in a sales test.

4. An opinion test can be upset by a split vote.

Here is how a split-vote error can occur. Suppose women are asked to select the better of two ad layouts, namely (1) layout with picture of a child versus (2) layout with picture of a home. Let us say that the score is 60 percent for the child picture and 40 percent for the home picture. *Result*: Child picture wins.

Suppose, however, you decide to "refine" the test by substituting two layouts with child pictures in place of one layout with a child picture because you want to try a boy picture versus a girl picture. The layout with the home picture remains the same.

You now show the housewives three layouts and ask which they like best. The 60 percent of the housewives who previously voted for the child picture will now split their votes and you will get a result like this:

30 percent for boy picture
30 percent for girl picture
40 percent for home picture

Result: Home picture wins. Note that the result of the three-way test reverses the result of the previous two-way test.

The proper way to do the preceding test is in two stages, as follows:

1. First you should test a home picture versus a child picture.

2. Then, in a separate set of interviews, you should test a boy picture versus a girl picture.

You may say at this point, "Why should I do an opinion test if it can sometimes produce a wrong answer?"

There are several things to consider in this regard.

1. An opinion test is quick and easy and frequently gives you the right answer.

2. An opinion test is inexpensive.

3. Due to pressure of closing dates, an opinion test is sometimes the only testing method you will have time for.

4. Some ad pros claim that only an actual sales test is worthwhile. But even a sales test can sometimes produce a wrong answer due to hidden factors you do not know about.

5. An opinion test gives you a chance to talk to the people who are voting on your ads. You may learn things you didn't suspect. You may uncover new copy ideas you forgot to include.

The value of opinion testing can be summed up as follows: An opinion test, if properly handled, can help you get nearer to the truth, although it may not always give you the absolute truth.

One company president used an opinion test as a sales device. He wanted to reach certain influential executives with his sales message so he prepared several ads and mailed sets of proofs to a list of prospects. In an accompanying letter, the president said, "Will you please look at the enclosed ads and then check on the enclosed postcard the headlines of the ad you think I should run in the trade press?"

In this way, the president induced a number of his best prospects to read several of his ads even before the ads were published.

4. MAIL-ORDER SALES TEST

A national advertiser recently asked this question: "In testing ads by mail response, when should you use a coupon, and when should you use a hidden offer?"

Answer: You should use a hidden offer when you don't want too many replies and when you want to avoid replies from curiosity seekers. (See page 243.)

You should use a coupon when you want a lot of replies, and when the replies are of real value to you. For example:

1. When the coupon is an order blank and represents an actual mail-order sale.

2. When the coupon secures a lead for a sales representative.

3. When you want to distribute a large number of booklets or samples.

4. When the coupon is a questionnaire and you want to find out the age or business position or other information about your readers.

The coupon stimulates replies as follows:

1. By calling attention to your offer.

2. By making it easy for the reader to reply.

3. By giving the readers a reminder they can tear out and carry with them to your place of business.

Among the most frequent users of testing via coupons are the mail-order advertisers who sell books, novelties, audio and video recordings, or other merchandise by including a coupon order form in each ad.

In the case of these advertisers, every ad is a sales test. The testing method consists of trying several different ads and then repeating over and over the ads that bring the most sales per dollar of space cost.

Mail-order advertisers test not only copy, but media, various positions in media, space size, and seasonal variation.

Here are examples of some of the selling devices included in the coupons of mail-order ads:

> Send check or money order.
> Charge my credit card.
> Bill me.
> Enroll me as a member.
> Send me booklet, sample or catalog—free or for [small amount]
> (Sales are made by direct mail follow-up.)

5. Testing Ads and Mailings with Coupons Plus Calls by Sales Representative

Some items are too high in price to be sold via mail order coupons. For example, an office machine, as shown in Figure 18.2, home improvements, life insurance policies, mutual funds, and correspondence courses. In such cases the coupons offer free literature and a sales representative calls on the prospect. Here are typical coupon offers.

> Please send free book, "How to Succeed."
> Without Obligation, send booklet "How to Fence Your Home."
> Send information on Life Insurance.

This plan gives you a double check on the selling power of each ad you test. First you count the number of coupons each ad produces, and second, you count the number of sales resulting from each ad.

Over a period of time, you can also determine the quality of the coupons you receive. You may find that certain publications bring higher quality leads than others. You may discover that ads featuring a free offer in the headline will bring lower quality leads than ads that subordinate the free offer.

6. Testing Ads with Coupons that Offer Samples or Literature

Most consumer advertisers do not wish to follow up coupon leads with telemarketing or a call by a sales representative, for example, advertisers of beauty products, household products, drug products, or the majority of vacation trips. These concerns do, however, have an interest in distributing literature or samples and in checking on the pulling power of their copy. There are two approaches to this type of testing:

BELOW:
Previous control that the IQ TEST
mailing outpulled by 138 percent

Figure 18.2: *A gifted mailing . . .* Sometimes it takes an IQ Test to get prospects to think about your product. Pitney Bowes' reps wanted *well-qualified* leads. To get them, the IQ mailing demonstrates how smart PB's "Smart Image" copiers are by asking office managers to give their photocopiers (not themselves) the "IQ Test Enclosed." The brief letter that begins and ends with a free gift offer, the 60-second fun-to-score test, and the colorful score sheet and reply card resulted in overwhelming success. IQ outpulled the less involving "Can You Afford . . ." control by 138 percent in response while converting to sales at a higher rate! *1st Place, 1995 CADM TEMPO Award.*

1. You can use a copy-testing plan in which you select a publication that is typical of your entire list of publications and pretest all new ads in that publication. After tabulating results, you can run the best-pulling ads in your entire list of publications.

2. You can use a less specialized approach in which you key all your coupons and keep a record of coupon returns and cost per coupon. You can study these records from time to time in order to learn which ads and which publications are getting the highest response.

Here are sample offers taken from magazines. Note that they have a cash requirement in order to screen out curiosity seekers.

> Please send free 30-day supply of vitamins. I enclose $2.50 for packing and postage.

> Free . . . terry-cloth apron with purchase of sponge mop. A $2.95 value, it's yours by sending a paid receipt (or sales slip) with 50¢ to cover mailing.

> Enclosed is $1 for custom-made drapery swatches and directions for measuring.

Here are some typical offers of literature. Some have a cash requirement and some are free.

> Send for Free Vacation Guide

> Free! Travel Planning Map of America

> Please send your book, "How to Build a Flexboard Garage." I enclose 50¢ in coin.

> Enclosed is 50¢ for my copy of "Planning and Decorating Your Dream Bathroom."

7. TESTING ADS WITH HIDDEN OFFERS

Question: When should you test your copy with a hidden offer instead of featuring your offer in a coupon?

Answer: (1) When you do not want too many replies, (2) When you want to avoid replies from professional coupon-clippers, and (3) When you want to find out if anyone is actually reading your ad.

When you are going to test a series of ads, the first matter to be decided is which offer to use. One advertiser said, "I'd like to test my copy, but I don't know what to offer."

The fact is that on almost all propositions you can use one of the following offers:

1. A sample of the product.

2. A booklet about the product or service.

On certain propositions, it is difficult to get sufficient replies. On others, it is so easy to get replies that you may have to take steps to reduce their number.

HARD-TO-GET REPLIES

An advertising agency copywriter wanted to test a lot of different selling appeals for a headache remedy. He put together some small all-type ads measuring 75 lines (5-1/3″) by two columns. Each appeal to be tested was featured in the headline of one of these ads. For example:

Ad No. 1. Quick Relief for Nervous Headache

Ad No. 2. Why Thousands Use this Headache Remedy

The agency wanted to get at least a hundred replies from each test ad. Experience shows that a hundred replies is about right. If you average only ten replies per test ad, the results may not be dependable. On the other hand, if you average a thousand replies per test ad, you may find that the cost of mailing out samples is unnecessarily high.

The ad manager was dubious about including an offer of a free bottle of the headache remedy. She said, "We may be swamped with requests for free bottles. Let's offer a free booklet instead."

The agency preferred to offer a sample of the product so that the test would approach the characteristics of an actual sales test. They prevailed on the ad manager to permit a test of a low-pressure offer in a single ad. The pulling power of the offer was reduced in three ways as follows:

1. Instead of offering a full-size bottle, the ad offered a sample bottle.

2. Instead of offering the sample bottle free, the copy required the reader to send 50¢.

3. The offer was completely hidden in the last paragraph of the copy. There was no subhead featuring the offer.

An all-type ad containing this offer was run in a single newspaper with half a million circulation. The copywriter waited nervously for results. He feared that his client, the ad manager, would be annoyed if the ad brought too many replies.

Result: The ad brought only two replies.

The next step was to run an ad containing the following offer: "Just tear out this ad and send it with your name and address and we will mail you a regular $1-size bottle absolutely FREE." *Result*: The ad brought slightly over a hundred replies, which was about the amount desired. The ad agency then proceeded to run other ads with different headlines in order to test the comparative pulling power of various sales appeals.

Regarding this test, one copywriter said: "Hidden offers of food samples or soap samples sometimes pull hundreds or even thousands of replies. Why is it so difficult to get people to write for a headache remedy?"

Answer: A headache remedy appeals to a narrower audience than does an offer of food or soap. Also, if people do not have a headache, they may not bother to read a headache ad. And if they do have a headache, they will probably go to a drugstore and buy a remedy. They will not wait several days to have the remedy delivered by mail.

On the other hand, the desire for food and soap is universal and continuous. All your readers know that they will be able to use a sample of these items regardless of whether the sample arrives in three days or in three weeks.

For another example of such a test—this one in Singapore—see Figure 18.3.

HOW TO GET MORE REPLIES FROM HIDDEN OFFERS

If your booklet or sample offer does not pull sufficient inquiries, you can sweeten the offer by including the promise of a free gift.

In testing lamp bulb ads, it was found that a hidden offer of a booklet did not pull a sufficient number of requests. Therefore the offer was made more attractive by including a free gift. This method worked well. Here is the offer:

> A handsome, double-action automatic pencil and extra leads . . . and an interesting booklet about light and seeing . . . will be sent to you free if you tear out this ad and send it to us with your name and address.

In another case, an airline wanted to test a series of 100-line, all-type ads for airplane trips to Bermuda. The ads were tested in a single newspaper of 600,000 circulation. The advertiser found that a hidden offer of a booklet pulled fewer than 50 replies per ad. This was not considered sufficient.

Figure 18.3: *Creating a database that's more than skin deep.* No reliable database existed for testing the promotion of skin care creams to Singapore's teenaged girls. The campaign, featuring a contest and prize drawings, ran in lively teen-media print ads and point-of-sale flyers. The 5,000-name goal was doubled, permitting more than expected test groupings and faster than expected results. The campaign was a double winner. It determined the best approaches for product sales, and also how to keep a valuable database current and continually productive. *Winner, 1995 ECHO Award.*

The advertiser sweetened the offer by including an offer of a free pair of sunglasses and a free map of Bermuda in addition to the free booklet. The offer was described as a "Free Bermuda Vacation Kit." This offer brought more than enough replies for a copy test—more than 400 replies per ad.

The "free kit" idea was also used successfully in copy tests for other limited-appeal propositions. For example, a "Free Painter's Kit" brought plenty of replies in testing house paint ads. A "Homeowner's Kit" had good pulling power in testing ads for building materials.

HOW TO DESCRIBE A BOOKLET ATTRACTIVELY

In testing ads for an investment service, it was found that the line "Send for a free booklet" did not pull sufficient replies. By including the following attractive description of the booklet, the number of requests was increased more than 500 percent:

> Where can I find out about investments that pay dividends? What do they pay? Where can I get facts?
>
> An 18-page booklet has been prepared to answer such questions. This free booklet gives you facts in simple language.
>
> It tells you what you own when you own stock. It tells you what dividends are . . . and how often you may expect to receive them.
>
> Did you know there is a way to reduce investment risks? That's in this booklet, too. Plus a list of companies whose stocks have paid a cash dividend every year for 20 to 103 years. The booklet includes some stocks that sell for less than $20 a share.
>
> If you are interested in extra income, send for this booklet—whether you have $200 or $5,000 to invest. Write for your free copy today. Booklet will be sent by mail. No obligation.

OTHER WAYS TO INCREASE REPLIES

Use a Sunday newspaper: If you are testing ads in a daily paper and you do not get enough replies, you can switch to a Sunday paper. Sunday papers pull better because almost all have larger circulation than their dailies and people have more time to answer ads on Sunday.

Use more circulation: If you are testing your ads in a paper with 250,000 circulation, you can switch to a comparable paper with 500,000 circulation. This should double the number of your replies.

Use additional newspapers: If you are testing your ads in a single newspaper, you can add additional newspapers to bring the number of replies up to a sufficient quantity.

Use bigger ads: If you are testing ads of 100-line size, you can increase the size of your ads to 200 lines or to 500 lines. Bigger ads bring more replies.

Of course, in any ad, you can increase replies by featuring the offer in a headline or in a subhead. However, that method is not recommended because the featuring of the offer tends to invalidate a copy test by focusing attention on the offer instead of on the sales appeal you are testing.

Summary: Following are briefly stated recommended methods for increasing hard-to-get replies in a hidden-offer copy test:

1. Offer the sample or booklet free instead of charging.
2. Set a value on the offer, such as "regular $1-size."
3. Sweeten the offer by adding a free gift.
4. Describe the offer attractively by listing its good features.
5. Run your test ads in a Sunday newspaper instead of in a daily.
6. Run your test ads in a publication with larger circulation.
7. Run your test ads in additional publications.
8. Increase the size of your test ads.

8. A CONTINUING SALES TEST BY MAIL

Some advertisers make a continuing, year-round sales test of their advertising by including a mail order offer in every ad and in every publication. A key number is included in each ad so that the advertiser can trace the source of every mail order that comes in.

As a rule, the mail orders received by this method do not pay the cost of the space, but they do give the advertiser a chance to make comparisons. For example:

1. You can compare the pulling power of one ad versus another.
2. You can compare the pulling power of one publication versus another.

3. You can keep records that will tell you in which months of the year your ads pull best.

4. You can find out in which positions in publications your ads do best.

Here is the last paragraph of a *Wall Street Journal* ad using this method. Note the key number at the end of the ad. This particular key number (NYT 1-10) stands for *New York Times*, January 10.

> The *Wall Street Journal* is the complete business DAILY. Has largest staff of writers on business and finance. The only business paper served by all three big press associations. It costs [amount] a year, but you can get a Trial Subscription for three months for [amount]. Just tear out this ad and attach check for [amount] and mail. Or tell us to bill you. Address: The *Wall Street Journal*, 200 Burnett Road, Chicopee, Mass. 01021 NYT 1-10.

9. TESTING ADS BY TELEPHONE RESPONSE

The following story illustrates how to handle this type of test:

> "I talked with our chief engineer, and he says the best feature of our new air conditioner is that it gets rid of humidity," said the sales manager of an appliance company. "If the air in a room is kept dry, the human body cools itself."
>
> "I see," said the ad manager.
>
> "Maybe we should talk about getting rid of humidity in our ads. I remember an old saying—It isn't the heat, it's the humidity."
>
> "That doesn't sound like a very exciting ad campaign."
>
> "Well, I must admit that our sales reps do not use the humidity appeal very much. They talk about cooling the air. They tell customers how to keep a room cool in hot weather. I wonder which appeal we should use in our ads, coolness or humidity?"
>
> "We can try both appeals. We can run an ad on humidity and put in a telephone number and ask people to telephone for information. We can keep track of how many telephone calls we get. Then we can run an ad on coolness and keep a record of how many telephone calls that ad brings."
>
> "Where will you run the ads?"
>
> "In a daily newspaper."
>
> "The ad that runs on the hottest day will be the winner. You know how people crowd into our showrooms on hot days."

"All right, we'll run each ad several times. We'll alternate the ads—first an ad on coolness, then an ad on humidity. Then coolness, then humidity. That will average out the weather factor."

"Good idea. Now, how about having the phone calls switched to our showroom? Then, when somebody telephones we can have the call handled by one of our sales reps. We can make some sales and test the ads at the same time."

"Fine," said the ad manager.

RESULTS OF THIS TEST

Two ads were prepared. The ads were set in type in editorial style with no pictures. Each ad measured two columns by 100 lines. In the last paragraph of each ad was a telephone number and a sentence urging the reader to telephone for further information.

Here are the headlines of the two ads. See if you can guess which ad brought the most telephone calls.

No. 1. Get rid of that humidity with a new room cooler that also dries the air.

No. 2. How to have a cool, quiet bedroom—even on hot nights.

These ads were run alternately, about once a week, in a newspaper with half a million circulation. A record was kept of the number of telephone calls produced by each ad.

It was not long before the pattern of results became apparent. The second headline, "How to have a cool, quiet bedroom—even on hot nights," averaged two and a half times as many calls as the first one, "Get rid of that humidity."

As a result of this test, the humidity appeal was dropped from the ad headlines and the coolness appeal was featured in all ads during the rest of the summer. Sales results were excellent.

OTHER EXAMPLES

A finance company wanted to test "hard-sell" ads versus "soft-sell" ads. Here are examples of the two different campaigns:

Hard-Sell:

Headline: How You Can Get a Loan of $200

Copy: The copy stressed quick, private service and no inquiries of friends, relatives, or employer. A list of figures showed the various amounts you could borrow and a monthly pay-back plan.

Soft-Sell:

Headline: When Can a Loan Help You?

Copy: The copy employed a philosophical approach and presented arguments such as these: "Sometimes a loan proves helpful. Sometimes it only gets one in deeper. Don't borrow unless a loan will improve your position. We make loans to those who can use funds constructively."

These ads were tested in newspapers. One ad contained a panel of copy that said: "For quick information on loans, simply telephone [telephone number] and ask for Miss Miller." All telephone calls to Miss Miller were credited to that ad. The other ad contained an identical panel of copy except that the line "Ask for Miss Miller" was changed to read "Ask for Miss Johnson." All telephone calls to Miss Johnson were credited to the ad containing the name Miss Johnson.

In this test, the ad with the headline, "How you can get a loan of $200" brought two and a half times as many telephone calls as the other ad.

In commenting on the results of this test, the account executive said: "The headline `When can a loan help you?' is a philosophical headline. When people are in trouble, they don't want philosophy—they want money! And so they respond better to the ad, 'How you can get a loan of $200.'"

Here are some other situations in which ads were tested by including an urge to telephone for information and by keeping records of which ads produced the most telephone calls.

An engineering concern ran help-wanted ads in the classified section of newspapers and included a telephone number in the copy. Each ad urged the job applicant to telephone for information and told the name of a certain individual to ask for. For example: Ask for Mr. Digby, Ask for Mr. Thompson, and so on. This method was used to test the pulling power of different copy approaches and also to test the pulling power of different newspapers.

A private school used the same method to test which ads were most effective in getting phone calls from prospective students. The school also used this method to determine which day of the week was best. *Result*: Sunday was found to be better than weekdays.

An office products manufacturer used this method, not only to test copy, but as a productive source of leads for sales representatives to call on.

10. TESTING ADVERTISING APPEALS BY MAIL

"How can we keep our competitors from learning about our new campaign if we run a copy test in newspapers?" said the advertising manager of a soap company.

"We can avoid testing in big cities. We can run our test ads in a small city like Peoria," said the account executive.

"I'm afraid of that. This new X-appeal has never been used to sell soap. I don't want it to leak out in advance of our national campaign. You know, our business is very competitive. If we run X-appeal ads in Peoria, our competitors will know about it in a few days."

"We can skip the copy test," said the account executive.

"No, I want to get a comparison of the pulling power of the X-appeal ads versus our current Y-appeal ads. I want some evidence to show to our management."

"We can do an opinion test among housewives. We can have interviewers show X-layouts and Y-layouts and ask women to vote for their preference."

"No, a lot of women might be embarrassed to vote for the X-appeal ads. The ads are a bit shocking. But I think they have sales appeal."

"We could do a copy test by mail."

"How would that work?"

"We would buy a list of names and addresses of typical housewives from a mail-order-list broker," said the account executive. "We could buy a good-sized list—10,000 names. We could get up mailing pieces based on our ads. Or we might mail actual proofs of ads. We could include an offer in the ads—and a reply card. We would mail X-appeal ads to half of the women on the list and Y-appeal ads to the other half. The reply cards would be keyed—Dept. X and Dept. Y—so that we could tell which appeal pulled best."

"What should we offer?"

"A sample of the soap."

"Free or for money?"

"Either way. If we charge 50¢ for the sample we would have to enclose return envelopes instead of postcards. And we would have to mail a larger number of letters in order to get sufficient replies. On the other hand, if the sample is offered free, we could use a smaller mailing and enclose postcards for reply."

"Should the postcards have the offer printed on them?"

"No, because some women might read the offer before reading the ad. They might even send for the offer without reading the ad. That would upset our test. The postcards should merely have blank spaces for the housewife to write in her name and address. Then the copy test would operate in proper sequence. There would be a hidden offer in the copy in the ads. Only those women who were sufficiently interested in the ads would read the copy and discover the hidden offer."

"How much would a copy test like that cost?"

"About five thousand dollars."

"How long would it take?"

"About two weeks."

TYPICAL EXAMPLES

The preceding incident illustrates a method of copy testing that has been used from time to time over the years.

One example is the case of a cigar manufacturer who wanted to test six different appeals. Six headlines were written, and each headline featured a different appeal. To save on mailing costs, double postcards were used instead of letters. Headlines and appropriate copy messages (containing a hidden offer) were printed on one side of the card, and the attached business reply card contained the manufacturer's name and address and space for the recipient's name and address. Here is the hidden offer:

> Sign your name on the attached postcard, mail it now, and we will send you three cigars with our compliments. We want you to know how good they are. And if you want more later—and we feel sure you will—your nearest cigar store has them.

One of the cards containing a new appeal in the headline pulled nearly 50 percent more replies than any of the other cards. This appeal was used subsequently as the basic theme of a successful ad campaign.

A package-goods manufacturer also used mailings to test the pulling power of several different appeals. Five appeals were tested. Each appeal was featured in the headline on 2,000 postcards making a total mailing of 10,000 postcards to housewives. Under each headline appeared three paragraphs of copy about the product. This was followed by a final paragraph containing the hidden offer, as follows:

> To get your free package, simply sign the attached card with your name and address and drop it in the mail. No stamp is needed. There is no obligation, of course. But don't delay. Put the attached card in the mail now.

Food manufacturers, drug manufacturers, and correspondence-school advertisers have also used this method of pretesting basic appeals or proofs of ads before running the ads in publications. The offers used have been samples of the product or booklets about the product or service.

11. OPINION TESTS BY MAIL

If your copy-testing problem is one that can be helped by an opinion test, you can, if you wish, do your opinion test by mail instead of by personal interview. For example, you can send out two thousand letters printed on a special letterhead with a heading such as the words "Research Bureau." Here is a typical letter:

RESEARCH BUREAU
Room 1891
590 Lexington Ave., New York, N.Y. 10017

Dear Friend:

The other day I made a statement that I was immediately challenged to prove.

I said that it wasn't necessary to go and see people in order to ask them questions. I claimed that if you wrote to them in the right sort of way, they would be glad to answer.

Will you help me prove that I am right? All you need do is compare the six roughly sketched advertisements attached to this letter and decide which one of them would be most likely to interest you.

Then enter your choice at the bottom of this sheet, using the initial that appears under the ad. After you have chosen number one, decide which ad is second, which third, and so on until you have entered all six in the spaces provided.

Do not return the ads themselves. Just enclose this letter containing your vote in the attached stamped and addressed envelope.

Gratefully yours,

Jane Thompson

My first choice is advt _____   My fourth choice is advt _____

My second choice is advt _____   My fifth choice is advt _____

My third choice is advt _____   My sixth choice is advt _____

Please indicate whether you are male _____ or female _____

12. TESTING BUS CARDS

A cosmetic manufacturer prepared two different bus cards featuring two different sales appeals. Let us designate these as Card A and Card B.

Card A featured the social popularity the user of the product would gain by using the cosmetic. At the bottom of the card was printed a line in small type that said, "For a trial bottle, send 50¢ to Dept. A." Below this line was printed the address of the manufacturer.

Card B featured a specific skin ailment the cosmetic would help to relieve. At the bottom of the card was printed the offer of a trial bottle for 50¢. The only difference was that the reader was instructed to write to Dept. B instead of to Dept. A.

As you may know, in buying showings of bus cards or subway cards, it is possible to buy small showings or large showings, as follows:

1. If you buy a half-showing, your bus card will be placed in every other bus on a certain bus line. In other words your card will appear in half the buses (or in half the subway cars, in the case of subway advertising).

2. If you buy a full showing, your card will appear in every bus or in every subway car.

The cosmetic advertiser bought two half-showings on a certain bus line. In one of the half-showings she placed Card A. In the other half-showing she placed Card B. In this way, each card received identical exposure under identical conditions. The test was continued for two months, and during that period this advertiser received 65 percent more replies from one card than from the other card. Incidentally, the results of this test agreed with a mail-order test in newspapers in which this manufacturer tested the same two appeals.

13. SALES TESTING IN SELECTED CITIES

A question sometimes asked by students of advertising in regard to testing ads is: "Why don't you just run the ad or ads you wish to test in newspapers in a single city and measure the sales results?" The answer is that this method sounds simple, but in actual practice may be expensive, time-consuming, and subject to errors. For example:

1. If you are selling an old and established product, the sales of your product will continue to a certain extent with or without additional advertising.

2. If you sell through wholesalers, it may be a long time before any extra sales (resulting from your newspaper ads) will be reflected in your factory shipments to wholesalers. Current users won't buy your household cleanser, for example, until their present supply is used up. Corner grocers or supermarket managers won't reorder until their stock runs low. The wholesaler won't send an order to your factory until inventory is nearly exhausted. Hence, an ad campaign in Peoria might be successful in making those who read your ad want your product, but you would not know about it until months later.

3. It is difficult to measure one advertising appeal against another by this method because both appeals will probably sell some merchandise. You have to find two equally matched cities so that you can advertise one appeal in one city and another appeal in another city and compare the difference in sales results. No matter how carefully you try to match two cities, you may find that your test is adversely affected by conditions you cannot control, or even by hidden conditions you are unaware of at the time.

In spite of the difficulties of sales testing in selected cities, this method has been used for many years in what have proved to be reliable test markets and will continue to be used because the results are measured in actual sales.

If you wish to test two different advertising appeals in selected cities, here are some precautions that may help to give you an accurate measurement.

1. Don't just test one ad (Ad A) versus another ad (Ad B). the difference in sales results would probably be too small to measure. You should prepare two campaigns, namely Campaign A and Campaign B. Run Campaign A for a long time (two to six months) in one city or in a selected group of cities. Run Campaign B for the same length of time in a different city or in a selected group of cities.

2. Instead of running small ads once in awhile, you can speed up results by running big ads frequently. In other words, during the test period you can overadvertise in order to accentuate the difference in the selling power of Campaign A versus Campaign B.

3. You should try to find a quicker and more sensitive measure of sales results than your factory shipments to wholesalers. For example, you can send out survey reporters at regular intervals to visit certain typical stores. By arrangement with store owners, these survey reporters should count the packages of your product on shelves and keep running inventories that will reflect sales results quickly and accurately.

SALES TESTING A NEW PRODUCT

If you are launching a new product, you may find that sales testing is more practical than it would be in a case in which you are trying to increase the sales of an established product. For example, one man who invented a new patent medicine started sales testing in his hometown by running a new and different ad each week in the daily newspaper. The ad directed prospects to buy at the local drugstore.

Each week this man personally visited the drugstores in his town and counted the packages of his product on the shelves. During some weeks he found that he made no sales, and during other weeks he made a few sales.

Then one day he ran a newspaper ad based on an entirely different sales appeal. As a result, he discovered that during that particular week the supply of his product was entirely sold out.

This discovery, in a single city, of an effective sales appeal was the beginning of a patent-medicine advertising campaign that later became well-known throughout the United States.

14. COOPERATIVE SALES TEST

In trying to discover a method for sales testing some ads, a manufacturer said to himself, "If I owned a department store, I could easily test the selling power of various different ads for my product. I would simply run the ads, one each week, in a daily newspaper in my city and keep a record of the sales resulting from each ad.

"Of course, there might be a few inaccuracies in this method. For example, one ad might run in a better position than another ad. And there might be some cumulative sales effect of a whole series of ads. Nevertheless, if one of my ads made an outstanding sales record, I would know it. And I could double-check the results by repeating that same outstanding ad at a later date."

While thinking about this problem, the manufacturer had this idea: "Perhaps I don't need to own a department store in order to use this method. Maybe I can induce a department store manager to cooperate with me in testing the selling power of some ads. I will tell him that I will pay the cost of running some ads in the daily newspaper if he will do me the favor of reporting to me the sales results from each ad. The ads will feature my merchandise and will be signed with the name of his store."

He tried this method and found it to be successful. Department store managers were approached on the basis of "I'll do a favor for you (pay for some ads urging people to go to your store) if you will do a favor for me (tell me the sales results)."

The same method has been used with chain drugstores in large cities in order to test the selling power of various ads for drugstore items. Ads were run in newspapers once a week. Each week's ad features a different selling appeal in the headline. And each ad was signed with the name of a certain drugstore chain. This caused the sales results to be concentrated in stores owned by that particular drug chain. This concentration of sales in a few stores owned by the same chain made the sales results easier to measure than if the sales results were scattered through dozens of independent stores.

Note that this method of "cooperative" advertising is regulated by federal law. Before starting any "co-op" plan, get clearance from a legal expert in this field.[1]

15. READERSHIP TESTS BY INTERVIEW

Suppose you ran an ad in the daily newspaper in your city and you wanted to find out how many people saw your ad. Suppose that the day after your ad appeared you decided to call on your friends and neighbors and ask them if they saw your ad.

---

[1] For an expanded discussion of "Co-op" advertising, see *Do-It-Yourself Advertising and Promotion, Second Edition* by Fred Hahn and Kenneth Mangun.

Let us say that you had to call on ten neighbors before you found one who had noticed your ad. You would then say to yourself "One out of ten is 10 percent. The newspaper in which my ad appeared has 20,000 circulation. Therefore, my ad was noticed by 10 percent of 20,000 people, or a total of 2,000 people."

This method is the readership method of testing the effectiveness of advertising. The preceding example is, of course, an oversimplification of the method. In actual practice, you have to improve the efficiency of a readership test by using refinements such as the following:

1. Don't call on friends. They are likely to try to please you by saying that they noticed your ad even though they did not actually notice it.

2. In interviewing people, don't point to a particular ad. It is better to turn the pages of the newspaper and say, "Did you notice anything on page 2? Did you notice anything on page 3? As I turn the pages of the newspaper, please point out anything you may have noticed." You can go through the entire newspaper in this way or you can save time by confining your interview to a few pages. In any event, you will get an idea of how your ad compares in attention value with other ads in the newspaper.

3. If you wish, you can ask additional questions. If a person says he or she saw a certain ad, you can then say, "Did you read any of it?" If the person says yes, you can ask further questions such as, "What part of the ad did you read? Did you buy the product advertised? Do you intend to buy the product? Did the ad make you want to buy the product?"

4. To increase the reliability of a readership test, it will be necessary for you to interview many more than ten people. It will be necessary to interview hundreds of people and this will require the hiring of a staff of survey reporters—men or women who will go from house to house and ask the questions you want asked.

In actual practice, the readership method of ad testing is usually done by hiring the services of a professional organization specializing in this work. These specialized companies make readership tests of ads in both magazines and newspapers—as well as for radio and television—and prepare detailed reports showing the percent of readers who said they saw or read various advertisements. You can buy these readership reports and have them mailed to you at regular intervals. This type of service is usually too expensive for an individual to buy. It is usually bought by advertising agencies or by large companies that invest millions of dollars in advertising.

The readership method of measuring the effectiveness of advertising has advantages and disadvantages. For example, one advantage is that you can get reports on the readership of all the ads in a publication including your competitors' advertising. A disadvantage is that an ad that gets a high rating by this method may not necessarily produce many sales. It may be an attention-getting ad without being a selling ad.

16. READERSHIP TESTS BY MAIL

Sometimes readership tests are done by mail instead of by personal interview. For example, here is an extract from a letter that was sent out by the publisher of a magazine:

> Your regular copy, Mr. [Name] of our July issue was mailed to you several weeks ago. You have undoubtedly had an opportunity to read it by this time.

> We will be sincerely grateful if you will cooperate with us in a study we are making among a few selected readers.

> What we would like to know particularly is which advertisements interested you when you went through this issue. We are also interested in your reading of editorial material. An extra copy of the July issue is enclosed. You will also find enclosed a special editor's pencil and a postage-paid return envelope.

> Will you kindly draw a line down the middle of each ad and each editorial item that interested you?

> If you have not seen this issue at all, please mark a large X on the front cover and return it anyway. The editor's pencil is yours to keep as a souvenir.

> We will also welcome any comments you wish to make on specific editorial items or advertisements.

> Thank you very much for cooperating with us in this study. Your help will be of great value to us and to our advertisers.

17. SPLIT-RUN COPY TESTING IN PUBLICATIONS

"Here are two mail order ads I'd like to test," said an advertising manager to his assistant. "I'd like to find out which ad is the better puller."

"Where shall we test them?" asked the assistant. "In a magazine?"

"No, let's test them in a daily newspaper. That way we can get a quick test. Magazines have longer closing dates."

"Which ad shall we run first?"

"That's a problem. I'm afraid that the ad we run first may have an unfair advantage. The first ad may grab the easy-to-get customers. The second ad will be left with slim pickings. The first ad may look like the winner on sales. But the second ad, although it gets fewer sales, may be the better of the two ads."

"I could argue the other way," said the assistant. "I've always heard that the effect of advertising is cumulative. Therefore, the first ad that appears will warm up the customers, but the second ad will get the most sales."

"Hmm," said the ad manager. "I wish this advertising business weren't so complicated! Isn't it almost time to go to lunch?"

VARIABLES IN COPY TESTING

The preceding story illustrates one of the variables that may affect a copy test, namely, the order of appearance of the ads. Some advertisers try to compensate for this variable by testing ads in two newspapers and by reversing the order of appearance of the ads in the second newspaper. In the first newspaper, for example, Ad A runs on Monday and Ad B on Tuesday. In the second newspaper, Ad B runs on Monday and Ad A runs on Tuesday. Returns from the two sets of ads are averaged.

The position of an ad in a newspaper is another variable that affects copy testing. One ad may get top-of-page position on the women's page while another ad gets bottom-of-page position on a general news page. To avoid this variable, you can ask newspaper makeup people to cooperate by placing test ads in similar positions. For example, you can include in your insertion orders this instruction: "Both of these ads are to appear in the upper right-hand corner of the women's page."

The weather can affect a copy test, too. One ad may have the advantage of appearing on a rainy day when a lot of people stay home and have more time to answer ads. This variable can be compensated for by running your test ads in several widely separated cities.

HOW SPLIT-RUN COPY TESTING WORKS

The advent of split-run copy testing put an end to these troublesome variables. By means of split-run testing, it became possible to test two different advertisements on the same day and in the same position by running each ad in one-half of the circulation of a newspaper. An explanation of how this is possible follows.

The presses that print certain newspapers print from cylinders on which each page of the newspaper is placed twice on each cylinder. Hence, a complete revolution of the cylinder prints two copies of a single page.

When advertisers want to use split-run testing in the newspaper, they provide the paper with two advertisements of the same size. One advertisement (A) is placed on one side of the cylinder, the next advertisement (B) is placed on the other side. Thus, a complete revolution of this cylinder prints two copies of the same page, a different advertisement occupying the same space on each page.

All newsdealers, no matter where they are located, receive a supply of newspapers in which Advertisement A and Advertisement B are equally divided among *consecutive* copies. Thus, in every locality and neighborhood into which the newspaper goes, whether delivered to homes or sold by news dealers, exactly the same number of papers containing Advertisement A and Advertisement B reach the newspaper readers. This kind of test is known and ordered as an "A/B Split Run."

The importance of this in testing is immediately apparent. Every variable that might affect the result of the test is removed. Each advertisement is tested under conditions exactly alike. Both advertisements reach readers simultaneously in the same geographical areas and under the same weather conditions. Both advertisements occupy the same position in the newspaper and are surrounded by the same editorial matter. Absolutely the only variable to which the advertisements are subjected is the one the advertisers themselves puts in for the purpose of testing one against the other.

VARIOUS USES OF SPLIT-RUN TESTING

Split-run copy testing in newspapers is one of the greatest inventions ever devised for the benefit of scientific-method advertisers. Here are three reasons why:

1. The method is quick. You can test two ads on a Monday, for example, and in most cases you will know as early as Tuesday or Wednesday which is the winner.

2. The method is accurate. No longer do you need to say, as a result of a test, "Ad A is about twice as good as Ad B" (or about half again as good as Ad B, whichever the case may be). You can now say, for example, that "Ad A is 43 percent better than Ad B."

3. You can test fine points. This method is so accurate that you can test small differences between ads. For example, the following small differences between ads were tested.

Test No. 1. Two drug-product ads were tested that were identical except that in Ad A the headline was printed above the picture and in Ad B the headline was printed below the picture. Ad B pulled 8 percent more replies. David Ogilvy in *Ogilvy on Advertising,* emphasizes the importance of this point by asking why anyone would give up 20,000 potential readers in a 250,000 circulation publication just to place a head-line over the picture.

Test No. 2. Two beauty-product ads using pictures of the same girl model were tested. The ads were identical except that in Ad A the girl was smiling and in Ad B the girl had a serious expression. Ad A pulled 25 percent more replies.

Test No. 3. Two all-type automotive ads were tested. The copy was identical in both ads except for a change in headline wording as follows:

Headline of Ad A: Save one gallon of gas in every ten
Headline of Ad B: Car Owners! Save one gallon of gas in every ten

Ad B pulled 20 percent more replies.

Test No. 4. Two financial ads were tested that were identical except that Ad A contained the subhead "Send for Free Booklet" above the coupon and Ad B omitted the subhead. The ad with the subhead above the coupon pulled 5 percent more replies than the other ad.

Split-run copy testing can be used for mail-order tests, coupon tests, hidden-offer tests, readership tests, layout tests, illustration tests, and store-sales tests. Advertisers have only scratched the surface of the possibilities of split-run testing. Just think, in a single day in a typical large city, you can put a certain ad (Ad A) into the hands of 250,000 people and you can put a different ad (Ad B) into the hands of another 250,000 people under identical conditions. This is accurate sampling on a massive scale and at low cost. To do large-scale sampling of this kind by other research methods would present enormous difficulties and cost staggering sums of money.

There are more than 1,000 split-run newspapers in the United States, listed by SRDS, (formerly the Standard Rate and Data Service). You can do split-run copy testing in any of these papers. You encounter no more difficulty than the scheduling of ads, the answering of replies, and the tabulating of results. And the cost is merely the cost of the newspaper ads plus a small mechanical fee charged by newspapers for split-run testing.

Many magazines also offer split-run testing. *TV Guide* has more than 80 editions in which copy can be split-run tested. Due to long closing dates (a month or two in advance of publication date), you cannot get a quick split-run test in magazines, but you can make copy testing a regular part of your advertising campaign.

HOW TO TEST A WHOLE SERIES OF ADS BY SPLIT-RUN

An advertising manager was talking to an agency media specialist about split-run copy testing. "I can see how you are able to test two ads by split-run. You just run each ad in half the circulation of a newspaper on the same day and count the replies," said the advertising manager. "But can you test more than two ads—for example four ads or ten ads?"

"Yes, you can test four ads by doing three split-run tests a week apart," said the media expert. "For example, let's say that during the first week you do a split-run test in a daily newspaper and Ad A gets 100 replies and Ad B gets 150 replies. The next week you can test two more ads, for example, Ad C versus Ad D. Let's say that Ad C is the winner. Now you have two winners—Ad B is the winner of the first test and Ad C is the winner of the second test. During the following week you can split-run test the two winners against each other and find out which ad is the best of the entire series of four ads."

"How would you test ten ads?" said the ad manager.

"You can divide the ten ads into groups—four ads plus four ads plus two ads—and test the groups separately. Then you can test the winners of the groups against each other. It's the same plan as they use in intercollegiate track meets where a lot of athletes are competing. First you have preliminary contests to weed out the obviously hopeless contestants. Then you have the semifinals and then the finals.

"A slightly different plan can be used if desired. Suppose you have ten ads, numbered from one to ten. Let's say that on a certain Monday you split-run test Ad Number One versus Ad Number Two. You count the replies and by Thursday you find that Ad Number One is the winner. Now, thanks to short newspaper closing dates, you have time to schedule your winner Ad Number One versus Ad Number Three on the following Monday. Again you count replies and you find out which ad is the winner of this second split-run test. You then schedule the winner on the second test against a new, untested ad on the third Monday. You can continue this process every Monday until all of your ads have been tested and you emerge with an overall winner."

"It takes a lot of time, doesn't it?" said the ad manager.

"Well, it takes ten weeks to test ten ads. And the process can go on indefinitely. This plan has the advantage that it gives the copywriters time to study the results as the test progresses. If they learn that a certain appeal is doing well, they can create and test new ads that accentuate that appeal. In other words, as the test progresses, the writers are given a sense of direction in which to travel."

A QUICK WAY TO TEST ADS BY SPLIT-RUN

"Is there any faster way to test a series of, say, ten ads?"

"Yes, there is a plan that lets you test ten ads in ten days instead of ten weeks."

"How does it work?"

"You select one of your ads and use it as a Control Ad or measuring stick. Every day you run your Control Ad in half the circulation of a split-run newspaper, and every day you run one of the ads you want to test in the other half of the circulation. For example, your schedule might start off like this:

Monday: Ad Number One versus Control Ad
Tuesday: Ad Number Two versus Control Ad
Wednesday: Ad Number Three versus Control Ad

"You can continue this process until you have split-run tested all ten ads against the same Control Ad."

"How do you tabulate the results in order to select the winning ad?"

"Well, as a rule, some ads pull more replies than the Control Ad and some pull fewer replies than the Control Ad. The winning ad is the one that exceeds the Control Ad by the greatest percentage. Your tabulation of results might look like this:

Ad Number One is 20 percent better than the Control Ad

Ad Number Two is 35 percent poorer than the Control Ad

Ad Number Three is 60 percent better than the Control Ad

And so on.

"Obviously, Ad Number Three is the best up to this point and Ad Number One is the second best. After all ten ads in the series have been tested against the Control Ad, you can rank the entire series in order of merit, from one to ten. In some tests it has been found that the best-pulling ad will outrank the Control Ad by several hundred percent."

"Doesn't a test of this kind tend to wear down the pulling power of the ads as the test progresses?"

"Sometimes it does. Sometimes the tenth pair of ads in a series will pull only half the total of the first pair. You can help to avoid this wearing down of pulling power by using small-sized test ads, for example, 100 lines each. Small-sized ads do not wear out their pulling power as fast."

"Does this wearing down of pulling power upset the test?"

"No, it doesn't. Many times we have repeated, at the end of a series of test ads, the same pair of test ads that we ran at the beginning, in order to double-check the results. The percentage of difference between the two repeated ads has been approximately the same as at the beginning of the test. In other words, you get the same percentage results no matter at what point in the series a certain pair of ads appears."

HOW THIRTY-SIX HEADLINES WERE TESTED

"What is the largest number of ads you have tested in a short time by this method?" said the ad manager.

"In one instance we tested 36 ads in two weeks. We wrote a piece of patent medicine copy containing two elements: (1) a complete sales talk for the medicine, and (2) a hidden offer of a sample bottle of the medicine for $1," said the media specialist.

"Then the copy department wrote 36 different headlines for this single piece of copy. We wanted to know which headline would induce the most people to read the ad. The copy was set in type—no pictures—in single-column size and 75 lines deep. We then set the 36 headlines in type, one for each headline. This gave us our total of 36 ads to test.

"Four newspapers that offer split-run testing were selected. Let us call them Newspapers A, B, C, and D.

"We picked a single Control Ad (any ad in the series can be used as a control) and scheduled this Control Ad to run in half the circulation of Newspaper A on ten different days—Monday through Friday, for two weeks. Each day, in the other half of the circulation of Newspaper A, we ran one of the 36 ads we wanted to test. In this way we tested ten ads in two weeks. Likewise, during the same two weeks, we tested ten different ads in Newspaper B using the same Control Ad as a measuring stick. In Newspaper C, we tested ten more ads using the Same Control Ad, and in Newspaper D we tested in the same way the remaining six ads in our total of 36 ads.

"The net result was that in a period of two weeks we tested 36 different headlines against the same Control Ad and then ranked the entire list in order of pulling power. One of the headlines exceeded the Control Ad by 300 percent and another by 200 percent. The selling appeals contained in these two winning headlines were used as the basis of a successful national campaign."

GENERAL COMMENTS ON TESTING

As previously stated, advertising is not an exact science like chemistry. If you tell chemists that you are going to mix certain chemicals in certain proportions, they can predict the result accurately. However, if you tell advertising professionals that you are going to run a certain advertisement in a certain publication, they cannot tell you exactly what results you will get. They can give you only an approximate opinion based on their own past experience.

Of all branches of advertising, mail-order advertising comes the nearest to being a science. Given a tested piece of copy and a tested publication, an experienced mail order pro can often predict results surprisingly well. It is for this reason that a study of mail order methods is valuable to the general advertiser.

Compare for a moment the present-day situation in advertising with the manufacturing situation. Would a manufacturer of electronic products install a new type of insulation without first subjecting it to all sorts of tests? Certainly not. Would an automobile manufacturer buy a trainload of new axles or enamel or fabric without pretesting? The answer is no. Yet scores of manufacturers are buying trainloads of advertising, and the only test to which the advertising is submitted is their own personal opinion or the opinion of a subordinate. Advertising will never produce the results it can produce until some sort of testing is brought into the picture.

FOUR IMPORTANT FACTORS IN EVERY ADVERTISING CAMPAIGN:

1. Copy—what you say in your advertisements. This includes the appeal used and the method of expressing that appeal.

2. Media—which magazines, newspapers, broadcasting facilities, or other media you select to carry your message to the public.

3. Position—what position your advertisements occupy in publications; which day of the week or what time of day you select for your broadcast messages.

4. Season—in which months of the year you run most of your advertising.

Any one of these factors can cause a wide difference in results from advertising. As mentioned earlier, Caples once saw one ad bring in 19-1/2 times as much business as another ad. Yet both advertisements appeared under similar conditions and both cost the manufacturer the same amount of money. This is an extreme case. Let us be conservative and say that in an average advertising campaign consisting of a dozen advertisements, some of the advertisements will produce two or three times as much business as others.

Certain publications will do the same, that is, produce several times as much business as others. As for the position of your ad in a publication, certain special positions often add 50 percent to 100 percent to inquiries and sales. And as for season, it is not unusual for a mail-order advertiser to receive twice as many orders from a January advertisement as from an August advertisement, both advertisements costing the manufacturer the same.

Consider the tremendous effectiveness of an advertising campaign that gets all these factors right—copy, media, position, and season. The advertisers who get these factors right are multiplying the effect of their advertising dollar. They make one dollar do the work of ten dollars.

The advertisers who get these factors wrong—especially copy and media—are throwing a large part of their advertising appropriation away.

Regardless of what method of testing you use, the important thing is to have some method of testing. Testing enables you to throw opinions overboard and get down to facts. Perhaps there is some particularly effective appeal in your sales story. Perhaps you do not realize how effective this appeal would be if featured in advertising. Testing will enable you to find out. Perhaps you are spending money on some hopeless appeal. Testing will point the way to the discarding of this appeal.

Testing enables you to guard against an advertising manager or copy chief whose pet ideas may be hurting your advertising. Testing enables you to guard against an advertising agency whose idea of agency service is merely to turn out pretty layouts and stereotyped copy. Testing enables you to guard against mistaken ideas that you yourself may have in regard to advertising. And finally, testing enables you to keep in touch with trends in advertising. What was good advertising a few years ago may not always be good advertising today.

Trends change. Sometimes the attitude of the public changes. When advertisers come out with a new idea they may be able to cash in on it for a while. Then other advertisers copy their methods. The idea is no longer new. It becomes common. The public gets used to it and tires of it.

There is, however, one rule that never changes:

Test everything on a small scale before you spend money on a large scale. Testing enables you to keep your finger on the public pulse. It enables you to sense trends in advance. It enables you to separate the wheat from the chaff, the sheep from the goats, the winning ideas from the duds. It enables you to multiply the results you get from the dollars you spend in advertising.

If I were starting life over again, I am inclined to think that I would go into the advertising business. Advertising covers the whole range of human needs. It brings to the greatest number of people actual knowledge concerning useful things. It is essentially a form of education. It has risen with ever-growing rapidity to the dignity of an art.

Franklin D. Roosevelt

INDEX